THE UNIVERSITY OF WINCHESTER

Martial Rose Library
Tel: 01962 827306

KT-146-626

2 5 JAN 2010

2 4 JAN 2011 - 8 MAY 2014

- 3 MAY 2011

1 7 JUN 2011

To be returned on or before the day marked above, subject to recall.

WITHDRAWN FROM
THE LIBRARY

UNIVERSITY OF
WINCHESTER

KA 0342412 X

Young Citizens and New Media

Routledge Studies in Social and Political Thought

12. The Age of Reasons
Quixotism, Sentimentalism and Political Economy in Eighteenth-Century Britain
Wendy Motooka

13. Individualism in Modern Thought
From Adam Smith to Hayek
Lorenzo Infantino

14. Property and Power in Social Theory
A Study in Intellectual Rivalry
Dick Pels

15. Wittgenstein and the Idea of a Critical Social Theory
A Critique of Giddens, Habermas and Bhaskar
Nigel Pleasants

16. Marxism and Human Nature
Sean Sayers

17. Goffman and Social Organization
Studies in a Sociological Legacy
Edited by Greg Smith

18. Situating Hayek
Phenomenology and the Neo-liberal Project
Mark J. Smith

19. The Reading of Theoretical Texts
Peter Ekegren

20. The Nature of Capital
Marx after Foucault
Richard Marsden

21. The Age of Chance
Gambling in Western Culture
Gerda Reith

22. Reflexive Historical Sociology
Arpad Szakolczai

23. Durkheim and Representations
Edited by W. S. F. Pickering

24. The Social and Political Thought of Noam Chomsky
Alison Edgley

25. Hayek's Liberalism and Its Origins
His Idea of Spontaneous Order and the Scottish Enlightenment
Christina Petsoulas

26. Metaphor and the Dynamics of Knowledge
Sabine Maasen and Peter Weingart

27. Living with Markets
Jeremy Shearmur

28. Durkheim's Suicide
A Century of Research and Debate
Edited by W.S.F. Pickering and Geoffrey Walford

29. Post-Marxism
An Intellectual History
Stuart Sim

30. The Intellectual as Stranger
Studies in Spokespersonship
Dick Pels

31. Hermeneutic Dialogue and Social Science
A Critique of Gadamer and Habermas
Austin Harrington

32. Methodological Individualism
Background, History and Meaning
Lars Udehn

33. John Stuart Mill and Freedom of Expression
The Genesis of a Theory
K.C. O'Rourke

34. The Politics of Atrocity and Reconciliation
From Terror to Trauma
Michael Humphrey

35. Marx and Wittgenstein
Knowledge, Morality, Politics
Edited by Gavin Kitching and Nigel Pleasants

36. The Genesis of Modernity
Arpad Szakolczai

37. Ignorance and Liberty
Lorenzo Infantino

38. Deleuze, Marx and Politics
Nicholas Thoburn

39. The Structure of Social Theory
Anthony King

40. Adorno, Habermas and the Search for a Rational Society
Deborah Cook

41. Tocqueville's Moral and Political Thought
New Liberalism
M.R.R. Ossewaarde

42. Adam Smith's Political Philosophy
The Invisible Hand and Spontaneous Order
Craig Smith

43. Social and Political Ideas of Mahatma Gandhi
Bidyut Chakrabarty

44. Counter-Enlightenments
From the Eighteenth Century to the Present
Graeme Garrard

45. The Social and Political Thought of George Orwell
A Reassessment
Stephen Ingle

46. Habermas
Rescuing the Public Sphere
Pauline Johnson

47. The Politics and Philosophy of Michael Oakeshott
Stuart Isaacs

48. Pareto and Political Theory
Joseph Femia

49. German Political Philosophy
The Metaphysics of Law
Chris Thornhill

50. The Sociology of Elites
Michael Hartmann

51. Deconstructing Habermas
Lasse Thomassen

52. Young Citizens and New Media
Learning for Democractic Participation
Edited by Peter Dahlgren

Young Citizens and New Media

Learning for Democratic Participation

Edited by
Peter Dahlgren

Routledge
Taylor & Francis Group
New York   London

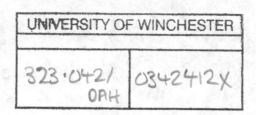

UNIVERSITY OF WINCHESTER

323·042/
OAH   0342412X

Routledge
Taylor & Francis Group
270 Madison Avenue
New York, NY 10016

Routledge
Taylor & Francis Group
2 Park Square
Milton Park, Abingdon
Oxon OX14 4RN

© 2007 by Taylor & Francis Group, LLC
Routledge is an imprint of Taylor & Francis Group, an Informa business

Printed in the United States of America on acid-free paper
10 9 8 7 6 5 4 3 2 1

International Standard Book Number-13: 978-0-415-39599-1 (Hardcover)

No part of this book may be reprinted, reproduced, transmitted, or utilized in any form by any electronic, mechanical, or other means, now known or hereafter invented, including photocopying, microfilming, and recording, or in any information storage or retrieval system, without written permission from the publishers.

Trademark Notice: Product or corporate names may be trademarks or registered trademarks, and are used only for identification and explanation without intent to infringe.

Library of Congress Cataloging-in-Publication Data

Young citizens and new media : learning for democratic participation / edited by Peter Dahlgreen.
   p. cm. -- (Routledge studies in social and political thought ; 52)
   Includes bibliographical references and index.
   ISBN 978-0-415-39599-1 (hardback : alk. paper)
   1. Youth--Political activity. 2. Mass media and youth. 3. Digital media--Social aspects. I. Dahlgren, Peter, 1946-

HQ799.2.P6Y64 2007
323'.042083--dc22

2007015917

Visit the Taylor & Francis Web site at
http://www.taylorandfrancis.com

and the Routledge Web site at
http://www.routledge.com

Contents

Acknowledgments   ix

1   Introduction: Youth, civic engagement and learning via new
    media   1
    PETER DAHLGREN

PART I
Youth, media, and democracy: Late modern landscapes   19

2   From big brother to *Big Brother*: Two faces of interactive
    engagement   21
    STEPHEN COLEMAN

3   Changing life courses, citizenship, and new media: The impact
    of reflexive biographization   41
    HENK VINKEN

4   Civic learning in changing democracies: Challenges for
    citizenship and civic education   59
    W. LANCE BENNETT

PART II
Situating young citizens' media use   79

5   Young people's identity construction and media use: Democratic
    participation in Germany and Austria   81
    UWE HASEBRINK AND INGRID PAUS HASEBRINK

6   Interactivity and participation on the internet: Young people's
    response the civic sphere   103
    SONIA LIVINGSTONE

7   Patterns of Internet use and political engagement among youth   125
    JO-ANN AMADEO

8   Finding a global voice? Migrant children, new media and the
    limits of empowerment   149
    DAVID BUCKINGHAM AND LIESBETH DE BLOCK

PART III
Media, engagement, and daily practices   165

9   Democratic familyship and negotiated practices of ICT users   167
    MAREN HARTMANN, NICO CARPENTIER, AND BART CAMMAERTS

10 An indispensable resource: The Internet and young civic
    engagement   187
    TOBIAS OLSSON

11 Mobile monitoring: Questions of trust, risk, and democracy in
    young Danes' uses of mobile phones   205
    GITTE STALD

12 Social networks of young political activism and cultural
    practices   227
    DOMINIQUE CARDON, FABIEN GRANJON, AND JEAN-PHILIPPE HEURTIN

Contributors   248
Index   253

Acknowledgments

The chapters of this book were first presented at a colloquium held at Lund University in late September 2004, as an extension of a research project on young citizens and new media that I headed together with Tobias Olsson.

I wish to express my gratitude to the Research School LearnIT, a part of the Knowledge Foundation of Sweden, for the funding of the project and of the colloquium. In particular my thanks go to Roger Säljö, head of LearnIT, for initially proposing this event.

Peter Dahlgren

1 Introduction

Youth, civic engagement, and learning via new media

Peter Dahlgren

In the discussions and debates about the difficulties facing the established Western democracies today, many issues come to the fore, but certainly one of the key themes is the trend towards declining civic engagement. While there are of course exceptions—and certainly the current uncommonly polarized climate around the policies of the Bush administration in the US is a case in point—extensive international evidence suggests that the citizens of today's liberal democracies show less involvement in political issues, are less inclined to vote, have less party loyalty, and demonstrate lower levels of participation in civil society than in the past. Turning to younger people, the picture on the surface, at least, generally looks even bleaker: they manifest the same patterns, only more strongly. When it became clear in the mid-1990s that the Internet was on its way to becoming a mass phenomenon, it did not take long for many commentators to make a hopeful connection: if democracy is in trouble, then perhaps the Internet can be of help, given not least that young people in particular were quickly being drawn towards it. It was becoming apparent that many in the younger generation were growing up with the newer information and communication technologies (ICTs) (e.g., Livingstone, 2002), of which the net was the foremost. Moreover, they were quickly mastering the tools offered in this new digital environment, and using them to learn about, relate to, and engage with the social world. Thus, it was hoped that they would also be using these tools to learn civic engagement.

Even with our admittedly limited historical hindsight we can still see that much of this early optimism was a bit hasty. There is no simple technological solution for democracy's dilemmas, and the availability of communication technology is no guarantee that it will be used for civic purposes. Yet, if the optimists overshot the mark, so too did the pessimists who scoffed at the notion that the Internet would play any significant political role. Today few would simply dismiss the idea that the Internet has become an important feature of political society. Also, many would agree that this impact extends to young citizens. While political uses of the net remain comparatively small in comparison with the many other areas of use, a picture is emerging that suggests that the net is of central importance even here. The

Internet is contributing in various ways to how many young people learn to become citizens, how they develop the role of civic agents, and even to the manner in which they engage in politics.

This volume brings together these overlapping concerns about the general state of democracy, questions of political engagement among younger citizens, and the role that the new information and communication technologies (ICTs) might play in the processes whereby young people learn to engage in the life of democracy. There have been a number of contributions in this area (e.g., Montgomery et al., 2004; Suorant, 2003; Bell, 2005; Delli Carpini, 2002, as well as works by several of the authors in this collection); yet more needs to be done. In this introductory chapter I first offer an overview of some of the key themes. I begin with some general perspectives on political engagement/disengagement and the role of the media, and socio-cultural change more generally, in altering the conditions of democracy. I then move on to some reflections more specifically on young citizens and politics. Thereafter I address the somewhat ambivalent picture that has emerged in regard to what we can expect from ICTs in these contexts. The final section previews the chapters that follow, indicating the main contributions of each to the central themes.

POLITICAL DISENGAGEMENT, MEDIA, AND SOCIO-CULTURAL CHANGE

In Western democratic societies over the past few decades, not only has there been varying degrees of decline in voter turn-out and in party loyalty, but also a disinterest in larger ideological visions. Expressions of cynicism and contempt for the political class are not unusual. If we look beyond the political realm towards engagement in the broader civil society of associations and civic networks, even here the general pattern seems to one of decline. In the US context, Putnam's (2000) oft-cited text presents key arguments, even if many aspects of this thesis have met with criticisms (e.g., Edwards et al., 2001). In accounting for the declining participation in traditional party politics, observers refer to a number of the institutional aspects of modern democracy, such as the often stale and unresponsive character of established political parties; the social distance between citizens and their representatives; and the growing, unaccountable power of the corporate sector. The evolution of the media landscape is also often pointed out as an important factor: the increasing conglomerate character of the media industries, coupled with neo-liberal deregulation, tends to intensify the demand for large and short-term profits, and thereby push aside most normative considerations (not least journalistic values) that may not immediately support the economic goals (Baker, 2002; McChesney, 2004; Bagdikian, 2004; Nichols et al., 2005). Journalism has been evolving in ways that evoke anxiety both within the profession and among researchers

(Franklin, 2004; Gans, 2003; Downie and Kaiser, 2003; Fallows, 1997). In particular, the drift towards infotainment, tabloidization, and sensationalism is seen as weakening the knowledge base of citizens.

A traditional view would also assert that this erosion of the boundaries between journalism and non-journalism—especially with popular culture—signals an unambiguous decline in the quality of news. This trend not only hampers civic participation, it also across time constitutes a deformed civic socialization: citizens are 'groomed' by the news media to expect little that is of serious political use, while at the same time they are acculturated to be addressed as spectators or consumers rather than citizens, thereby deflecting or undermining their identities—and likelihood to act—as citizens (Mindich, 2005). Milner (2001) demonstrates with extensive international comparisons that the availability—and use by the public—of high quality journalism tends to correlate with higher levels of participation in democracy.

The debates on tabloidization (e.g., Sparks and Tulloch, 2001), however, indicate that there are many aspects involved and that simple categorical positions on these matters can be problematic. Such discussions begin to relocate the issues from within journalism to a view that sees journalism and its evolution in terms of broader socio-cultural changes. With the ubiquity of popular culture and entertainment, and with the cultural shifts in late modern society, it may well be that a perspective that simply reasserts the traditional form and content of the news media is travelling down a path that will soon exit from the historical scene, as the trends in news consumption suggest. While new forms of journalism are emerging, it is not clear to what extent they can compensate for the deficit in traditional political knowledge, and these trends thus remain troubling.

In the meantime, the new media culture offers—especially for young people—many areas of popular engagement other than politics. In this regard, the media manifest and amplify a number of socio-cultural trends that bear on the issue of civic engagement and disengagement, though it is not easy to specify any simple causal relationships (cf. Gibbins and Reimer, 1999), even if these more overarching tendencies at least they can be said to coexist with political disengagement. In the proliferating literature on late modernity (cf. Beck and Beck-Gernsheim, 2002; Bauman, 2002, 2000; Giddens, 1990) one can glean a number of intertwined trends that have particular relevance for young people's civic engagement . Among the most pertinent are:

- *The fragmentation of shared common public cultures*: Society is becoming more pluralistic and differentiated along several lines: class, ethnicity, patterns of media consumption, cultural interests, lifestyles, etc. This development points to the emergence of small, disparate islands of communicative and cultural spaces. While such pluralism can be lauded in some ways, it can also hinder democracy's dynamics.

- *Mediatization of everyday life*: The media are not only ubiquitous, they also increasingly play a more important role in the socialization of the young, while the impact of traditional institutions such as family, school, church, neighbourhood are in relative decline.
- *The centrality of consumerism*: Beyond the material and symbolic aspects of consumption, we have the emergence of a way of life (Miles 1998) that resonates with a cultural template for which life strategies, large and small, are for the most part individual rather than collective. The role, identity, and activities of the consumer have become pervasive and taken for granted, while those of the citizen become marginalized.
- *Individualism becomes more pronounced*: This can be seen in part as an outcome of the above; social horizons tend to emphasize personal life, the graspable local milieu; the involvement with abstract 'isms' declines. Identity formation becomes all the more a focused, ongoing project, where the viability of previous models of life trajectories can no longer simply be assumed.

The consequences of these transformations run deep, and the stability and efficacy of democracies come into question. The ensuing entropy encompasses at times antithetical tendencies. On the negative side we can list chaos, inefficiency, unpredictability, etc., which can serve to deflect engagement. On the positive side, we would place such trends as the increase in the range of political voices, new modes of political engagement, and even understandings of what constitutes politics, as tendencies that might be seen as openings that invite participation. The drift towards loosening and disorganising the established patterns of political communication can thus potentially extend civic engagement and be seen as democratic gains. Yet, again, it must be acknowledged that from a systems perspective, too much dispersion and poly-vocal input at some point begin to undercut political functionality and hamper governance. Democratic systems are not infinitely elastic.

Thus, the contemporary situation is ambiguous; the newer forms of extra-parliamentarian political engagement and commitments, with a focus on daily life, personal values, and single issues, offer a counterpoint to the narratives of decline (e.g., Bennett, 2003, 2004). For example, in the case of Sweden, Sörbom, (2002), using life course interviews, finds that political commitments at the personal level have in fact grown in the past decades, while commitments to parties and traditional social movements have declined. In an ambitious international comparison, Norris (2002) provides a perspective that emphasizes variation in regard to electoral politics, and a degree of optimism about the newer forms of politics. She concludes that while participation in elections has declined in many established Western democracies, it has remained fairly stable in others. Moreover, it is clearly on the increase in many of the newer democracies. In regard to the growth of new politics, she suggests that we are seeing the emergence of important new patterns of civic engagement:

> ...political activism has been reinvented in recent decades by diversification in the *agencies* (the collective organizations structuring political activity, the *repertoires* (the actions commonly used for political expression), and the *targets* (the political actors that participants seek to influence). The surge of protest politics, new social movements, and internet activism exemplify these changes. If the opportunities for political expression and mobilization have fragmented and multiplied over the years...democratic engagement may have adapted and evolved in accordance with the new structures of opportunities, rather than simply atrophying. (Norris, 2002: 215–216; italics in original)

YOUNG CITIZENS, DEMOCRACY, AND POLITICS

Looking further at young citizens, Bruhn (1999), in a Swedish study with results typical of much such research, finds that they have today a low trust in politics and politicians, though they still affirm their support of democracy. Young citizens feel remote from the formal political system; that which is discussed does not seem relevant to them personally. Young people say often that they have difficulty identifying with the political actors, who are usually much older and normally do not seem to have insight into the life situations of young people. Also, even among those who do hold some political views there is a strong feeling that contemporary political life seems to hold few clear alternatives; it appears as various shades of grey.

There is a general sense among many that politics consists of too much unproductive bickering, at times cast in a mode of speech that is difficult to follow. At the same time, young people tend not to have detailed political information. They are not serious readers of newspapers—they tend to skim political articles—neither do they sit dutifully and watch TV news. Research on mass media journalism and young people suggests that while the young are tuning out, it is partly because they feel the news is not addressing them (e.g., Buckingham, 2000). However, among those of middle class background, many have a high competence in handling information via the new media, giving them a sense of self-confidence and social competence.

In terms of socialization, Bruhn (1999) also notes that many young people say that their parents seldom talk about politics, or even emphasize that they don't wish to influence their children, that people in the younger generation have to come to their own conclusions. Thus, the 'passing on of political tradition' within the family seems to be loosening. Neither do they reflect much class-identification. They do value having influence, and tend to demand participation and desire community if they become engaged in social issues, but party politics tends not to fulfil these needs for them. In a wide-ranging study emphasizing civic competence and skills, Youniss et al. (2002), in noting similar patterns internationally, underscore that these developments can be confronted through a variety of initiatives from various corners: from the family, educational institutions, the business sector, government, civil society organizations, the media, as well as from researchers.

Certainly there is much that can be done, and one can anticipate varying degrees of success. Yet a fundamental question is exactly how one defines the problem in regard to young citizens. Is the goal to 'bring them back into the fold'—that is, to strive to generate the kind of civic behaviour that has characterized liberal democracy in the past? Or does one re-think the preconditions and attributes of democracy in light of the social and cultural changes that characterize the present historical juncture? It would seem that the former course hold out a delimited promise for the future. And the latter course is characterized by a lack of clarity and considerable and uncertainty. The disinterest in party politics is a problem, since most visions of democracy are hard pressed to see how it could function well without their presence. And extra-parliamentarian forces can certainly enhance democratic vitality. How the present mix will evolve cannot be predicted, but we can assume that liberal democracies are unavoidably heading forward into somewhat unfamiliar circumstances.

While it is difficult to get any solid numbers of those involved in alternative politics (not least due to the often transitory character of membership), impressionistically it seems that alternative forms of engagement are on the rise, even if the participants remain a rather small segment of the population. Various social and cultural movements, single issue activists, networks, transnational linkages, NGOs, etc., are emerging outside the boundaries of conventional party politics. Analytically, the various modes of alternative politics seem to address certain needs for young people that conventional politics does not fill. The boundary between the political and the personal is no longer so rigid, and such issues as globalization and economic justice, the environment, human rights, gender, sexual orientation, what we eat, etc., often blend political perspectives with personal normative involvement. Politics becomes not only an instrumental activity for achieving concrete goals, but also a performative and expressive activity, a way of asserting group values, ideals, and belonging in public spaces. The private domain can thus become a springboard for political concerns and engagement, and issues of identity are often intertwined with societal engagement. Various labels have been used to describe this phenomenon: life politics, lifestyle politics, new politics, or alternative politics.

An important implication here is the potential for engagement that surfaces: if 'politics' is increasingly not the bounded terrain defined by politicians, then it can potentially emerge anywhere on the socio-cultural landscape. This is not the same as saying that 'everything is political', rather it points to a situation where politics is in the process of being both decentralized and decentred. As Norris says in the quote above, we witness within democratic politics the emergence of new agencies, repertoires, and targets. However, while we find cause for some optimism here, we should not forget that racist and other undesirable anti-democratic elements are also present. Also, we should not forget that many of the key decisions that shape society and people's lives are still taken within the confines of conventional politics, and it would be indeed problematic for democracy if the young continue to abandon this terrain. And finally, while the non-hierarchical mode of organization in many such groups is commendable, the tendencies toward loose (and at time undependable) membership may put such groups at a disadvantage in their confrontation with more conventional political forces.

NEW MEDIA: AN AMBIVALENT ROLE

At the same time that the discussions about the poor health of democracy intensified during the 1990s, a media revolution was taking place: new information and communication technologies (ICTs), with the Internet at the forefront, were beginning to profoundly impact all areas of social life (cf. Lievrouw and Livingstone, 2002; Burnett and Marshall, 2003; Wellman and Haythornthwaite, 2002; Bakardjieva, 2005). The new media are contributing to profound changes that include reconfiguring our sense of place and our subjective experience of everyday life. That ICTs are reshaping modern life is of course not news, but there remains ambiguity as to the extent to which they are enhancing democracy (cf. Anderson and Cornfield, 2003; Jenkins and Thorburn, 2003). One's understanding—and perhaps even appreciation—of this ambiguity grows as one's insight into the complexity of democracy's difficulties deepens.

In the case of formalized e-democracy, for example, the consequences of modest experiments to formally incorporate the Internet into the political system have not been overwhelming (Clift, 2003). These efforts to incorporate citizens into discussions and policy formulations via ICTs usually have a decisive top-down character (cf. Malina, 2003, for a discussion of the UK circumstances), with discursive constraints that derive from the elite control of the contexts. It should be noted, however, that at the local level, there often remains a certain lack of clarity about the explicit models of democracy that guide the experiments. This suggests that the actual forms that e-democracy may take can still be negotiated and customized to some extent (Grönlund, 2003).

Simplifying somewhat, we can say that two contending perspectives have emerged in regard to the role of the Internet in democratic life. One view posits that while there have been some interesting changes in the way democracy works, on the whole, the import of the Internet is modest; the net is not deemed yet to be a factor of transformation. In an international collection, for example, Gibson et al (2003) underscore that parliamentarian parties use the Internet largely for enhanced top-down communications efficacy, but that civic participation via party politics per se has largely not been augmented thus far. A few years ago Margolis and Resnick (2000: 14) concluded that what we see on the net is largely an extension of offline political life. In their view, while the major political actors may engage in online campaigning, lobbying, policy advocacy, organising, and so forth, democracy as such is not transformed. This evidence about the minimal impact of ICTs on politics cannot be lightly dismissed, but what should be emphasized is that this perspective is anchored in sets of assumptions that largely do not see beyond the formal political system, and the traditional role of the media in that system. While the problems of democracy are acknowledged, the view held is that the solutions lie in revitalizing the traditional models of political participation and patterns of political communication.

Other scholars alternatively take as their point of departure precisely the understanding that we are moving into a new, transitional era in which the certitudes of the past in regard to how democracy works have become problematic. Democracy is seen to be, precariously, at a new historical juncture, and it is precisely the emergence of newer forms of political participation, especially among the young, that gives credence to this perspective. In the arena of new politics the Internet has become not only relevant, but central: it is not least its capacity for the 'horizontal communication' of civic interaction that is important. Both technologically and economically, access to the net (and other ICTs, such as mobile phones) has helped facilitate the growth of large networks of activists (cf. Cammaerts and Van Audenhove, 2004; Cardon and Granjou, 2002; van de Donk et al., 2004; Danaher and Mark, 2003; McCaughey and Ayers, 2003; Jordan and Taylor, 2004; de Jong et al., 2005). There is not that much research available yet on these new forms of engagement, but initial findings suggest a variety of different organisational forms, usually very loose and horizontal in character, with a good deal of transitory membership. This implies a very different kind of organisational structure, as well as a view of membership, compared to traditional parties. The embryonic patterns taking shape now may, with historical hindsight, in the future prove to have been quite significant, as a body of new literature suggests.

LEARNING CIVIC ENGAGEMENT

To talk about civic engagement is to see citizenship as something beyond legal categories and formal attributes; it implies that citizenship is also a form of social agency. To render citizenship in terms of agency leads us to a number of questions. First, it leads us to query how such modes of agency can be learned by the subjects themselves. This requires that we attend to the specific attributes and contexts of such learning; that is, it does not take place only in 'civics classes' or other formal pedagogic settings (although these could certainly be of relevance). Rather, such learning must be seen as emerging from the practices of enacting citizenship, in the 'natural' settings where people participate in political matters—i.e., 'learning by doing'. Thus, a number of preliminary attributes about learning for democratic participation are relevant here:

- It is largely non-linear and non-hierarchical (as opposed to more traditional modes of formal instruction);
- It takes place in diverse social environments that relate to or prepare for some form of democratic participation, with varied technical resources;
- It is largely driven by the subjects' own motivations, which in turn are highly contextual.

Secondly, we would inquire about the circumstances that that can impinge on these learning processes, and on the role of civic agency—circumstances that promote (or hinder) people's sense of themselves as civic agents. If citizenship has mostly been conceived in terms of legal frameworks, and been framed by the histories of the nation-state, in recent years it has also become an object of contemporary social theory (cf. Isin and Turner, 2003). For our purposes, a major strand of such studies highlights the subjective side of citizenship, as a dimension of our identities (cf. Preston, 1997; Isin and Wood, 1999; Clarke, 1996; Mouffe, 1993, 1999). To see oneself in these terms suggests that a decisive subjective factor is involved, a dimension that we can call civic identity. Whether or not the vocabulary of 'citizen' or 'citizenship' per se is of personal relevance is not the key, rather this identity has to do with a sense of belonging to—and perceived possibilities for participating in—societal development. As civic agents people can imagine themselves acting in political contexts, where they sense that their engagement, together with that of others, would be meaningful.

How people actually come to see themselves as civic agents can take many different routes, under many different sets of circumstances, but as I have suggested elsewhere (Dahlgren, 2003, 2007), it can be analytically helpful to understand civic agency and identity in terms of larger, encompassing civic cultures. We can think of civic cultures as cultural patterns in which identities as citizens are an integrated part, supported by a number of important elements such as relevant knowledge, democratic values, trust, practices, and skills. Civic cultures, to the extent that they are compelling, are internalized, intersubjective, operating at the level of being taken for granted, everyday realities, empowering and supporting civic agency.

We can think of such cultures as resources, as storehouses of assets that individuals and groups draw upon and make use of in their activities as citizens. Robust civic cultures are of course nothing that democracies can take for granted; rather they usually need to be further developed.

Linking together learning with civic cultures that can foster agency, we can analytically understand that such agency, as well as the knowledge, values, trust, practices, and skills that support it, should be conceptualized in broad terms, not just limited to cognitive processes. Such learning can potentially proceed via socio-cultural processes, in many settings and circumstances (see, for example, McInerney and van Etten, 2002, 2004). A socio-cultural perspective on learning emphasizes how the development of knowledge, skills, practices, and so on circulate in society, with old ones evolving, and new ones emerging. Such learning is dependent on prevailing social circumstances and cultural patterns, especially communication, and the dynamics between individuals and groups. Technical tools of course play a big role, and computers (e.g., Säljö, 1999) and the Internet are obvious technologies in this regard, not least since they help generate social networks where various kinds of learning—including for civic agency—can take place.

PLAN OF THE BOOK

The chapters that follow take up and weave together in various ways these themes of young citizens' democratic engagement and new media, and how these media can offer new possibilities for learning civic agency. They differ in their approaches and in their emphasis, with some chapters conveying analytic overviews, while others focus on more detailed situations. The first section, 'Youth, Media, and Democracy: Late Modern Landscapes', introduces a number of key topics that are followed up in later chapters. Here the emphasis is on understanding the present situation in terms of overarching socio-cultural changes.

Stephen Coleman's discussion offers a provocative starting point. Instead of simply defining the problem as residing with the young who refuse to shoulder their civic responsibility, he problematizes some of the key assumptions about youth engagement in democracy. The 'public' has from the start been a source of anxiety for liberal democratic thought. For example, it becomes difficult to maintain the notion of the 'free will' of citizens as the foundation for democracy when they manifest indifference towards democratic responsibilities, or, alternatively, when they seemingly collaborate with manipulative forces. Moreover, Coleman argues that democracy has long treated 'engagement' in an uncritical manner. In Orwell's novel *Nineteen Eighty-Four*, Big Brother stands as a dystopian metaphor for an authoritarian power to which people acquiesce and which they praise. On the other hand, the reality TV series *Big Brother* clearly mobilizes popular engagement and participation in ways that evoke alarm in some corners (and envy from traditional political parties). Yet, based on his research, Coleman suggests that there are important lessons for democratic politics to be learned from the multimedia interactivity and popular engagement that characterize the program. Also, it becomes apparent that the communicative mode of mainstream democratic politics is out of step with contemporary horizons of experience and cultural frameworks of many citizens.

Henk Vinken in chapter 3 offers an analysis of the formation of young people's subjectivity in late modern societies, and this in turn provides a foundation for understanding their turning away from traditional politics and looking for new alternatives. He argues that the basic structures of young people's life courses—and career paths—have become 'detraditionalized', being more fluid, forcing them to make more decisions not only about what to do, but also who to be. This involves increasingly intensive 'reflexive biographization', that is, a continual confrontation with oneself in the face of a fast-shifting socio-cultural terrain, where not least, job markets offer many unanticipated changes. In this context, young people are developing more autonomy than in the past; individualization is a key concept here. Traditional political organizations, for example, are experienced as restrictive, offering mainly pre-defined roles for them. The new media play an extremely important role in all this; it is not least via the Internet where young people are working through their identities, developing their autonomy, and engaging in the society around them. Not surprisingly young people find the traditional models of citizenship on offer rather restrictive. Hence, the net offers spaces not only to develop themselves, but also to find new ways of defining and engaging in politics.

Lance Bennett's contribution, chapter 4, offers first an overview of international data on civic disengagement among young people. He then notes that the challenge for civic education today is to convey the knowledge, skills, and values associated with citizenship in a time when a number of the cultural patterns and identity mechanisms that have been central for democracy are evolving. He conceptualizes the tension with the analytic construct of the traditional Dutiful Citizen vs. the new Actualizing Citizen. Bridging the gap between them is no easy task, as the ambivalent results of an ambitious civics development project in Australia suggest. Bennett maintains, however, that we can still conceptualize the important elements for more effective civic education. With reference to a variety of research, he develops a communication model of civic learning consisting of several concrete pedagogical steps that enhance identities, skills, and knowledge. Such a model is anchored in concrete issues and experiences that students can relate to, and involves critical analysis of political communication in the mass media, face-to-face deliberative encounters, as well as skills in the use of ICTs. Bennett is specific in pinpointing the particular learning role that the new media can play.

UNIVERSITY OF WINCHESTER
LIBRARY

The second section, 'Situating Young Citizens' Media Use', looks at a number of national settings and particular contexts. Uwe Haebrink and Ingrid Paus Hasebrink in chapter 5 begin with summaries of young people's views on democratic participation as well as their use patterns of the mass media and ICTs in Germany and Austria. In particular, they indicate the newer elements that define youth civic engagement, and relate these to the media. From there they pick up and develop further some of the themes introduced by Vinken in chapter 3: using a variety of data, they probe the dynamics of identity formation in relation to the media and the emerging contours of contemporary society. They underscore, among other things, that research must take as its point of departure the horizons of young people themselves. Thus, for example, it is important that the domain of politics not be treated a priori as distinct from and unrelated to other realms of experience, since this is at odds with perceptions prevalent among the young. In this light, the authors also highlight what they see to be some problematic limitations in the research literature concerning the processes of meaning construction by young people. They introduce the multi-dimensional notion of 'practical meaning' in order to attain better focus in the research on young people, their media use, and civic engagement.

Sonia Livingstone in chapter 6 also emphasizes the importance of using a broader conception of politics, and of focusing on the new heterogeneous communications environment. She observes that it is not just the commercial sector but even families and the public sector that are, in their respective ways, promoting the use of the Internet among youth. In looking at how young people aged 12 to 19 are responding to these invitations and to hopes for their democratic participation, Livingstone finds that there is some engagement among youth. It takes a variety of forms and must be understood in terms of a number of basic social variables. Internet access per se does not seem to recruit political participation. She also finds considerable disengagement, sometimes even in the face of explicit efforts to stimulate involvement. The situation is complex, but she observes, for example, that many young people often find civic websites rather uninspiring compared to the commercial ones they normally frequent. On a deeper and more troubling level, her research shows that disengagement among youth is in part anchored in feelings that while they are being invited to participate and to express themselves, nobody is really listening: no dialogue emerges, and ultimately nothing comes of it.

Making use of a wide array of international data, Jo-Ann Amadeo in chapter 7 examines patterns of Internet use and its relationship to civic engagement and the development of civic identity among young people. After looking at some basic trends in the US, she then suggests that civic engagement can be promoted via the early development of civic identity, and explores the literature that develops this view. With this conceptual horizon, she then turns to the massive study of the civic profiles and media use among 14-year-olds that was recently carried out in 28 countries by the Amsterdam-based consortium International Association for the Evaluation of Educational Achievement (IEA), She selected three countries where a significant number of 14-year-olds use the Internet to follow the news: Chile, Denmark, and England. She notes how such factors as gender and differences in levels of literacy in the home impact on net use for news, yet the really interesting findings have to do with the possibilities for civic learning. Though use of the Internet for political news remains relatively low in absolute terms, Amadeo highlights how the net is important in this regard. The Internet is seen as an important feature in larger socio-pedagogical contexts that can facilitate 'communities of practice' in the everyday lives of young people. Such learning is a collective activity, a net-facilitated 'doing' that also promotes civic identity.

In a vein that can be seen as a cautionary counterpoint to some of the guarded optimism expressed in several of the chapters, David Buckingham and Liesbeth de Block in chapter 8 report on a six-country European action-research project. It involved a group of migrant and refugee children—from several different countries and with a number of different mother tongues—in each of the participating countries, who used digital media to express themselves and communicate between the groups. The guiding notion was to help 'give voice' and empower these dislocated children via their own media productions, and to ascertain how and to what extent the media function in this regard. In a candid and self-reflexive manner, Buckingham and de Block trace the successes and especially the difficulties encountered. They clarify how the adult-led research situation, for instance, positioned the children as migrants/refugees, and encouraged them to make 'statements' about their experiences and situation. This not only pre-defined the horizons of expectation, but also privileged documentary and factual media genres, while the children often leaned towards less direct forms of expression. There were a number of unresolved tensions in the project, but the authors conclude that the media's potential to empower must be understood as highly contingent on how they are used, as well as on the institutional, pedagogic, and social circumstances. Empowerment does not simply flow per se from the use of media technology.

The third section of this volume, 'Media, Engagement, and Daily Practices', begins with chapter 9 by Nico Carpentier, Maren Hartman, and Bart Cammaerts. Their contribution explores how the use of ICTs in the home is negotiated in the context of family life. They assert that democratic learning is to a great extent an informal process, based in everyday practices. The social sphere of family life, as a micro social sphere, is thus an important setting in which young people become socialized to democratic—or undemocratic—ways of dealing with authority, reaching compromises, and making decisions. What they call 'democratic familyship' is characterized by dialogic negotiation and a degree of balance in power relations. As both symbolic and material objects in the home, ICTs often generate family conflict. In their study of how North Belgian young people negotiate the issues of acquisition, access, and expertise that arise in the processes of the domestication of ICTs, the authors find that consensus-seeking is fairly strong. While the character of family democracy can be shaped by several major social variables, the authors found that discussions about ICTs were shaped by such factors as parental familiarity with these technologies and their perceptions of their social importance. Discourses of education could often be used for justifying decisions, yet it was also evident that the generational bias in terms of expertise played a role in modifying the balance of power on these issues within some families.

The use of the Internet by young citizens is the theme of chapter 10 by Tobias Olsson. His study focuses on young, engaged citizens in Sweden between 16 and 19 years of age who are active in the youth organizations of the parliamentary political parties. The question that guided the study was how the Internet is used for democratic learning. Thus, the research targeted young people who were politically active and routine users of the net, rather than 'representative' respondents. These young people are strong in material, social, and discursive resources. There is no evidence that they came to politics as a result of net access, but it is clear that their skills with ICTs enhances their civic learning and efficacy. Olsson finds that the net serves four basic functions in the daily, routine political practices of these young activists: daily use of the net (1) a tool for monitoring society; (2) a resource for organizational coordination; (3) a resource for participation in the internal public spheres of their own party; and (4) a tool for participation in the public spheres of antagonistic political parties. The learning processes lie thus not only in the accumulation of new information and the development of new knowledge, but also in the development of civic communication skills.

In chapter 11, Gitte Stald turns her attention to the use of mobile phones among young Danes. Mobile phones have become ubiquitous; they are not only connecting people instantly, they are also implicated in a variety of social practices and identity processes. Moreover, they link with and extend other media: the spread of high-capacity, multi-function phones is progressing quickly, and they become portable multi-media consoles that facilitate not just contact with one's social network, but even access to the whole world, as it were. In her ambitious extensive study of young Danes, Stald finds that while most uses of mobile phones are initially motivated by personal practicalities, the social and political implications of this technology loom very large, and many young Danes are coming to see the phone as an explicit civic tool. They express little concern about such risks as surveillance, and in their use they demonstrate a generalized trust. The connectedness offered by the mobile phones has important implications for democracy. If we recall that democracy involves informal socio- cultural participation beyond the formal aspects, the mobile phone provides a potentially empowering link that just about all citizens can make use of. Moreover, there are emerging explicitly societal and political uses; for example, voting and opinion polling. Given the explorative and innovative uses which especially young people develop, one can only speculate about the role that mobile telephones will have in the coming years.

Dominique Cardon, Fabien Granjon, and Jean-Philippe Heurtin report in chapter 12 on their research on ICT-dependent social networks among young people. They bring together two separate studies for purposes of methodological and theoretical development, providing summary descriptions of the routine practices of several respondents. The first study maps the personal networks of young people that derive from leisure and cultural activities, while the second focuses on young people who are active in the alter-globalization movement. Their premise is not only that networks are important for the social capital and learning that help facilitate political engagement, but also that political activism can be treated as a form of cultural practice. Like Olsson's study, they selected young people from relatively privileged backgrounds, though their respondents were a bit older. Their findings generate a typology of three basic network models, which reflect what they call polarization, distribution, and specialization. Comparisons of these models between the two spheres show that they follow very similar social logics. Further, the authors suggest that while personal relations have always been significant for political protest groups, the newer, network-based movements, which are organizationally quite loose and rather fluid in terms of membership, manifest thinner forms of affinity. Lastly, they also see a sequential progression of the network models according to life phases, with polarization more typical of people in their teens, and specialization more common among those in their late twenties.

REFERENCES

Anderson, David A. and Michael Cornfield, eds. (2003) *The Civic Web: Online Politics and Democratic Values*. Lanham, MD: Rowman and Littlefield.

Bagdikian, Ben (2004) *The New Media Monopoly*. Boston: Beacon Press.

Bakardjieva, Maria (2005) *Internet Society: The Internet in Everyday Life*. London: Sage.

Baker, Edwin (2002) *Media, Markets, and Democracy*. New York: Cambridge University Press.

Bauman, Zygmunt (2000) *Liquid Modernity*. Cambridge: Polity Press.

Bauman, Zygmunt (2002) *Society Under Siege*. Cambridge: Polity Press.

Beck, Ulrich and Elisabeth Beck-Gernsheim (2002) *Individualization: Institutionalized Individualism and its Social and Political Consequences*. London: Sage.

Bell, Brandi L. (2005) 'Children, youth and civic (dis)engagement: digital technology and citizenship'. CRACIN Working Paper No. 5. Toronto: Canadian Research Alliance for Community Innovation and Networking. Online: http://www.cracin.ca

Bennett, W. Lance (2003) 'Lifestyle politics and citizen-consumers: identity, communication and political action in late modern society', in John Corner and Dick Pels, eds., *Media and Political Style: Essays on Representation and Civic Culture*. London: Sage, pp. 137–150.

Bennett, W. Lance (2004) 'Communicating global activism', in Wim van de Donk et al., eds., *Cyberprotest: New Media, Citizens and Social Movements.* London: Routledge, pp. 123–146.

Bruhn, Anders (1999) 'Ungdomarna, politiken och valet', i *Valdeltagande i förändring.* SOU 1999:132.

Buckingham, David (2000) *The Making of Citizens: Young People, News and Politics.* London: Routledge.

Burnett, Robert and P. David Marshall (2003) *Web Theory: An Introduction.* London: Routledge.

Cammaerts, Bart and Leo Van Audenhove (2004) *Transnational Social Movements, the Networked Society, and Unbounded Notions of Citizenship.* Report: ASCoR, University of Amsterdam.

Cardon, Dominique and Fabien Granjou (2002) 'La radicalisation de l'espace public par les media-activistes'. 7th congrès de l'Association française de science politique, Lille, Sept.

Clarke, Paul Barry (1996) *Deep Citizenship.* London: Pluto.

Clift, James (2003) 'E-democracy: Lessons from Minnesota', in David A. Anderson and Michael Cornfield, eds., *The Civic Web: Online Politics and Democratic Values.* Lanham, MD: Rowman and Littlefield, pp. 157–165.

Dahlgren, Peter (2003) 'Reconfiguring civic culture in the new medimilieu', in John Corner and Dick Pels, eds., *Media and Political Style: Essays on Representation and Civic Culture.* London: Sage.

Dahlgren, Peter (2007) *Media and Civic Engagement: Citizens, Media and Communication.* New York: Cambridge University Press.

Danaher, Kevin and Jason Mark (2003) *Insurrection: Citizen Challenges to Corporate Power.* London: Routledge.

de Jong, Wilma, Martin Shaw, and Neil Stammers, eds. (2005) *Global Activism, Global Media.* London: Pluto Press.

Delli Carpini, Michael X. (2002) 'Gen.com: youth, civix engagement, and the new information environment', *Political Communication* 17 (4), 341–349.

Downie, Leonard, Jr. and Robert G. Kaiser (2003) *The News About the News.* New York: Vintage.

Edwards, B., Foley, M.W., & Diani, M., eds. (2001) *Beyond Tocqueville: Civil Society and the Social Capital Debate in Comparative Perspective.* Hanover, NH: University Press of New England.

Fallows, James (1997) *Breaking the News.* New York: Vintage Books.

Franklin, Bob (2004) *Packaging Politics: Political Communication in Britain's Media Democracy*, 2nd ed. London: Edward Arnold.

Gans, Herbert (2003) *Democracy and the News.* New York: Oxford University Press.

Gibbins, John and Bo Reimer (1999) *The Politics of Postmodernity.* London: Sage.

Gibson, Rachel, Paul Nixon, and Stephen Ward, eds. (2003) *Political Parties and the Internet: Net Gain?* London: Routledge.

Giddens, A. (1990) *The Consequences of Modernity.* Cambridge: Polity Press.

Grönlund, Åke (2003) 'Emerging electronic infrastructures: exploring democratic components'. *Social Science Computer Review* 21 (1) 55–72.

Isin, Engin F. and Patricia K. Wood (1999) *Citizenship and Identity.* London: Sage.

Isin, Engin F. and Bryan S. Turner, eds. (2003) *Handbook of Citizenship Studies.* London: Sage.

Jenkins, Henry and David Thornburn, eds. (2003) *Democracy and New Media.* Cambridge, MA: MIT Press.

Jordan, Tim and Paul A. Taylor (2004) *Hacktivism and Cyberwars: Rebels with a Cause?* London: Routledge.

Lievrouw, Leah A. and Sonia Livingstone, eds. (2002) *Handbook of New Media: Social Shaping and Consequences of ICT's.* London: Sage.

Livingstone, Sonia, (2002) *Young People and New Media.* London : Sage.

Malina, Anna (2003) 'e-Transforming democracy in the UK: considerations of developments and suggestions for empirical research'. *Communications: The European Journal of Communication Research* 28 (2) 135–155.

Margolis, Michael and David Resnick (2000) *Politics as Usual: The Cyberspace 'Revolution'.* London: Sage.

McCaughey, Martha, and Michael D. Ayers, eds. (2003) *Cyberactivism: Online Activism in Theory and Practice.* London: Routledge.

McChesney, Robert (2004) *The Problem of the Media: US Communication Politics in the Twenty-First Century.* New York: Monthly Review Press.

McInerney, Dennis and Shawn van Etten, eds (2002) *Sociocultural Influences on Motivation and Learning.* Greenwich, CT: Information Age.

McInerney, Dennis and Shawn van Etten, eds. (2004) *Big Theories Revisited: Research on Sociocultural Influences on Motivation and Learning.* Greenwich, CT: Information Age.

Miles, Steven (1998) *Consumerism as a Way of Life.* London: Sage.

Milner, Henry (2001) *Civic Literacy: How Informed Citizens Make Democracy Work.* Hanover, NH: University Press of New England.

Mindich, David T.Z. (2005) *Tuned Out: Why Americans Under 40 Don't Follow the News.* New York: Oxford University Press.

Montgomery, Kathryn, Barbara Gottlieb-Robles, and Gary O. Larson (2004) *Youth as e-Citizens: Engaging the Digital Generation.* Washington, D.C.: Center for Social Media, School of Communication, American University. Online: http://www.centerforsocialmedia.org/ectitizens/youthreport.pdf

Mouffe, Chantal (1993) *The Return of the Political.* London: Verso.

Mouffe, Chantal (1999) 'Deliberative democracy or agonistic pluralism?' *Social Research* 66, 745–758.

Nichols, John, Robert McChesney, Tom Tomorrow, and Tim Robbins (2005) *Tragedy and Farce: How the American Media Sell Wars, Spin Elections, and Destroy Democracy.* New York: The New Press.

Norris, Pippa (2002) *Democratic Phoenix: Reinventing Political Activism.* Cambridge: Cambridge University Press.

Preston. P.W. (1997) *Political/Cultural Identity.* London: Sage.

Putnam, Robert (2000) *Bowling Alone: The Collapse and Revival of American Community.* New York: Simon & Schuster.

Säljö, R.(1999) 'Learning as the use of tools: a sociocultural perspective on the human-technology link', in Karen Littleton and Paul lights, eds., *Learning with Computers: Analyzing Productive Interaction.* New York: Routledge, pp. 144–166.

Sörbom, Adrienne (2002) *Vart tar politiken vägen?. Om individualisering, reflixivitet och görbarhet I det politiska engagemanget.* Stockholm: Almqvist& Wiksell.

Sparks, Colin and John Tulloch, eds. (2000) *Tabloid Tales: Global Debates Over Media Standards.* Lanham, MD: Rowman and Littlefield.

Suorant, Juha (2003) The world divided in two: digital divide, information and communication technplogies, and the ‚youth question'. *Journal for Critical Education Policy* Studies 1 (2).

van de Donk, Wim, Brian D. Loader, Paul Nixon, and Dieter Rucht, eds. (2004) *Cyberprotest: New Media, Citizens and Social Movements*. London: Routledge.

Wellman, Barry and Caroline Haythornthwaite, eds. (2002) *The Internet in Everyday Life*. London: Blackwell.

Youniss, James, Susan Bales, Verona Christmas-Best, Marcelo Diversi, Milbrey McLaughlin, and Rainer Silbereisen (2002) 'Youth civic engagement in the twenty-first century'. *Journal of Research on Adolescence* 12 (1) 121–148.

Part I

Youth, media, and democracy: Late modern landscapes

2 From big brother to *Big Brother*

Two faces of interactive engagement

Stephen Coleman

This paper traces the history of an abiding anxiety of modern, mass society. From Orwell's panoptic dystopia (*Nineteen Eighty-Four*) to Endemol's multi-mediated spectacle (*Big Brother*), the image of the deluded, disciplined, and ductile public has haunted the liberal imagination. Democratic power is legitimised through mass participation, but when voluntary engagement takes the form of collusion with manipulative authority, power ceases to be accountable and the autonomous citizen begins to look more like a slavish subject. This is an enduring paradox of political freedom: how does one explain the happy slave, the willing dupe, and the popular tyranny? Why—and how—do people participate in their own disempowerment and degradation as citizens?

My argument in this paper is that too often 'engagement' is discussed and promoted in an uncritically normative fashion, as if to engage is an inherently good thing. Non-participation and disengagement are over-simplistically explained in terms of irresponsibility (the need to conquer 'apathy') and cognitive incapacity (the need to teach 'citizenship'). It is my purpose here to problematise engagement by questioning its historical genealogy, its contested meanings, and its ideological functionality. Youth disengagement is a specific manifestation of a wider social preoccupation, illuminating precisely because, as in many cases when adults exhort the young to behave in certain ways, normative intentions are inadvertently revealed.

PARTICIPATORY NORMS

To engage is to act as a free moral agent. The enslaved cannot choose to engage, for they cannot disengage. Engagement is a voluntary encounter with power: a moral interaction between different dimensions within the structure of social control. Voting for a politician, joining a party or pressure group, watching news, talking politics, demonstrating on the streets, and breaking unjust laws all entail a choice to react to power rather than simply succumb to it. Such choices are partly determined by identifiable social and psychological factors, notably socio-economic status, age, gender, personal efficacy, and the extent of interpersonal networks. But they are also explained by less tangible or measurable motivations, such as moral responsibility and selective responses to chance experiences.

There are consequences to engaging with politics. To engage is to have a voice, but not necessarily to be heard. It is to count in a world where the inert are invisible, but it is also to be counted by the surveillant gaze of authority. Engaging is a risk—of being ignored, challenged, or classified. Engaging is a chore—as Oscar Wilde once quipped, the trouble with socialism is that it takes up too many evenings.

Ever since the ancient Athenians, democrats have echoed the Periclean assertion that citizens have a duty to participate:

> Our concern for our private affairs is balanced by our involvement with the affairs of the city. Even people who are mostly occupied with their own business are extremely well informed on political matters. We do not simply regard a man who does not participate in the city's life as one who just minds his own business, but as one who is good for nothing. (Warner, 1954)

Rationales and motivations for participation vary, sometimes quite inconsistently, between different actors. From the perspective of state authority, public participation in politics can serve several functions: legitimising power, informing government of grass-roots needs, educating citizens for civic behaviour, incorporating vocal minorities into the governing process, and contributing to collaborative responses to social risk and complexity. For citizens themselves, participation can be instrumental (obtaining specific outcomes), communitarian (performing social duties), or expressive (articulating cultural moods or identities.)

Since the 1950s, social scientists have attempted to define and measure political culture, with levels of public participation in formal politics providing a key criterion of good health. Almond and Verba's famous definition of 'the civic culture' as a congruence between the civic attitudes of the public and the effective working of the political system is typical of the way in which participation has been regarded as a stabilising norm (Almond and Verba, 1963).

In the case of youth participation, the normative discourse is even more pronounced. As embryonic citizens, the capacity and willingness of young people to engage politically is critical to the future quality of civic culture. Galston (1995) has identified three reasons for the necessity of youth political engagement. Firstly, it enables 'legitimate generational interests' to be articulated. Secondly, young people have a duty 'to uphold reasonably just institutions' and a 'communitarian' obligation to match responsibilities to rights. Thirdly, 'political engagement helps develop capacities that are intrinsically...important'. Although the first reason is vaguely instrumental, the other two are moral injunctions: they are about nurturing better citizens. Government-sponsored schemes to promote youth participation encourage such activities as voting, party-joining, and newspaper-reading, but discourage activities such as strike action, posting political graffiti, and resisting 'bad' laws. Governments do not simply seek to create engaged citizens; they want to produce virtuous citizens engaged in approved forms of participation (Galston, 1995).

This is where liberal anxieties begin. If participation is about adherence to norms, who sets these norms and how are they enforced? What sort of ideological constructions underlie injunctions to participate? For Rousseau, 'the basic problem was to secure the voluntary integration of individual and social action'. His enthusiasm for public participation was based upon the belief that 'as long as several men in assembly regard themselves as a single body,...the common good is everywhere apparent, and only good sense is needed to perceive it' (Watkins, 1953). The indivisibility in Rousseau's thought between individual perspectives and collective truths exposes him to the charge of being the father of 'totalitarian democracy' (Talmon, 1952). Other political thinkers have seen participation as a means of steering the uneducated masses towards a higher consciousness. J.S. Mill supported public discussion because it would help 'the manual labourer, whose employment is a routine, and whose way of life brings him in contact with no variety of impressions, circumstances or ideas' to feel for and with his fellow citizens, and becomes consciously a member of a great community (Mill, 1991, p. 328).

The liberal conception of the engaged citizen as a rationally autonomous agent in pursuit of open-ended goals is at odds with the participatory practices of most liberal democracies, in which political participation has been relegated to the function of a docile civic duty.

PARTICIPATORY PATHOLOGIES: COLLUSION AND SEDUCTION

If the dutiful passivity of liberal citizenship disappointed the expectations of some democratic theorists, the neurotic, regressive and instinctually pathological behaviour of the illiberal mob accorded precisely with critiques of what Ortega y Gasset called 'the brutal empire of the masses' (Ortega, 1930). In Orwell's *Nineteen Eighty-Four*, to participate was to enter a grotesque orgy of repressed sado-masochistic urges:

> People were leaping up and down in their places and shouting at the tops of their voices in an effort to drown the maddening bleating voice that came from the screen. The little sandy-haired woman had turned bright pink, and her mouth was opening and shutting like that of a landed fish. Even O'Brien's heavy face was flushed. He was sitting very straight in his chair, his powerful chest swelling and quivering as

though he were standing up to the assault of a wave. The dark-haired girl behind Winston had begun crying out 'Swine! Swine! Swine!' and suddenly she picked up a heavy Newspeak dictionary and flung it at the screen. It struck Goldstein's nose and bounced off; the voice continued inexorably. In a lucid moment Winston found that he was shouting with the others and kicking his heel violently against the rung of his chair. The horrible thing about the Two Minutes Hate was not that one was obliged to act a part, but, on the contrary, that it was impossible to avoid joining in. Within thirty seconds any pretence was always unnecessary. A hideous ecstasy of fear and vindictiveness, a desire to kill, to torture, to smash faces in with a sledge-hammer, seemed to flow through the whole group of people like an electric current, turning one even against one's will into a grimacing, screaming lunatic. And yet the rage that one felt was an abstract, undirected emotion which could be switched from one object to another like the flame of a blowlamp. (Orwell, 1949)

This depiction of the emboldened and impotent crowd originates in the sociological theory of Le Bon, for whom crowds represented the antithesis of personal responsibility: 'An individual in a crowd is a grain of sand amid other grains of sand, which the wind stirs up at will' (Le Bon, 1895). In *Group Psychology and the Analysis of the Ego*, Freud praised Le Bon's 'brilliant psychological character-sketch of the group mind' and asserted that 'It is only through the influence of individuals who can set an example and whom masses recognise as their leaders that they can be induced to perform the work and undergo the renunciations on which the existence of civilisation depends' (Freud, 1974 [1921]). In the decade that followed, Le Bon's fear of the irrational crowd and Freud's image of the disintegration of repressive civilisation were translated into deadly realities in the crude participatory rituals of fascism and Nazism.

While not written as a direct response to the regimes of Hitler and Stalin, *Nineteen Eighty-Four* is clearly an attempt to explain the nature of mass collusion with abusive power. It does so in the context of two problematic post-war concepts: authoritarianism and totalitarianism. The former was first explored by Lasswell in *Psychopathology and Politics* (1930), Reich in *The Mass Psychology of Fascism* (1933), and Fromm in *The Fear of Freedom* (1942) (The seminal study by Adorno et al. was published after *Nineteen Eighty-Four*.) The latter term was popularised by Sigmund Neumann's 1942 study, *Permanent Revolution: Totalitarism in the Age of International Civil War*, although it had been first brought to Orwell's attention by Peter Drucker's *The End of Economic Man: A Study of the New Totalitarianism*, first published in 1939. Both of these concepts, although they were flawed as coherent accounts of social behaviour, were to have a profound and enduring effect upon popular attitudes towards political participation.

The concept of authoritarianism is central to Orwell's account of politics. In his review of Bertrand Russell's *Power* he stated that 'Bully-worship, under various disguises, has become a universal religion' (Orwell, 1968, p. 375). The value of authoritarianism as a concept is that it goes beyond the banal circularity of observing that powerful people want power, to a social-psychological exploration of the relationship between societal forces and psychic motivations. Bettelheim's account of the psychological complicity of Nazi victims and Fromm's conception of sado-masochism as a response to social powerlessness suggest that the abuse of power had less to do with psychopathic bullying than mutual relationships of need between dominating leaders and dominated followers. In his essay on 'Raffles and Miss Blandish' (1944) Orwell observes that 'The interconnexion between sadism, masochism, success-worship, power-worship, nationalism, and totalitarianism is a huge subject whose edges have barely been scratched, and even to mention it is considered somewhat indelicate'. *Nineteen Eighty-Four* is a vehicle for the literary exploration of the symbiotic dynamics of authoritarian politics. The consequence of this dystopia was not only to add a number of rich political terms to English vocabulary—newspeak, double-think, thought police, Big Brother—but to capture for popular thought the fear of omnipotent authority that demands not only complete obedience, but unconditional love. For, to need, admire, and desire one's oppressor is what makes oppression both endurable and unbearable.

Linked to the authoritarian anxiety was the contingently post-war angst about totalitarianism, defined by Carl Friedrich as political control on the basis of a totalising ideology by a single party, usually led by a single dictator, utilising a fully developed secret police which exercises monopolistic control over mass communications, operational weapons, and all organisations (Friedrich, 1954). A key element of totalitarianism is the all-seeing scope of the state, epitomised in *Nineteen Eighty-Four* by the ubiquitous and inescapable telescreens through which people are both seen in their every movement and exposed to the incessant propaganda of Big Brother. The crimes of 'ownlife' (being alone) and 'facecrime' (improper expressions in the omnipresence of Big Brother) were indicative of a world in which 'nothing was your own except the few cubic centimetres inside your skull' (p. 24). The totalitarian notion of participation is most clearly articulated by O'Brien when he tells Winston that 'Never again will you be capable of love or friendship or joy of living or laughter or curiosity or courage or integrity. We shall squeeze you empty, and then we shall fill you with ourselves.' The abject nature of participation in such a regime is summed up by Julia's advice to Winston: 'Always yell with the crowd. That's what I say. It's the only way to be safe' (p. 108). It is the individualist's aspiration to not be squeezed empty by organisational commitment and to seek identity and security beyond the yelling of the crowd that makes contemporary non-participation feel to many young people less like a retreat into apathy than an escape from acquiescence.

After *Nineteen Eighty-Four,* popular images of mass politics were never quite the same again. Two worries became negatively associated with entreaties to participate in politics: firstly, the belief that all dealing in power, whatever its explicit rationale, is morally corrupting and psychologically destructive, and that it attracts or produces defective character types; and secondly, that even the most benign political visions can turn into totalising regimes of power, in which monitorial technologies are used to maintain public discipline, and non-participation is seen as a form of dissent and subversion. It would be far too simplistic to suggest that these anxieties led directly to a decline in political participation, but what should be recognised is their contribution to the sense of participation-as-collusion that is now a prevalent basis for disengagement from formal politics.

Orwell's Big Brother was not the only dystopian image to cast doubt on norms of mass participation. As Margaret Atwood has observed, 'The twentieth-century could be seen as a race between two versions of man-made hell—the jackbooted state totalitarianism of Orwell's *Nineteen Eighty-Four,* and the hedonistic ersatz paradise of *Brave New World,* where absolutely everything is a consumer good and human beings are engineered to be happy' (Atwood, 2003). Huxley's vision was a dystopia of seduction rather than collusion, an assault upon dignity more than freedom. Like the 'housemates' in Endemol's twenty-first century *Big Brother,* the residents of *Brave New World* had succumbed to the narcoticising tyranny of fun. For the political elite, *Big Brother* has become a byword for the superficiality and fatuity of mass culture. Bernard Crick, Orwell's biographer, describes it as 'a brilliant show for the empty mob, a cunning synthesis of game show and debased, dumbed-down documentary' (Crick, 2000). A British government minister lamented before a global conference that 'Sadly enough I can tell you that in the UK, the televised *Big Brother* produced higher voting rates than the election to the European Parliament. We must face the fact that traditional democratic channels have lost much of their ability to engage people' (Stringer, 2001).

Although Big Brother and *Big Brother* reflect common anxieties about what it means to engage with mass culture, there are significant contrasts in the techniques and technologies that they use to connect with their publics. Orwell's Big Brother was a political leviathan, exercising power through dictatorial imposition, permanent surveillance, and fear. Endemol's *Big Brother* does not exercise power in the traditional political sense. Its authority is rooted within public habits and pleasures. Its surveillance appears as a drama of performative accountability. Its strength relies not on the public's fear, but its appetite for interactivity and feelings of control. Big Brother is emblematic of a largely obsolete model of hierarchical power, whereas the interactive, multimedia spectacle of *Big Brother* hints at new ways of envisaging and practising democratic participation.

GOVERNMENT AND GOVERNMENTALITY

Although Orwell's Ministries of Truth and Love are parodies of a men-
dacious totalitarian state, they are depicted as centralised, vertical, and
hierarchical models of government that would have been familiar to most
twentieth-century observers. The more recent transition from the concept
of government to governance reflects a radical reconfiguration of political
institutions and processes. Whereas governments in the past tended to be
exercising top-down authority via a well-recognised chain of command, the
exercise of power through governance is less institutionally centralised and
more diffuse, devolved, and collaborative. The turn towards governance
has occurred for a number of complex reasons: the emergence of information and communication technologies (ICT) that transcend bureaucratic
silos; the breakdown of traditional disciplines of command and control;
the globalisation and decentring of political and economic power; and the
entry of the state into aspects of life that are not typically political. The
organising force of governance is the network, but the energising force is
governmentality: reliance upon everyday habits and codes of unenforced
behaviour by a self-regulating citizenry.

The notion of governmentality, as first used by Foucault (1991) and theoretically developed by Rose (1999), describes the ways in which political
elites define, for themselves and others, the rationalities of governing social
conduct. These rationalities are observable at the molecular level of daily
conduct, where people act on the basis that behaviour must be governed and
self-governed. It is the self-disciplining nature of governmentality, operating at the levels of both psychological motivation and social interaction,
which makes it of particular interest to theorists of participation. For, if the
activity of citizenship entails a psychic embrace of the ideologies and protocols of governance, the need for coercive structures of governing diminish to the point of virtual obsolescence. If, for example, social ostracism
can perform roles hitherto reserved for judges and courtrooms, the need
for official and officious law enforcement diminishes. If 'neighbourhood
watch' can produce better results than policemen on the beat and self-help
groups can provide more valuable support for the socially excluded than
government bureaucrats, what need is there for the interventionist state? If
people are prepared to watch and watch out for one another, Big Brother
becomes redundant. But the condition for this devolution of responsibility
to 'active citizens' and 'active communities' is that they possess the moral
resources to govern in accordance with overarching rationalities of governmentality. The observation, nurturing, and collective shaping of such moral
resources and rationalities of governmentality is a key democratic imperative for twenty-first century democracy.

Big Brother can be seen as a laboratory for the observation of social and
moral interaction. A dozen people are put into a house filled with twenty

to thirty surveillance cameras. They are under the control of a disembodied voice called Big Brother who sets them tasks, punishes their disobedience, and hears their private confessions. Their one common objective is to win the support of the viewing and voting public—or, more accurately, to avoid their displeasure. The audience is invited to participate in resolving a number of questions. Which housemates are strategising and which are 'being themselves?' Who leads and who follows? How do they deal with anti-social and dissembling behaviour? How willingly do they obey, or even anticipate, the commands of Big Brother? What happens when the environment is altered by the provision of alcohol or the heating being turned up or the food supply limited? How far can private and illicit relationships survive when transparency is almost total? These are demanding and stimulating questions—perhaps more so than those which citizens are called upon to think about when making political choices. In response to the accusation that they are passive voyeurs of a dumbed-down cultural spectacle, *Big Brother* viewers see themselves as employing sophisticated skills of emotional intelligence and moral evaluation.(Coleman, 2003). At the same time, viewers are witnessing and making judgements about the interactions of people whose 'ordinary' origins make them in certain ways representative of the wider public. Just as participants in formal politics are urged to watch potential leaders in ritualised television debates and judge their fitness for office, the *Big Brother* audiences are called upon to judge the fitness of citizens like themselves for the consequences of sociality. Whereas Orwell's Big Brother imposed discipline upon citizens through a coercive state, *Big Brother* turns good behaviour into a permanent game: an ongoing test of social propriety.

SURVEILLANCE AND PERFORMANCE

Linked to the emergence of governmentality are new forms and functions of surveillance. In his classical study of nineteenth-century prisons, which he saw as a microcosm of the panoptic state, Foucault stated that 'The inmate must never know whether he is being looked at any one moment; but he must be sure that he may always be so' (Foucault, 1979, p. 201). Foucauldian surveillance is always associated with the curtailment of individual freedom.

With the rise of compact, affordable, mass produced technologies, such as camcorders and 3G phones, designed to enable personal recording of everyday events, surveillance has come to be seen as a form of positive expression. To record one's own digital account via a blog or vlog is to limit dependence upon the lens of the mass media as a portal to social reality. Personal media democratise surveillance in two ways: they extend the notion of accountability and open up opportunities for performative autonomy.

In the context of the panoptic state, accountability meant being accounted for: being counted, recognised, approved, and integrated. Interactive accountability enables the relatively powerless to hold power to account. The video recording of the LA police beating up Rodney King; the blog produced by the Baghdad resident, Salam Pax, before and during the bombing of Iraq; the incriminating pictures of soldiers torturing civilians after the occupation of Iraq, are examples of such democratic surveillance.

In *Big Brother* permanent surveillance is a route to fame and prestige. The public trusts people it has seen that much and that often. Stars line up to enter the 'celebrity' version of the show, sometimes as a way of boosting flagging careers, often as a way of building a unique relationship with the public. As we shall discuss later in this paper, some politicians are looking to the *Big Brother* format as a way of regaining public sympathy.

In another sense, surveillance technologies become a conduit for account-giving, creating space for ordinary people to represent themselves. Popular TV shows record the public falling off ladders, crashing their cars, learning to drive, emigrating to Australia, cleaning their houses, coping with terminal illnesses, surviving on desert islands, and swapping wives. Even where the cameras are inconspicuous, these shows are always performative events, in the sense that all social action is in some sense performed. In *Big Brother*, public exposure is given to 'private' performances, which originate as offstage discourses (Scott refers to them as 'hidden transcripts'), but end up as televisual spectacles.

FEAR AND INTERACTIVITY

Orwell's *Nineteen Eighty-Four* inspired fear in its readers. In his publisher's review, Fredric Warburg observed that 'This is amongst the most terrifying books I have ever read'. Diana Trilling, reviewing the novel in *The Nation,* stated that it 'exacerbates the emotions almost beyond endurance'. After the live dramatisation of *Nineteen Eighty-Four* on BBC television on 12 December 1954 *The Times* commented that it had 'made many thinking people uncomfortable' and a motion tabled in the House of Commons by five Tory MPs deplored 'the tendency, evident in recent British Broadcasting Corporation television programmes, notably on Sunday evenings, to pander to sexual and sadistic tastes'. In all of these responses, Orwell's dystopia was seen in the context of a simplistic stimulus–response relationship with its audience. Faced with the horror of a totalitarian people, the audience was immobilised by fear. Between Big Brother and *Big Brother* the control–reception balance between media producers and audiences has changed. The public is now offered an unprecedented degree of interactive power over mediated events.

At one important level, *Big Brother* reflects the principles of representative democracy. Those inside the house—be it the *Big Brother* house or the House of Commons—must present themselves to the public in the best light possible. Public opinion about who should be in and who should be out is sovereign. This opinion is aggregated from vast numbers of individual opinions. But unlike the representative democratic process, which is often seen by the *Big Brother* audience as opaque, inaccessible, and dull, participating in the *Big Brother* process is simple, entertaining, and has visible consequences. In a world where pushing buttons tends to be followed by manifest consequences, interacting with a game show is more like shopping online than walking to a polling station on a rainy day to cast a possibly wasted vote.

The global success of *Big Brother* owes less to its format as a game-show-cum-post-documentary (Corner, 2004) than its shrewd and innovative use of interactive multimedia. Remote viewers of *Big Brother* can participate in the regular eviction votes via their phones and text messaging; watch live, 24-hour streaming on digital TV and online; join online discussions and receive the latest news from the website; receive e-mail and SMS alerts; as well as watching the nightly edited TV package. The ethos of the show is that the public decides—a public comprised of millions of individual viewers who come together through technological aggregation and a pervasive network of daily conversations. (I walked through the shopping streets of Oxford the morning after the infamous episode in *Big Brother 5* when the police had been called into the house to prevent violent disorder, and lost count of the conversations about it that I overheard. It was a week before the European election, but nobody seemed to be talking about that.)

Interactivity is a much contested concept, but its attraction would appear to relate to its convenient technologising of hitherto onerous exchanges and the extent to which it passes control from communication centres to dispersed networks of users. Although interactivity might in some cases be 'a superficial sham leading...us into thinking we're taking part, we're having a say' (Iannucci, 2004), its appeal lies in the tangible relationship that is engendered between the remote individual and the drama of the main event. Technically, one is simply pushing a button or texting a vote; culturally, one is creating an instantaneous connection between the isolated individual and the meaningful aggregate. One is part of the show, able to play a part in determining its script and outcome.

DEMOCRATISING POLITICAL ENGAGEMENT

The ecology of politics has changed, but the rules of engagement remain the same. Hegemonic appeals to play the new game using the old rules deserve to be contested, for the rhetoric of re-engagement is misconceived in its implicit assumption that the terms of traditional political engagement are either sustainable or desirable from a democratic perspective. Much of what has constituted political participation in the past—voting in irregular elections; submitting periodic requests to elected representatives; joining mass, centralised parties; following politics in the press or broad-cast media as a spectator sport—is only compatible with a narrow and parsimonious conception of political democracy. Even some of the more autonomous strategies of participation—joining pressure groups, signing petitions, going on demonstrations—are rooted in pre-industrial modes of organisation and communication. Perhaps the public is behaving rationally in disengaging from such obsolete channels of expression.

A strategic alternative to exhorting and cajoling people—particularly the young—to join in the political process would be to develop viable new models of political participation, shaped around aspects of popular culture that currently generate public enthusiasm. Examples of such models might be football supporters' clubs, neighbourhood associations, music fanzines, reading groups, or medical self-help networks. Drawing upon Eliasoph's important recognition that political opinions are often not articulated in public for fear of appearing 'political' (Eliasoph, 1998) and Scott's obser-vation that the views and activities of the powerless are often submerged within 'hidden transcripts' of repressed expression, the proposal is to seek participatory energies in those places and spaces where people feel that they are safely and meaningfully engaged (Scott, 1990).

Participation in *Big Brother* is but one example of seeking participa-tory energies in popular culture. The suggestion here is neither that *Big Brother* somehow personifies contemporary popular culture, nor that political democracy should be adapted to reflect a game show. The critical research questions concern the composition, character, and motivation of the *Big Brother* audience and lessons that these might provide for political participation. My choice of *Big Brother* as a model for political participa-tion results from survey and qualitative research over three years into the *Big Brother* audience. In 2001–2002 I conducted five surveys designed to measure and contrast the socio-demographic characteristics and attitudes to politics and political engagement of 716 viewers (BBs), who regularly watched *Big Brother* and participated in its weekly 'eviction' votes, but had little or no interest in politics and 817 Political Junkies (PJs), who were very interested in politics (as identified by regular viewing of political coverage on TV or regular political discussion with friends or family) but did not watch *Big Brother*. In addition to the surveys, the two groups were invited to respond to open-ended questions about the nature of politics and about one another. Over 500 written responses were received (Coleman, 2003). In 2004 I conducted three surveys of regular *Big Brother* viewers and vot-ers, designed to find out about their voting habits and explore the correla-tion between support for a specific candidate and attribution of a range of character qualities to each candidate. During the 2005 UK general election I conducted a series of ten surveys of regular *Big Brother* viewers and vot-ers, designed to explore their experience of a political campaign and to encourage them to reflect upon the contrasts between voting to appoint a government and voting to evict a game-show contestant. The richness of the data arising from this research provides empirical support for the strategic recommendations outlined below (Coleman, 2005). These proposals for a more culturally democratised approach to political engagement should be read as principles intended to guide policy rather than any kind of policy blueprint.

DEMOGRAPHIES OF EXCLUSION

Firstly, it is necessary to ask who is participating and who is not. Political participation is largely dominated by people who are old rather than young and male rather than female. The average age of Labour and Conservative party members is over 60; only 5% of Labour Party members are under 35. According to the Electoral Commission, 'women are less likely than men to participate in campaign-orientated activities, such as contacting a politician and donating money to, working for, or being a member of, a political party.' Until 1997 there were more MPs called John in the House of Commons than there were women.

Many participatory opportunities, such as attending party meetings or polling stations, visiting political websites or standing in the street collecting signatures for a petition, are uninspiring and alienating for demographic groups comprising the majority of the population. The timing, location, language, and style of many political events make them more attractive to older males than younger females. By contrast, the profile of *Big Brother* participants is overwhelmingly female (72% of BBs in the 2002 survey were female, while 68% of PJs were male) and mainly young (36% of BBs were under 30 and 71% are under 40, whereas 64% of PJs were over 50 and 41% were over 60) (Coleman, 2003).

Rebalancing the demography of participation is essential if democracy is to engage more than unrepresentative minorities of the demos. Historically, included groups have resisted attempts to make participation more attractive to hitherto excluded sections of the population. In the late nineteenth century appeals to new working-class voters were seen as demeaning to political debate. In the early twentieth century newly-enfranchised women were accused of feminising the political agenda. Efforts to engage alienated youth are bound to be dismissed by some political 'insiders' as dumbing down. When the BBC published the results of its review of political coverage in 2002, in which it argued for a more accessible political discourse, the *Daily Telegraph*'s (2003) response was to observe that 'it is the telly folk who have decided there is a crisis in democracy and it is they who are calling the shots, not the reluctant politicians. Broadcasters are in the driving seat and politicians have been following like reluctant goats tethered to an accelerating bandwagon over which they appear to have no control'. Extending the demographic reach of democratic engagement is not simply a matter of increasing the numbers participating, but of making each individual who contributes to those numbers feel needed, wanted, and appreciated (Rogers, 2004).

TECHNOLOGIES OF PARTICIPATION

With the exception of online activism, which is still marginal in most democracies, most forms of political participation have hardly changed within the last half century. Former Leader of the House of Commons, Robin Cook's observation that 'for anybody under 40, polling day is the only point in the year when they actually see a pencil stub, and that's probably why it's tied to a piece of string, because it's so rare and they might pocket it as a souvenir' captures well the archaic mechanics of contemporary political participation (Cook, 2002).

Interactive ICT, when used imaginatively, can provide users with a richer sense of involvement in events. Voting in *Big Brother* tends to be an integrated part of a wider cultural engagement, which includes visiting the website (56% of viewers), engaging in online discussion in the web forum (16%), and talking to friends and workmates about the series (76%) (Coleman, 2005).

There are likely to be three consequences of more interactive political participation. Firstly, information costs will be reduced. Non-participation is often the result of not knowing about available opportunities or being able to make political choices. As information becomes easier to collect, challenge, and disseminate virally, the threshold of entry to political activity will be lowered. Secondly, interactive communications will give rise to more sociable participatory spaces in which people can join in at times of their own choosing and meet others in a safe and egalitarian environment. Thirdly, because the emergence of leaderless and inclusive communication networks is compatible with the emerging trends of globalisation, they will allow social activism to take place in new ways (Bennett, 2005). In this sense, one can at least speak of 'the vulnerable democratic potential' of interactive ICT (Blumler and Coleman, 2001).

SURVEILLANCE AS ACCOUNTABILITY

As argued above, although surveillance is usually associated with illiberal intentions, and even when initiated as a reciprocal relationship rarely entails symmetrical power relationships, there are some circumstances in which surveillance technologies can be used to hold power to account. It is clear from open-ended responses to the 2002 survey of *Big Brother* viewers that many BBs regard permanent surveillance of political representatives as a key democratic check on power:

Maybe it might help if politicians were to spend a long period in the public gaze—their ambitions, subterfuges, deceptions, etc., would slowly be revealed. (Survey respondent)

The main difference between *Big Brother* and MPs is the fact that the contestants in *Big Brother* were able to be watched 24 hours a day. MPs are only really in the public eye when in parliament. This leads to an element of distrust, as we do not know what MPs are 'up to' when we can't 'see' them. (Survey respondent)

The *Big Brother* contestants did not always realise they were being watched every minute of the day and as a consequence performed certain actions thinking they could not be detected. Some of them were extremely two-faced, siding with whoever they believed would further their ambition at that time. They were all found out and received their just rewards. One can easily see the similarities between MPs and the BB contestants. Perhaps MPs would do well to heed the lessons taught in the BB series. (Survey respondent)

The democratic potential of surveillance depends not simply on making the exercise of power transparent, but the public's ability to dissect power in its own way, according to its own judgements. In this sense, democratic surveillance assumes a rhizomatic quality, weakening the hold that politicians and other power-holders have over their own images and the aspects of themselves that are exposed for public scrutiny and consumption.

THE SIGNIFICANCE OF AFFECTIVITY

In the light of what has been described as the 'affective turn' in social science, a number of new studies have explored the symbolic and emotive construction of citizenship. Contrary to the clinical depiction of the citizen in rational choice theory, citizens can be regarded as more than atomised bundles of interests and preferences in search of instrumental representation. Much of what it means to be a civic actor depends upon the ambivalences of self-identity and reflexive apprehensions of power and its diverse narratives. Models of citizenship constructed around people's instrumental interests and normative duty to participate have tended to miss the experiential and affective elements of what it means to be a sentient social participant, as opposed to a political consumer or free-floating ego.

In *Big Brother* there is a shameless interest in evaluating affectively registered characteristics such as authenticity, trustworthiness, integrity, honour, and decency. Critics of such judgements refer to *Big Brother* as a vulgar popularity contest based upon emotion rather than rationality. *Big Brother* participants defend themselves in two ways: firstly, by arguing that the kind of 'emotional intelligence' required to make character judgements is more sophisticated, nuanced, and multi-dimensional than the choices entailed in adhering to a political manifesto; and secondly, by pointing to the hypocrisy of the politically engaged, who routinely make judgements based on the characters of political leaders. The implication is that political competition would be improved by more explicit and elevated talk about who can and cannot be trusted. A series of surveys during the 2004 *Big Brother* series showed that certain qualities—namely, respect and trustworthiness—counted far more voters' decisions about who to vote for than others—such perception of candidates' wisdom or likelihood of getting on in the world (Coleman, 2005). The elitist response that it would be disastrous for formal politics to take such judgements seriously is disingenuous, for politicians and party strategists are already deeply interested in these judgements, at least in private. Indeed, given that citizens are sentient and emotional as well as rational and instrumental (and often at the same time), there is something profoundly undemocratic about seeking to exclude such forms of opinion from the democratic process.

PLAYFUL PARTICIPATION

Politics is pervaded by what Nichols has called (in a different context) 'a culture of sobriety' (Nichols, 1991). There is something buttoned-up, pompous, and arcane about the way that most people imagine they are supposed to participate in politics. The most common term used by young people to describe politics is *boring*. To some extent this is inevitable, because fair and constitutionally-established procedures, often addressing complex, parochial, or technical issues, are intrinsically arid. Arguably, it is good for social stability if politics is relatively dull.

But the failure of political culture to adopt entertaining participatory forms is not inevitable. It is partly a consequence of the demographic concentration of older males, whose tastes are not inspiring to younger females; partly a result of lack of imagination in using new technologies that could help to invigorate politics; but partly also an effect of an over-rationalist, sometimes morally puritanical conception of politics that has become dominant in the past fifty years. It was not always so. Songs, social events, carnivals, clubs, and inspirational oratory were once integral features of democratic culture. To engage in politics was to enter a cultural community. As politics has become more managerial and consumerist and less ideologically partisan, its internal dramas have come to resemble boardroom feuds more than moral crusades. (And when managerial-consumerist politics occasionally pretends to be crusading it comes across as hectoring and insincere.)

The *Big Brother* model of participation has been touted as a way of introducing an element of fun into politics. In Australia, Channel 7 is planning to run a series called *Vote For Me* in which the public nominates independent candidates for election to the Senate. Channel 7's advertising for the series states that

> We want to hear your policy ideas to see if you've got what it takes to be a Federal Senator. Our viewers will select our best applicants by SMS and telephone voting and *Sunrise* will follow the selected applicants' campaigns every step of the way up to the election.

Barry Harradine, an independent Senator for Tasmania, and the longest-standing Senator in Australian history, has argued that Channel 7 is 'reducing the Senate to a game show' and that '*Vote for Me* could just turn into a popularity contest where one or more of the six candidates is elected purely because they have become TV personalities' (*Online Opinion,* 12 July, 2004*)*. In Canada, a new reality show has recruited three former Primer Ministers to judge contestants on their political performances. While there are significant regulatory issues to be debated in relation to such projects, it is unhelpful for debate to proceed on the basis that certain participatory activities, such as election campaigns, are sacrosanct. In may be that democracy entails a trade-off between the sobriety of settled tradition and the appeal of more entertaining, even if riskier, modes of engagement.

ENGAGING YOUTH AND ENGAGING WITH YOUTH

The etymology of engagement is revealing. The earliest English usage of the word was in the context of pledging or betrothing one's allegiance, entering into an agreement for service, or being bound by a contract or formal promise. In short, there is an historical relationship between being engaged and being bound to someone else. Only in more recent usage has engagement come to be associated with the active and autonomous choice to commit to a cause or activity. In any attempt to sell political activism to young people, an honest distinction must be made between seeking to engage them, in the sense of entangling or ensnaring them in obligatory relationships, and engaging *with* them, in a collaborative, mutually respecting sense.

Engaging *with* young people entails a willingness to enter their spaces on their terms; to communicate in mutually accessible language, without condescension; and to produce a shared political agenda, without trying to impose conventional norms. In short, it involves engaging with calls for new conceptions of active citizenship and democratic participation. Bang argues that models of participation should recognise the countless 'lay citizens' who are 'free to be more everyday, indirect, emotional and spontaneous in their conventional communication and therefore less systematic, articulate, programmatic, risk assessing etc than is required for participating in the strategic type of communication characteristic of authorities' (Bang, 2000,

p. 15). In her writing on citizenship, Eliasoph seeks to transcend the 'image of political conversation that disconnects it from everyday life, makes political conversation seem to be a rare, scary activity that should happen only in special circumstances, that will disrupt meetings and rip friends apart and intimidate neighbours and evacuate meetings of healthy community volunteers and ruin good jokes and not do any good.' (Eliasoph, 1998, p. 2) In observing how people engage in talk about child rearing or appropriate content for library story hours, Eliasoph draws attention to the implicitly political threads that pervade spaces and moments of apparent political disengagement. Bang proposes a focus 'on the day-to-day experiences and actions of laypeople' in order to 'find political spaces of potential public relevance' (2000, p. 7).

As in my own research on *Big Brother*, Bang, Eliasoph, and others are seeking alternative spaces of engagement in which the discreet articulations and energies of the ostensibly inert can be discovered. Often, such alternative spaces are Goffmanesque backstages in which hidden transcripts are produced.

In the most recent UK series of *Big Brother*, views were expressed and conflicts arose in relation to the rights of asylum seekers, the identity of transsexuals, anarchism, the power of Big Brother to withhold a contestant's suitcase, and the morality of wasting food. These debates spread into the official *Big Brother* web forum which was flooded with tens of thousands of messages, the form and style of which was radically different from that of conventional online political discussion. Engaging in, and with, such discussion is a challenge that the political class has yet to take up. Perhaps the politically active are being disingenuous in their enthusiasm for engaging with youth, when what they really want is for youth to be engaged. Indeed, perhaps the more ambitious objective is not to engage youth in politics, but to engage the political class with youth.

REFERENCES

Adorno, T., Frenkel-Brunswick, E., Levinson, D., and Nevitt, S. (1950) *The Authoritarian Personality*. New York: Harper & Row.

Almond, G. and Verba, S. (1963) *The Civic Culture: Political Attitudes and Democracy in Five Nations*. Princeton, NJ: Princeton University Press.

Atwood, M. (2003) 'Orwell and me', *The Guardian* 16 June.

Bang, H. (2000) 'The everyday maker: building political rather than social capital', in P. Dekker and E. Uslaner, eds., *Social Capital and Participation in Every Day Life*. London: Routledge.

Bennett, L. (2005) 'Communicating global activism: some strengths and vulnerabilities of networked politics', in W. van de Donk, B. D. Loader, P. G. Nixon, and D. Rucht, eds., *Cyberprotest: New Media, Citizens and Social Movements*. London: Routledge.

Blumler, J. and Coleman, S. (2001) *Realising Democracy Online: A Civic Commons in Cyberspace*. IPPR/Citizens Online: http://www.citizensonline.org. uk/site/media/documents/925_Realising%20Democracy%20Online.pdf.

Coleman, S. (2003) *A Tale of Two Houses: The House of Commons, the Big Brother House and the People at Home.* London: Hansard Society/Channel Four.

Coleman, S. (2006) 'How the Other Half Vote: Big Brother Viewers and the 2005 General Election', *International Journal of Cultural Studies*, 9(4): 457z–479

Cook, R (2002) 'Intent on change: radical Robin returns to the fray: Robin Cook interviewed by Jackie Ashley'. *The Guardian*, 7 January.

Corner, J. (2004) 'Foreword', in E. Mathijs and J. Jones, eds., *Big Brother International: Formats, Critics and Publics.* London: Wallflower Press.

Crick, B. (2000) 'Big Brother belittled: George Orwell's warning has been treated with cynical contempt', *The Guardian*, August 19.

Daily Telegraph (2003) *'Is big brother the future of British government'?* 8 June.

Drucker, P. (1940) *The End of Economic Man: A Study of the New Totalitarianism.* London: Basic Books; Heinemann.

Eliasoph, N. (1998) *Avoiding Politics: How Americans Produce Apathy in Everyday Life.* Cambridge: Cambridge University Press.

Foucault, M. (1979) *Discipline and Punish.* New York: Vintage Books.

Foucault, M. (1991) 'Governmentality', eds. Burchell, Gordan, and Miller, in *The Foucault Effect: Studies in Governmentality.* Hemel Hempstead: Harvester Wheatsheaf.

Freud, S., (1953–74) *The Standard Edition of the Works of Sigmund Freud,* ed. James Strachey. London: Hogarth.

Friedrich, C. (1954) *Totalitarianism.* New York: The Universal Library.

Fromm, E. (1941) *The Fear of Freedom.* London: Routledge & Kegan Paul

Galston, W.A. (1995) 'Liberal virtues and the formation of civic character,' in Mary Ann Glendon and David Blankenhorn, eds., *Seedbeds of Virtue.* Lanham, MD: Madison Books

Harradine, B. (2004) *Online Opinion,* 12 July 2004.

Iannucci, A. (2004) 'Poke, prod, press or push...it's your choice', *Sunday Times*, 24 April.

Lasswell, H. (1930) *Psychopathology and Politics.* Chicago: University of Chicago Press.

Le Bon, G. (1895) *The Crowd: A Study of the Popular Mind.* London: Transaction. (1995 edition)

Mill, J.S. (1991) *John Stuart Mill On Liberty and Other Essays,* ed. John Gray. Oxford: Oxford University Press.

Neumann, S. (1942) *Permanent Revolution: Totalitarism in the Age of International Civil War.* London: Pall Mall Press.

Nichols, J. (1991) *Representing Reality.* Bloomington: Indiana University Press.

Ortega y Gasset, J. (1930) *The Revolt of the Masses.* New York: Norton. (1993 edition)

Orwell, G. (1944) 'Raffles and Miss Blandish', *Horizon.*

Orwell, G. (1949) *Nineteen Eighty-Four, a Novel.* London: Secker and Warburg.

Orwell, G. (1968) *The Collected Essays: Journalism and Letters of George Orwell. An Age Like This (Volume 1),* eds. S. Orwell and I. Angus. London: Secker and Warburg.

Reich, W. (1933) *The Mass Psychology of Fascism.* New York: Farrar, Straus, and Giroux.

Rogers, B. (ed.) (2004) *Lonely Citizens,* the Report of the IPPR Working Party on Active Citizenship. London: Institute for Public Policy Research.

Rose, N. (1999) *Powers of Freedom.* Cambridge: Cambridge University Press.

Scott, J (1990) *Domination and the Arts of Resistance: Hidden Transcripts. New Haven, CT:* Yale University Press.

Stringer, G. (2001) 'Putting government online, bringing citizens online', *Third Global Forum—Fostering Democracy and Development Through e-Government*, Naples, Italy, 15–17 March.

Talmon, J. (1952) *The Origins of Totalitarian Democracy*. Harmondsworth: Middlesex: Penguin Books. (1986 edition)

Trilling, D. (1949) 'Review of *Nineteen Eighty Four*',*The Nation*, 8 June.

Warner, R. (translator) (1954) *Thucydides' History of the Peloponnesian War*. Harmondsworth, Middlesex: Penguin.

Watkins, F. (1953) *Rousseau: Political Writings*. Edinburgh: Thomas Nelson.

3 Changing life courses, citizenship, and new media

The impact of reflexive biographization

Henk Vinken[1]

DE-STANDARDIZED LIFE COURSES

Life course developments are crucial for young people's contemporary forms of civic engagement. Life courses are about discrete transitions in people's lives, such as the transition from school to work, from childlessness to parenthood, from being excluded from voting to being able to vote. Life course regimes in advanced societies have changed fundamentally. During the late industrial or 'Fordist-welfare state phase' (from 1955 to around 1973), life courses became standardized: there was a male breadwinner, a nuclear family, and early marriage, and with standardized transitions from one stage to the next. There were distinct life phases of schooling (stable contract), employment, and retirement; with covered risks (sickness, disability, old age); a linear increase in wages and savings over the life course; and, from a subjective point of view, a life course orientation directed at progression and accumulation, and conformity to a (gendered) division of roles both in the public and private sphere (Mayer, 2001). Identities in this ideal type life course regime description were stable and well-defined or, perhaps better, one-dimensional (i.e., either private or public).

In the post-industrial or post-Fordist life course regime we witness increasing differentiation and heterogeneity as transitions are delayed, prolonged, and there is increased age variance. Interruptions in education and work are normal, are even part of the institutional framework in which periods of on-the-job learning, other types of a time-out (caretaking in the home or in the wider family or world travel), and temporary job contracts are regulated. We found in a study within the Dutch context that work itself is not stable, not in terms of lifelong commitments to one type of job or employer, and not in terms of guaranteed cumulative, progressive growth (Ester and Vinken, 2000, 2001). Collective social provisions, including pension entitlements at a given age are under threat. The late-industrial clear-cut gender roles are contested, at least at the cultural level. It is regarded as a normal if not compulsory choice for women to work outside the home all their lives. Not working outside the home (and 'just' being a housewife) is a choice that has become hard to support. Although the problems are far from being exclusively modern, combining paid work out-side the home with family life is in reality even harder for today's women both because of gender roles in contemporary families and because in many societies governments only reluctantly invest in daycare facilities.

Finally, we also found that with the rise of ICT and the 24-hour society, distinctions between work and non-work time are blurred. This of course influences the very idea of a transition from a non-working to a work-ing life and again to a non-working life (Ester and Vinken, 2000, 2001; Vinken and Ester, 2001). Increasingly these types of developments, pri-marily highlighting rising insecurities and unpredictabilities, particularly in the domains of work and the economy, and of family and social life, have inspired authors in the realm of civic engagement. Bennett (1998), for instance, dwells on these types of notions when explaining the rise among younger people of lifestyle politics at the expense of politics based on stable group formations. Of course, some of the same arguments can be found in Bennett's chapter in this volume when discussing the characteristics of the Actualizing Citizen. As I will indicate more thoroughly later in this chapter, there is also a strong link between these rising insecurities related to profound life course changes and Coleman's BB's (see Coleman in this volume), the mostly younger generation members who prefer to participate in *Big Brother* and not in traditional politics.

In short, sociologists agree with the idea that since the mid-1970s, life courses in late-modern societies have become de-standardized (e.g., Fuchs, 1983; Held, 1986; Kohli, 1985; Mayer, 2000, 2001, 2004; Heinz and Mar-shall, 2003). The traditional three-phased life course model is believed to have lost ground in these societies (i.e., first a period of preparation and education, then a time of work and family life, and then, finally, years of rest and disengagement from society). Life courses have changed. In terms of timing, it is clear that some people postpone many transitions (e.g., hav-ing children) while they experience certain transitions earlier and earlier (e.g., having intimate relationships). The sequential order of transitions is changing as well, so it seems; for instance, we see people starting a full-time course of study after retirement, having children before marriage, or having a 'real' job before having finished their education. Moreover, transitions seem to have become 'reversible': choices people have made are revoked and replaced by other choices. For example, after a short career in the working world, some 'realize' that becoming a student (again) might be more rewarding. The combined result of all these factors is that con-temporary people experience transitions at different moments in time, and thus at any given point, more people of similar ages are in very different life phases.[2]

My argument here is that the de-standardization of the life course goes hand in hand with a process of reflexive biographization of the life course, a process with key consequences for younger people's ideas on identity, citizenship, and democratic engagement. Moreover, interactive media are especially crucial in the process. It is argued that a biography of citizenship is produced, characterized by the focus on change and challenge, and played out in the leisure and consumption domain using interactive media, which help build generational consciousness among younger people in advanced societies. In this chapter I hope to lay out some elements that may help to draw up a future research agenda, particularly for empirical studies regarding the democratic engagement of young people. These elements take into account that young people today live in a world in which life courses are biographized and a world, therefore, that encourages engagement in a wide variety of life domains and a broad range of social networks, and for which the tools and platforms of the new media in particular are a condition sine qua non.

REFLEXIVE BIOGRAPHIZATION

According to German social scientist Hermann Veith (2002), socialization is changing and giving rise to the process of reflexive biographization of the life course. Socialization, he argues, is no longer a matter of *Vergesellschaftung* (individuation by social integration). It is reversed and can only be understood as a process of subjective option-observation by individuals imagining their own path and taking a self-directed route to integrate into society and live the future life they wish to live. In other words, socialization shifted from developing individuality by taking part in society, to, regardless of 'real' participation, developing competences to imagine one's own future and to imagine one's personal choices by selecting from the seemingly ever growing number of available options for participating in society. This shift in socialization may seem plausible, particularly for individualizing societies where classic institutions and their representatives seem unable, or at least highly reluctant in their communications towards younger people, to determine, direct, and control the choices young people (should) make. The emphasis is on a battery of psychological strongholds, on first developing individuality, building self-esteem and personality, discovering one's true inner self, unraveling one's own unique motives, before making definite choices, and especially before making choices that pin people down on an irreversible trajectory.

The point is not that this is not the whole story and that it denies that people are directed, determined, and controlled by institutions (e.g., school, church, family, neighbourhood); that they undergo true-felt constraints from the real social categorizations they are part of (class, gender, education); and that they are dependent on previous choices they themselves and the ones they interact with have made (the so-called 'path' and 'other'— dependencies in the life course). Rather, people, at least in individualizing societies, are increasingly less willing to acknowledge and value these types of outside control, direction, and determination. Interpreting and legitimizing one's choices with this outside dependency perspective is what runs against the culture of individualism (Elchardus, 1999).

Veith argues that the consequence of the changing focus of socialization is that the life course undergoes what he terms a 'reflexive biographization'. People's biography or their individual paths through life, have become the central theme on which people focus in their life course. Again, rather than actual participation in society in the conventional sense, what is central is to take up different roles in life itself, the projection of one's future biography, one's plans for one's future, the options themselves that one may or may not explore, the consequences as well of choosing any of the multitude of options; these are the themes that take up the bulk of energy people spend today. To put it in modernist dichotomous terms: in the late-industrial era, people participated in society (went to work, got married, had children, etc.), and by doing so they learned to project the next steps to take in life following each stage; they became aware of the life plan that revealed itself to them, and were confronted with the consequences of choices they made or forgot to make. This way they learnt what it was they had wanted from life (and what in reality they had received from life), and what their own strong and weak points were or the nature of their own individuality. In post-Fordist days people seem to first focus on who they are, or better, who they want to become; they focus on making a list first of both their weak and strong points, to try to predict consequences of choices they want/do not want to make, to explore an overall plan of life, before even participating. Participation (work, marriage, parenthood, and citizenship) itself is postponed, in other words, or, and I will get back to this later, participation is at best seen as a temporary 'challenge' so long as it of the type that keeps options open to other, new, yet unimagined forms of participation.[3]

The key word is *reflexivity*, which is first of all a process of self-confrontation with the unplanned, unmanageable, and unintended elements of one's life, and therefore seems to build much more on non-knowledge (what we don't know) than on knowledge (what we know).[4] This differentiation is relevant for the idea of reflexivity competences. Investments in planning, organizing, evaluating, and re-adjusting one's life course are likely to deal with just that part that is hardest to grasp: the unknown elements of one's future life course. Hence, competences for reflexivity not only include abilities or skills such as planning, evaluation, or adjustment, but also the capacity to continuously monitor one's thoughts and actions, to test and retest how one is doing at any given moment, and thus repeatedly to look at and validate one's initial grounds and reasons for one's thoughts and actions, to reformulate and change these if necessary, given new information or changed circumstances. The need, urge, and ability to stay constantly in touch with one's thoughts and actions results in a knowledge creating process, However, this increasingly takes place under the well-recognized condition that one's knowledge horizon will always

fall short, thus acknowledging that one's life course as well as one's competences will never be definitely finalized and fully developed.

Another basic principle of reflexivity is self-destruction (i.e., leaving previous accumulated experiences behind whenever necessary). People should
be willing and able to abruptly part from a given route in their biography
and take on a completely new one, leaving everything behind and taking nothing with them, comparable to some sort of scorched earth military policy. The late modern life narrative is therefore more like a set of
seemingly unrelated short stories of unexpected and unplanned twists and
turns into an unknown if not unknowable future, than it is an account of
one chain of well-designed, well-planned, logically associated, and neatly
stacked life events and rational choices.

Reflexive biographization of the life course itself is a process resulting
from forces of structure and agency.[5] On the one hand, people, young or
old, are increasingly forced to take their lives in their own hands, and are
thus going to lead a more biographized life course and to develop reflexive
competences. On the other hand, people of all ages, but perhaps more so
younger people, as I aim to show below, are seeking ways to control their
own particular future, thus increasingly focusing on their own biography
and investing in developing reflexive competences.

REFLEXIVE GENERATION

As can be seen in the chapters by Bennett and Coleman in this volume,
there is an increasing awareness that younger people have different citizenship perceptions from those of older people.[6] The generational perspective
in sociology, so it can be argued, builds on *reflexivity*. The reflexivity of
those who, in their formative years, have experienced disruptive socio-his-
torical events or discontinuous change in society is central in a sociological
view of generations. It was Karl Mannheim (1928/1929), who first framed
generations in a sociological way. It is surprising to note that present-day
social science has drifted away from his notions; that is, from the purely
sociological notions of generations. Though the generational perspective
is widely used in many value and life chance studies, methodologically the
'intergenerational' in these studies is usually restricted to comparing different
birth cohorts. A crucial sociological notion emphasized by Karl Mannheim
has been lost along the way. It is the notion that a generation is not simply
a numerical clustering of birth cohorts, but a group of contemporaries who
share a sense of *belonging* to a generation. They share this because they have
experienced common societal events and circumstances that marked their
formative period and that have lasting effects on their individual life courses.
From a sociological perspective, birth cohorts as such are not equivalent to
generations. A consciousness of the shared history and destiny is a necessary condition if a generation is to emerge, a generational consciousness that

separates one generation from the others. The sociological concept of generations originally refers to individuals who think of themselves as members of a generation and who (either implicitly or explicitly) express the extent to which this sense of belonging leads to unique experiences and unique endeavours further on in the life course (Diepstraten et al., 1999).

The Mannheimian conceptualization of a generation stresses that a generation is not a mere statistical birth cohort. To begin with, the term refers to individuals who are born in the same historical period, who live in the same socio-cultural space, and are aware of sharing similar experiences in their formative years. This conceptualization presupposes that generation members subjectively identify with their generation, are linked by a common biography, have an elementary sense of a joint destiny and of being different from other generations. Generation membership assumes generation *consciousness* and a cognizance that one's generation is *distinct* from other generations. Generation membership thus depends on the subjective views of people in a particular social and historical setting. Analytically this implies that objective and subjective aspects should both be taken into account in empirical generation research. Much of the generation research aims at assessing intergenerational differences by only examining differences between birth cohorts. A *subjective comparative* approach is needed to do justice to Mannheim's theory on the origins and emergence of generations. All things considered, this means that from a sociological point of view, birth cohorts are at best generation locations but by implication do not represent an actual generation.

Similar to what Bennett in this volume reports on US generations, we found that younger Dutch cohorts are also more likely than older ones (especially the ones framed as the Lost Generation or in US terms as GenX, people who were young in the late seventies and eighties of the last century) to display generational consciousness, to feel part of a separate generation, in particular in referring to their formative experiences with lifestyle diversity and with ITCs (Diepstraten et al., 1999). Generation membership and generation co-members are more important for the younger cohorts today, it seems. The biographization of the life course, as we have seen, is not taking place in a social void. Especially in intimate circles, such as generation co-members, the media are believed to have an impact (Zinnecker 2000, 2002). Sensitivity to the biographization phenomenon is also what was clearly established in a career orientation study among Dutch people aged 40 years of age and younger (Vinken et al., 2002, 2003; Vinken 2004). It shows that Dutch young people (aged less than 30 and compared to those aged 30 to 40) are well aware of the wide range of life course options, but other than for 30-something people, there was not a single career path for these younger people that they preferred more or preferred less: every option was fine.

Furthermore, they preferred a 'dynamic life course model', a model which is directed not at progress (getting ahead) or self-development (broadening one's capabilities) per se, but directed at variety, change, and continuous challenges. At the same time, their prime supporters in this model are people only from the direct social circle of intimates (partners and spouses, and to a lesser extent parents and peers).[7] Professional educators, teachers, career consultants, and others with an explicit pedagogic agenda are absolutely absent in the life course perceptions of young people.

These results are a forceful indication of the reflexive biographization of the life course. That young people feel like pursuing any type of career path and are predominantly favoring a life course of variation, change, and challenges is an indication that they want to explore their own individuality and follow the path of self-confrontation and self-destruction; on the one hand by postponing participation and a fixed choice (the choice for one single career path in this case), and on the other hand by perceiving participation in general as some sort of an adventure consisting of temporary commitments and unplanned and unpredictable events (see also Du Bois-Reymond, 1998). Of course, the rejection of outside control or even support is also in line with the reasoning related to the reflexive biographization of the life course. These young people claim to take control over their own life and believe they are able to deal with the challenges (and the uncertainties and difficulties) themselves; again, not completely on their own, but with their intimates, and certainly not with society's pedagogically inspired representatives.

With this intimate company they are likely, over the total life course, to develop a common consciousness of a shared history and destiny in which autonomously, but with the help of close relatives, directing the dynamics of one's individual biography and in a process of self-confrontation and self-destruction may be and may persist in being the central issue. This might result in the rise of a 'reflexive generation' not only *having* formative experiences regarding their relationship with their life course that are fundamentally different from the experiences of previous generations, but also—and necessarily so, given the rise of the reflexivity in the life course—*being aware* of the distinctiveness of their formative experiences.

CITIZENSHIP AND NEW MEDIA

New media, especially communication technologies such as mobile platforms and Internet platforms, are crucial in the process of reflexive biographization and generation formation. There is reason to believe that these technologies and developments are a powerful mix that redefines younger generations' notion of citizenship and their way of learning democratic engagement. It is important to analyze these suggested relationships without digressing into unfounded optimistic views on the blessings of the good young 'digital generation' (cf. Howe and Strauss, 2000; Tapscott, 1999; see Bennett in this volume for more examples) or the equally unfounded and almost maliciously negative perspectives of the 'anti-civic' post-Baby Boom generation (cf. Putnam, 2000; see for comments on both views Ester and Vinken, 2003; Vinken, 2004).

In general, first of all, Zinnecker makes an important point on the role of consumption and media use. Through consumption and media use by young people (both children and adolescents), Zinnecker argues that their traditional status of civic incapability (the idea of being a 'minor' itself) is transferred into, if not replaced by a model of equal competence of action. Especially the domains of leisure and consumption promote socialization of the self with the help of generation co-members aware of their shared history and destiny. When using new media (and engaging in leisure and consumption) young people are, virtual or real, regarded as fuller members of their community. In these domains they are no longer 'minors', but to the contrary highly admired 'experts', if not somewhat mistrusted geeks who mysteriously seem to outplay adults with the speed with which they adopt new technologies. More than the model of equal competence of action, as Zinnecker suggests, a model of a higher competence of action seems to apply.

This 'higher' competence is interesting in reference to concepts of citizenship. A minimal perception of citizenship (Evans, 1995) emphasizes that it is gained when civil and legal status is granted. The mobile and Internet platforms on which young people are regarded as more competent ignore the real-life limitations that accompany minimal citizenship. A maximal citizenship definition underlines that people define themselves as members of society. It refers to the consciousness of seeing oneself as a member of a shared democratic culture and can be said to even include questions of reflexivity and responsibility-taking. This definition, of course, emphasizes participatory approaches and considers ways to overcome the social disadvantages that undermine citizenship by denying full participation in society.

Yet, education for citizenship usually builds on minimal citizenship requiring 'only induction into basic knowledge of institutionalized rules of rights and obligations. Maximal interpretations require education which develops critical and reflective abilities and capacities for self-determination and autonomy' (Evans, 1995, p. 5). Citizenship is defined in terms of its formal aspects, such as voting for representatives and decision-making, which is deferred to adults and requires only passive participation or acknowledgement on the part of young people. Moreover, it builds on the assumption that education is preparing young people to have the skills they will need *in the future* as citizens. It tends to focus on political and civic elements in citizenship, in which 'the objectives should be to enable young people to discharge formal obligations of citizenship such as voting and compliance with laws' (Civics Expert Group, 1994, p. 6). To the extent that it remains within this framework, citizenship education offers only a minimal interpretation of citizenship. The effect of this approach can be counterproductive: 'Learning about democracy and citizenship when I was at school was a bit like reading holiday brochures in prison. Unless you were about to be let out or escape, it was quite frustrating and seemed pointless' (Hannam, 2000).

Minimal citizenship education, as well as many institutions, perceive youths as 'deficit' (incomplete and immature) versions of adults and impose an adult-centred view of appropriate involvement in which young people have had no determining role. Maximal definitions that emphasize the role individuals play in forming, maintaining, and changing their communities perceive younger generations as already valuable and valued citizens (see also Bynner et al., 1997).

The mismatch of a minimal definition of citizenship with the de-standardized and biographized life course reality of contemporary younger generations almost needs no further comment. This is especially so when we refer to a broader definition of citizenship and focus on the 'public' in the sense of referring to the public cause, of striving for public acknowledgement, of seeking to legitimise one's actions with arguments from the public sphere, and of identifying with, participating in, and taking responsibility in public life. This connects citizenship to 'public' issues, as Wuthnow (1991, pp. 22–23) says,

> ...public discourse must be thought of in terms broader than those of political debate alone. Its essential concern is with the collective, not necessarily in the sense of the entire society, but with the relationships among individuals, between individuals and communities, and among communities. Public discourse—or what is often referred to as the public sphere—is thus the arena of questions about the desirable in social conduct: How shall we live as a people? What do we hold as priorities? To what ends shall we allocate our time, our energy, our collective resources? Where do we locate hope? How do we envision the good?.

In this process young generations are involved too, most certainly so under the reign of de-standardized and reflexively biographized life course regimes.[8]

As stated, these regimes increasingly require, especially members of younger generations, to 'be flexible' and to reflect on their (future) positions in a wide range of domains in society, not only as regards education, work, or family life, but also as regards citizenship and democratic engagement. What kind of learning experiences enrich me, show me something new I do not yet know; help me to keep on moving; what is my passion, and so what kind of work do I want to do and with whom; with which kind of people do I like to work; do I want an intimate relationship and a family of my own or will this prevent me from living a full social and working life; what kind of public role do I like to play; what issues do I feel committed to, and with whom can I connect and play out this engagement? There are indeed many questions, but they are real for younger generations living the reflexively biographized life course, and the urgency of these questions for younger generations is highly underestimated in the present-day civic engagement debate. Classic minimal definition-based institutions and their corresponding forms of participation are not on a par with this life course reality, mainly because (paradoxically, considering the key issue of choice, for instance in the process of voting), they do not include agency or build on reflexivity. They represent a pre-determined world from which one is either excluded on legal grounds if one is too young or in which one can follow a pre-assigned route of participation, for instance in a voting process or a formally organized political (party) organization.

Furthermore, commitment to this type of participation usually requires a 'long march' through these institutions: for instance starting as a freshman-member, climbing up in the organizational hierarchy and being allowed to represent issues in these organizations after a few years, and in the process being forced to align with party strategies at the expense of individuality and reflexivity. To put it mildly, participation like this is most probably only weakly experienced as a form of action that allows for change and challenges, and as a form of participation that satisfies the urge for self-confrontation and self-destruction. As Coleman in this volume argues, the strengths of new forms of participation, in his case engaging in the voting process in Endemol's *Big Brother*, is that they build on pleasures and affectivity and appeal to interactivity and the feeling of control which are largely absent in the hierarchical power model of politics-as-is. Non-organizational engagement, by contrast, is more likely to be preferred and especially engagement that allows one to participate in changing and challenging commitments. Interactive media, such as mobile and Internet platforms, one may argue, may well provide these types of commitment.[9]

Scholarly literature on the Internet seems to suggest that at least the Internet may serve this role because it has strong ties to the basic cultural, social, and political characteristics of contemporary society (see the review by Ester and Vinken, 2003). The Internet emerges from these characteristics of today's society as well as strongly contributes to them. I will recapitulate some of these characteristics below and relate them to the issue of reflexivity and citizenship, in the mean time referring to the work of Bennett and Coleman in this volume.

Culturally, today's society provides space for autonomous construction of meaning and builds on individuals who function within multiple cultures. The Internet is a constitutive force because it adds to these particular features. It allows for the creation of multiple identities and symbolization of selves in a setting where no culture should be dominant, or at least that's the way the theory goes; in which, in other words, the individual can dream of imagining a continuously changeable and challenged self. Though the reality of the Internet might be more bleak, and many contemporary analysts (e.g., Jordan et al., 2003) argue that the Internet is becoming a closed, controlled, commercial space dominated by a small group from corporate business and government, the idea that the Internet is essentially an open space for controlling and enhancing one's own identity to fit modern-day society is not dead. The large number of initiatives to counterbalance the suggested increase in corporate and government control is proof in itself. Still, more than any other medium, the Internet culturally builds on the very value of enhancing the ability of people to self-organize and develop individuality, to engage in self-confrontation and self-destruction (e.g., enabling withdrawal from previously established identities and to opt in and opt out more easily), elements that are prominent in the contemporary life course model presented above.

Socially, contemporary society and its permeable institutions allow and demand that people develop partial commitments, establish 'weak tie' relationships, and combine diverse sets of social identities and roles based on shared interests rather than on social categorizations. The Internet, in turn, is the space that both promotes and pressures people to connect to and disconnect from relationships at high speed, to experience heterogeneity in these relationships, and indulge in supportive environments and communities without social burdens or inhibiting social cues. Moreover, it is built on the very idea of connectivity and interoperability of social networks, which gives many people the opportunity to engineer forms of social interchange that they have never had with previous media (Jordan et al., 2003).

These features of the Internet itself carry with them the significance people attach to connecting to others in a certain way (and not connecting to them in other ways). It allows the individual to engage in relationships and community life without running the risk of making irreversible commitments that would impinge on the desired openness and changeability of one's life course, which would especially counteract the call and desire for self-destruction. The Internet in social terms relates much more closely to Bennett's Actualizing Citizen (see his chapter in this volume) who favours loose networks of community action that are sustained through peer networks, which are also prominent in the modern life course and socialization models. Moreover, it at least entails a promise to be linked to the priority of having affective, pleasurable, and interactive relationships more than to power relationships that are aligned with classic social status, as Coleman indicates elsewhere in this volume. These are relationships, in other words, that build on intimacy with equals (such as generation co-members), as is important in the reflexively biographized life course.

Politically, present-day society confronts the citizen with a wide variety of agencies and organizations (political movements, parties, and interest groups) each with divergent repertoires of action and political expression, and each targeted to influence a diversified set of political actors. The Internet, in turn, offers the alternative avenues of engagement. The Internet is probably functioning more as an alternative reality, benefiting non-mainstream political actors, when political culture is less open for alternative political views. Therefore, the Internet can function as the ultimate alternative route to democratic engagement, especially in those societies that are less inclusive as regards participation of specific groups in society's decision-making platforms (young people, women, gays, ethnic minorities, etc.).[10] Moreover, it taps into the more urgently felt need to experience politics in highly personalized and localized terms, as Bennett in this volume frames contemporary political life. The Internet is the tool and platform for his Actualized Citizen, more than it will probably ever be for the classic Dutiful Citizen, who regards voting as the core democratic act and frames its part in political life as the obligation to participate in government centred activities.

That the Internet serves a purpose for those who are less welcome in traditional political circles is interesting also from a generational perspective. Based on French studies at hand, it can be argued that there is a strong generational dimension to the issue of civic engagement through the Internet. Even when only smaller groups of young people engage in these types of activities, they might well point to a transition away from the 'biography' of citizenship that was 'normal' for the older generation, one that needed stable identities, strong-tie relationships, and life-long commitments in formal institutions, associations, and established political homes. In France, but perhaps also in many other advanced societies, we witness a rise of insider–outsider polarizations of generations (Chauvel, 2002; Diepstraten et al., 1999). Many institutions in these countries are led by a homogeneous group of Baby Boomers (roughly, people born before 1955), not involved in securing issues that are important for younger generations. Younger people in France face great difficulties in participating in decision making, acquiring political know-how, and attaining the abilities necessary to participate in the collective bargaining for collective choices.

Moreover, decisions are made and planned by these institutions that have long-term negative effects for the younger generation, that seriously contrast with the comfortable, affluent, and high-opportunity past of the Baby Boomers, and do not affect the (shorter) future of Baby Boomers (especially as concerns demands for lifelong learning, employability at the workplace, individualization of social security, and slacking investments in provisions to combine work and family life). In France (Chauvel, 2002) there is an exceptional risk of 'dys-socialization': a growing gap between participative aspirations and the real social conditions among the younger generation, which provoke disappointment, disinterest, and anomie. The values transmitted by the 1960s generation on the benefits of participation, on the importance of self-development, on engineering your own life, and planning your future, conflict fundamentally with the practice of being denied access to participative society, the crumbling of the welfare system, and the realities of the educational system and labour market. In times of economic affluence this might not seem a major problem; in times of economic decline—as we are experiencing in many societies at the moment—this problem of dys-socialization becomes pressing.

The search by young people for other ways to make their political voices heard and to express their engagement, therefore seems not only a matter of 'choice' that aligns with modernity's need to 'keep all options open', it also seems a matter of generational exclusion from institutions that do not open up to youth. Also because of these developments younger generations may turn to mobile and Internet platforms to engage in democracy.

EPILOGUE

This chapter addresses the civic engagement consequences of sociological insights on changing life courses in advanced societies. Life courses have de-standardized and are increasingly subject to the process of reflexive biographization. Attempts to develop individuality (exploring one's unique motives), to engage in self-confrontation (being ready to continuously monitor and reformulate goals), and in self-destruction (leaving previous accumulated experiences behind whenever necessary) have led to a dynamic life course model in which change and challenge are central elements. In this life course model, people's intimate friends and the interactive media, which enable the continuous quest for individuality, self-confrontation, and self-destruction, have a more prominent role than for earlier generations. It is argued that younger people recognize the theme of change and challenge in the life course they and their contemporaries strive for, which promotes the formation of generational consciousness and might lead to an identifiable reflexive generation in the course of time.

Applied to young people's civic engagement, especially the one supported by interactive media, this means that the modern, dynamic life course model calls and allows for commitments to platforms (instead of organizations) that underline the value of self-organization, individuality, self-confrontation, and self-destruction, that allow interactivity and connectedness with intimate circles, and that reflect the political diversities that are real in many advanced societies. The Internet may especially serve the purpose of an outlet for those who not only choose to express themselves politically in this self-organized, personalized, and reflexive way, but also for those who are excluded from formal participatory paths. Many institutions of politics-as-is have cultures, routines, and programs that, intentionally or not, exclude younger generations from participation. These same institutions more or less contribute to the choice of the younger generation to follow alternative routes to citizenship and civic engagement.

An important aspect in the modern life course is the absence of pedagogically inspired institutions and agents. The importance of this aspect can hardly be underestimated, especially when thinking about ways to enhance younger people's civic engagement. The fundamental characteristic of self-organization in the modern life course indicates that there is little room for civic education organizations to influence the direction, quality, and quantity of younger generations' civic engagement. Even when recognizing the limited powers available, the least that could be done is to start from a broad definition of citizenship as it is pursued by younger generations and to tap into their life course realities.

This chapter attempts to show that it is time to thoroughly investigate these alternative types and platforms of engagements. In doing so it is especially important to take account of the sociological reality of the reflexively biographized life course that in advanced societies may very well serve as the basis for contemporary generation formation among today's younger cohorts. This element in turn changes the face of the democratic engagement of this future adult generation. Taking seriously the changing life course realities of younger generations in many advanced societies (in both the West and the East) is a first step.

NOTES

1. Tilburg University, PO Box 90153, 5000 LE Tilburg, the Netherlands; e-mail: h.vinken@uvt.nl. This chapter was prepared during my stay as a visiting professor at the School of Sociology, Kwansei Gakuin University, Nishinomiya, Japan. I thank members of the School of Sociology for their inspiring comments on earlier versions.
2. Some label the process of diverting from the linear and accumulative logic of life course transitions—stacking experiences as a necessary condition to being able to make and process new experiences in the life course—as the 'yoyo-ization' of the life course (Pais, 1995; Walther and Stauber, 2002) in which one combines and exchanges roles at a specific moment that once belonged uniquely to one or the other life course phase.
3. See Vinken (2004), for more on the issue of reflexive biographization and the (self-) socialization debate.
4. The concept of reflexivity only partly dwells in Beck (1994). Beck focuses much more on institutional levels when discussing reflexivity, not explicitly rejecting the idea that it is a process at work at other levels as well, but only giving relative attention to these other levels (see also Giddens 1991; Lash 1994).
5. Lash (1994: 119–135) also reflects on the balance between agency and structure and seems to bend towards the concept of structures forcing agents to be free.
6. Although it is not always clear in the studies Bennett cites that we are dealing with different generations, because these studies usually dwell on one-shot data making it impossible to disentangle cohort from aging effects; for example, that DotNets participate in protest politics twice as much as older cohorts could be a characteristic of young people of every generation and not a feature of this particular generation per se. It takes time series data to know this. Generational conclusions when lacking these data are not valid.
7. The role of partners and spouses reminds us of the large impact of interpersonal tie dependencies of life courses, which are directly dependent on the life

courses of the most immediate intimates in people's lives, as Mayer (2000, 2001) also argues.

8. There is an interesting recent example of relating changes in the transitions to adulthood to citizenship (Thomson et al., 2004). However, the report on this qualitative study does not dwell much on young people's attitudes and behaviours, referring to issues of the public cause and does not provide information on the role of new media in the process.

9. One must be aware that good, internationally comparative data is lacking. There are no international projects that address the importance of the Internet for younger generations' engagement, at least no projects that rise above the level of anecdote, case studies, and presentations of 'travellers tales'. Evidence on the rise of alternative forms of engagement is scattered and highly underdeveloped.

10. Of course the Internet as well as the mobile phone have many other uses, which in popularity easily outnumber 'political' use. The issue here is not that overall (across all nations) the Internet fails to include those who do not get involved in politics-as-is and thus that it does not impact overall patterns of political engagement (Dahlgren, 2001). It is likely that it is an alternative for those of the younger generation (as well as of other groups) who might consider involving themselves in politics in real-life (especially the higher educated segments), but who find the Internet a platform that serves their purposes better than real-life political engagement.

REFERENCES

Beck, U. (1994) The reinvention of politics: towards a theory of reflexive modernization. In U. Beck, A. Giddens, and S. Lash, eds., *Reflexive modernization,* Cambridge: Polity Press, pp. 1–55.

Bennett, W.L. (1998) The uncivic culture: communication, identity, and the rise of lifestyle politics. *Apsanet Psonline* (http://www.apsanet.org/PS/dec98/bennett.cfm)

Bois-Reymond, M., du (1998) 'I don't want to commit myself yet': young people's life concepts. *Journal of Youth Studies* 1 (1), 63–79.

Bynner, J., L. Chisholm, and A. Furlong, eds. (1997) *Youth, Citizenship and Social Change in a European Context.* Aldershot: Ashgate.

Chauvel, L. (2002) *Le destin des générations. Structure sociale et cohorts en France au XXe siècle.* Paris: Presses Universitaires de France.

Civics Expert Group (1994). *Whereas the People. Report of the Civics Expert Group.* Canberra: AGPS.

Dahlgren, P. (2001) 'The public sphere and the net: structure, space, and communication', in W.L. Bennett and R.M. Entman, eds., *Mediated Politics.* Cambridge: Cambridge University Press.

Diepstraten, I., P. Ester, and H. Vinken (1999) 'Talkin' 'bout my generation: ego and alter images of generations in the Netherlands'. *Netherlands' Journal of Social Sciences*, 35 (2), 91–109.

Elchardus, M., ed. (1999) *Zonder maskers. Een actueel portret van jongeren en hun leraren.* [Without masks. A current portrait of young people and their teachers.] Gent: Globe.

Ester, P. and H. Vinken (2000) *Van later zorg. Verwachtingen van Nederlanders over ontwikkelingen op het terrein van arbeid, zorg en vrijetijd in de 21ste eeuw. Het OSA Toekomst van de Arbeid Survey.* [Of later concern. Expectations of Dutch people about developments in the domains of work, care, and leisure in the 21st century. The OSA Future of Work Survey.] Tilburg: OSA.

Ester, P. and H. Vinken (2001) *Een dubbel vooruitzicht. Doembeelden en droombeelden van arbeid, zorg, vrijetijd in de 21e eeuw.* [A double focus. Gloomy and dreamy perspectives on work, care, and leisure in the 21st century.] Bussum: Uitgeverij Countinho.

Ester, P. and H. Vinken (2003) 'Debating civil society. On the fear for civic decline and hope for the Internet alternative'. *International Sociology*, 18 (4), 659–680.

Evans, K. (1995) 'Competence and citizenship: towards a complementary model'. *British Journal of Education and Work*, Autumn.

Fuchs, W. (1983) 'Jugendliche Statuspassage oder individualisierte Jugendbiographie?' *Soziale Welt*, 34, 341–371.

Furlong, A. and Cartmel, F. (1997) *Young People and Social Change.* Buckingham: Open University Press.

Giddens, A. (1991) *Modernity and Self-Identity. Self and Society in the Late Modern Age.* Stanford, CA: Stanford University Press.

Hannam, D. (2000) 'A democratic response'. Lecture at Forsokgymnaset, Oslo, Norway. (http://www.forsok.vgs.no/Hannam.htm).

Heinz, W.R. & V.W. Marshall, eds. (2003) *Social Dynamics of the Life Course. Transitions, Institutions, and Interrelations.* New York: Aldine de Gruyter.

Held, Th. (1986) 'Institutionalization and deinstitutionalization of the life course'. *Human Development*, 29, 157–162.

Howe, N. and W. Strauss (2000) *Millennials Rising: The Next Great Generation.* New York: Vintage Books.

Jordan, K., J. Hauser, and S. Foster (2003). 'The augmented social network: building identity and trust into the next-generation Internet'. *First Monday*, 8 (8). (http://firstmonday.org/issues/issue8_8/jordan/index.html)

Kohli, M. (1985) 'Die institutionalisierung des lebenslaufs'. *Kölner Zeitschrift für Soziologie und Sozialpsychologie*, 37, 1–29.

Laermans, R. (1993) Bringing the consumer back in. *Theory, Culture & Society*, 10, 153–161.

Lash, S. (1994) 'Reflexivity and its doubles: structure, aesthetics, community', In U. Beck, A. Giddens, and S. Lash, eds., *Reflexive Modernization. Politics, Tradition and Aesthetics in the Modern Social Order.* Cambridge: Polity Press, pp. 110–173.

Mannheim, K. (1928/1929) 'Das Problem der Generationen'. *Kölner Vierteljahresheft für Soziologie*, 7, 157–185/309–330.

Mayer, K.U. (2000) 'Promises fulfilled? A review of 20 years of life course research', *Archives Europeenes de Sociologie*, 41 (2), 259–282.

Mayer, K.U. (2001). 'The paradox of global social change and national path dependencies: life course patterns in advanced societies', in A.E. Woodward and M. Kohli, eds., *Inclusions and Exclusions in European Societies.* London: Routledge, pp. 89–110.

Mayer, K.U. (2004). 'Life chances and life course in a comparative perspective'. Pdf from website of Yale University Center for Research on Inequalities and the Life Course (CIQLE): http://www.yale.edu/socdept/CIQLE/CIQLE%20papers/mayer,%20Life%20Courses%20and%20Life%20Chances.pdf.

Pais, J. (1995) 'Young people and new social conditions: trajectories, prospects and crossroads'. Paper presented at the International Conference Young Adults in Europe, Tutzing, 3–5th May, 1995.

Putnam, R.D. (2000) *Bowling Alone. The Collapse and Revival of American Community.* New York: Simon and Schuster.

Tapscott, D. (1998) *Growing Up Digital: The Rise of the Net Generation*. New York: McGraw-Hill.

Thomson, R., J. Holland, S. McGrellis, R. Bell, S. Henderson, and S. Sharpe (2004) Inventing adulthoods: a biographical approach to understanding youth citizenship. *The Sociological Review*, 52 (2), 218–239.

Veith, H. (2002) 'Sozialisation als reflexiven Vergesellschaftung'. *Zeitschrift für Soziologie der Erziehung und Sozialisation*, 22 (2), 167–177.

Vinken, H. (2004) 'Civic socialization in late modernity: perspectives on young people's alleged withdrawal from civil society, in D. Hoffmann and H. Merkens, eds., *Jugendsoziologische Sozialisationstheorie. Impulse für die Jugendforschung*. Weinheim & Munchen: Juventa Verlag, pp. 253–267.

Vinken, H. and P. Ester (2001) Druk, drukker, drukst. Nederlanders over de toekomst van arbeid, zorg en vrijetijd. [Busy, busier, busiest. Dutch people on the future of work, care, and leisure.] *Vrijetijdstudies*, 19 (1), 21–42.

Vinken, H., P. Ester, H. Dekkers, and L. van Dun (2002) *Aan ons de toekomst. Toekomstverwachtingen van jongeren in Nederland. [The future is ours. Future expectations of young people in the Netherlands.]* Assen: Van Gorcum.

Vinken, H., P. Ester, L. van Dun, and H. van Poppel (2003). *Arbeidswaarden, toekomstbeelden en loopbaanoriëntaties. Een pilot-study onder jonge Nederlanders. [Work values, future perceptions, and life course orientations. [A pilot-study among young Dutch people]* Tilburg: OSA.

Walther, A. , B. Stauber et al., eds. (2002) *Misleading Trajectories. Integration Policies for Young People in Europe? An EGRIS Publication*. Opladen: Leske and Budrich.

Wuthnow, R. (1991) 'The voluntary sector', in R. Wuthnow, ed., *Between States and Markets*. Princeton, NJ: Princeton University Press, pp. 22–23.

Zinnecker, J. (1987) *Jugendkultur 1940–1985*. Leverkusen: Leske and Budrich.

Zinnecker, J. (2000) Selbstsozialisation. Essay über ein aktuelles Konzept. *ZSE, Zeitschrift für Soziologie der Erziehung und Sozialisation*, 20 (3), 272–290.

Zinnecker, J. (2002) 'Wohin mit dem "strukturlosen Subjektzentrismus"? Eine Gegenrede zur Entgegnung von Ullrich Bauer'. *Zeitschrift für Soziologie der Erziehung und Sozialisation*, 22 (2), 143–154.

4 Civic learning in changing democracies

Challenges for citizenship and civic education

W. Lance Bennett

The times they are a changing in long established European and North American democracies. Alarming numbers of young citizens seem to have turned their backs on government and conventional politics. It appears that contemporary politics in most societies increasingly fail to capture the interest and attention of young citizens, who are generally skeptical of politicians and party affiliation, and increasingly unlikely to vote. A study of voting turnout by age in 15 European democracies conducted by the Institute for Democracy and Electoral Assistance in Sweden concluded that youth voting decline is a serious and widespread problem for contemporary democracies looking to the new generation of citizens for participation, legitimacy, and support (IDEA, 1999).

To many observers, the civic deficit problem appears to run far deeper than voting. For example, Rahn (2004) finds a strong correlation between national integration in the global economy and diminished citizen identification with a range of civic activities and indicators of national citizenship. Some scholars have concluded that there is a distinctive Millennial Generation (roughly composed of those turning 21 around the turn of the century), and that this cohort is profoundly apolitical, as highlighted by a rejection of traditional citizen roles centered around civic duties such as voting. For example, 71% of British Millennials believe that voting makes no difference. The numbers of British youth who aspire to enter public service are dwarfed by nearly a fifty-to-one preference for entrepreneurial business careers (Pirie and Worcester, 1998). A follow-up survey in Britain in 1999 compared the Millennials to the general population and found that 40% of 18- to 24-year-olds in Britain were not even registered to vote, compared with just 8% of the general population (Pirie and Worcester, 2000). O'Toole (2004) observes that a media stereotype of the youth engagement crisis in Britain has evolved around the factoid that more young people voted on the reality TV show *Big Brother* than in the 2001 general election (in a personal communication, Stephen Coleman avers that the possibility of multiple voting on Big Brother may cloud this claim).

Even before it had reached the level of media myth, the severity of youth voting decline in Britain prompted the government to commission what has become known as the Crick Report (1998), which called for compulsory civics education in the secondary schools. The underlying question for Britain—and for this essay—is what should such education look like? A first step toward an answer is to understand the nature of the problem.

YOUNG CITIZENS AND POLITICS: ORIGINS OF A CROSS-NATIONAL TREND

A general survey on the status of young people in Europe revealed a remarkable convergence of trends reported by researchers in 15 European Union member states and three nations outside the EU (Instituto di Ricerca, Milan, 2001). A bulletin on the report posted by one of the participating research institutes sounded this alarm:

> Young people's and young adults' limited political participation—voting, membership in political parties, youth organizations, and representation in decision-making bodies—is considered a major problem in most Western European countries. Young people's declining political engagement and participation in society are perceived as a challenge for the future of representative democracy. (Deutsches Jugend Institut, 2003)

A survey of the "civic and political health of the nation" in the United States concluded that the American Millennials might be better termed the "DotNets," both out of their strong self-identification as a generation and their preferences for communicating through various digital interactive media, factors that seem important for thinking about civic education initiatives. Like their European counterparts, the American DotNets are turned off to conventional politics and government, but highly involved in issue activism, political consumerism, and protest activities (Keeter et al., 2002).

Some observers contextualize such trends in less alarmist terms based on theories of social change, arguing that recent generations have entered a time of more personalized, less institutionally (e.g., party, union, church) organized politics in which citizens participate by other means through "self-actualizing" or "self-reflexive" involvement in personally meaningful causes guided by their own lifestyles and shifting social networks (Inglehart, 1997; Giddens, 1991).

If we apply such perspectives on social change and political identity to the question of what defines the Millennials as a generation with similar cross-national political tendencies, we might consider first that they entered society at the height of the current wave of economic globalization. Among other things, this period has been defined by high levels of labor market dislocation (more frequent career changes, less employment security, periods of unemployment and underemployment) and an overriding sense of generalized risk (Bennett, 1998; Beck, 1999, 2000). Unlike earlier periods of modern era change, the contemporary experiences of risk and dislocation are negotiated by individuals largely through independent identity management strategies. The Millennials are less guided by encompassing ideologies, mass movements, party and governmental support structures, and other factors that might help individuals focus on government and politics in times of strain.

Living in these disrupted social contexts, young citizens find greater satisfaction in defining their own political paths, including: local volunteerism, consumer activism, support for issues and causes (environment, human rights), participation in various transnational protest activities, and efforts to form a global civil society by organizing world and regional social forums (Bennett, 1998; O'Toole, 2004). Bang (2003) has called this a generation of "everyday makers" who define their own sense of politics according to networks of personal relationships aimed at adding value to their lived experiences. Observers like O'Toole and Bang argue that new generations of citizens are simply redefining what they mean by politics, and that social scientists should embrace this shift. Others counter that citizens greatly diminish their political capacity when they replace familiar public action repertoires centered on government and collective identities with narrower discourses fashioned from highly personalized and localized concerns (Eliasoph, 1998).

When politics becomes so personal, public policies that try to embrace the Millennials may fail because governments tend to deliver collective solutions, and collective solutions do not fit personalized problems. Consider, for example, the reaction of a 19-year-old black woman (one of O'Toole's respondents) to an effort by the British Labor Party to address economic and social dislocation among young people:

> ...this New Deal thing that Tony Blair has come up with, it's not for everybody, it does not suit everybody's needs. It basically puts everybody in a little box and expects them to go either this way or that way. It doesn't work for everybody... You have to treat people as individuals, not just a little group so that everybody does have the opportunity to do something. (O'Toole, 2004, p. 18)

Some observers contend that changing definitions of citizenship are a natural feature of democratic life (Schudson, 1998). This is surely true. However, the compelling issue remains that the turn away from such defining democratic activities as voting may also represent a serious threat to the core of democratic civic culture (Putnam, 2000). In addition, the redefinition of politics in highly personal and localized terms raises questions about whether procrustean governments can appeal to their new generation citizens on the terms those governments were primarily designed for delivering collective solutions to broadly defined social problems. These concerns present clear challenges for thinking about and designing effective civic education programs that may appeal to the young citizens who go through them, and at the same time serve the interests of democracy in changing societies. Since there appear to be very different brands of citizenship in play within the same societies, how can civic education address and reconcile these differences without forcing unappealing, one-size-fits-all models of political consciousness and behavior on entire cohorts of young citizens?

THE CHALLENGE FOR CIVIC EDUCATION

The challenges to civic education in this picture are obvious. Most policy makers define and fund civic education programs (which are run primarily in the schools) based on highly conventional citizen models which center around the idea of the "Dutiful Citizen" (DC). At a minimum, the DC is expected to learn about the basic workings of government and related political institutions, to understand the values of the national civic culture, to become informed about issues and make responsible voting choices. The challenge for civic education, simply put, is how to integrate and adapt these conventional DC virtues to the changing civic orientations of the new "self- Actualizing Citizen" (AC) who may see her political activities and commitments in highly personal terms that contribute more to enhancing the quality of personal life, social recognition, self esteem, or friendship relations, than to understanding, support, and involvement in government. Table 1 offers a preliminary contrast between the AC and DC models of citizenship.

One can debate endlessly whether Millennials are effectively engaged, and whether democracy can prosper, with the rise of AC politics that exclude the core DC value and action repertoire. While this debate may make an interesting academic exercise, it does not serve the interests of civic education particularly well. Whatever the merits of the respective positions, both dimensions of citizenship seem important to address and integrate in effective approaches to civic education. To put it crudely, older generation educational policy-makers—who may tend to see only the DC virtues—must somehow engage with the political consciousness of a new civic generation experiencing an historic set of social changes that appear to be occurring on a transnational level. To make matters even more challenging, making this AC/DC connection must somehow facilitate the ongoing transformation of democratic societies and institutions.

Simply arguing for one model over another will not serve much purpose. Civic identifications and practices, if they are to be adopted, must have some anchors and inducements in the lived experiences of individuals both inside and outside of the education and socialization settings in which they

Table 1 The divided citizenry: The traditional civic education ideal of the Dutiful Citizen (DC) vs. the emerging youth experience of self-actualizing citizenship (AC)

Actualizing citizen (AC)	*Dutiful citizen (DC)*
Diminished sense of government obligation—higher sense of individual purpose	Obligation to participate in government centered activities
Voting is less meaningful than other, more personally defined acts such as consumerism, community volunteering, or transnational activism	Voting is the core democratic act
Mistrust of media and politicians is reinforced by negative mass media environment	Becomes informed about issues and government by following mass media
Favors loose networks of community action—often established or sustained through friendships and peer relations and thin social ties maintained by interactive information technologies	Joins civil society organizations or expresses interests through parties that typically employ one-way conventional communication to mobilize supporters

are introduced. The Dutiful Citizen continues to have obvious appeal, particularly to educational policy makers, based on the reasonable perception that citizen activities centered on voting and (at least somewhat) informed opinion are necessary to instill in new generations in order to ensure the viability of democratic polities. At the same time, recognizing that young citizens today may have substantially different social and political experiences than their elders did at comparable stages of life also seems important to incorporate into models of civic education. In short, effective civic education models need to address substantive changes in citizen roles, while finding ways to motivate young people to find ways to engage meaningfully and effectively in civic life.

What can civic education do for the AC citizen who simply fails to make the connection between personal political concerns and the distant DC world of government and elections? While there is no obvious standardized solution for this dilemma, this analysis offers a set of heuristics based on communication logics that enable young learners to participate in defining their personal political world as part of the learning process, and to find more meaningful pathways that lead to conventional politics and government. This idea of a civic education paradigm that bridges the two ideal types of citizenship reveals an obvious normative assumption: I see little to recommend some postmodern notion of democracy that obviates government or citizen engagement in favor of privileging individually generated conceptions of public life. Even if AC citizens become engaged in substantial transformations of government, citizenship, and democracy, they must be equipped to accomplish those ends in knowing and effective ways. In short, the basic challenge for civic education is finding compelling ways to integrate the two citizenship models without forcing one into the other. The illustrative case of civic education in Australia highlights some of the issues and the dilemmas in addressing this challenge.

CASE IN POINT: AUSTRALIA

Australia offers an interesting national case both because of the awareness in the policy community of generational changes among young citizens, and because of the difficulty of incorporating this awareness into the classroom curriculum. Part of the policy innovation and implementation problem no doubt stems from the fact that there are so many sites of civics curriculum coordination and breakdown—as is the case in many nations. For example, the Civics Education Research Group at Canberra University (2004) lists 45 distinct sites of input and coordination—from international organizations such as the International Association for the Evaluation of Educational Achievement (IEA), to national governmental policy agencies involved with citizenship, education, and immigration, to numerous state education boards and private councils. At the same time, the issues confronting the Australian civics project have been fairly well defined by The Australian Council of Education Research (ACER) following participation in the landmark IEA study of 90,000 14-year-olds in 28 nations (Torney-Purta et al., 2001).

Australian students scored around the middle of the international distribution in terms of overall civics skills scores. The authors of the ACER report conclude that despite this passing performance on the skills and knowledge tests, the data revealed a deeper problem. The adequate performance of Australian students on basic civic knowledge and skills measures did not translate into a desire to engage in the corresponding activities of civic life defined by the IEA study as "conventional citizenship" (which I term the DC side of the citizen divide). This is a form of what Rahn (2004) describes as the disconnection between identification and engagement, or the "being and doing" aspects of citizenship. Among the disturbing findings: 83% felt that joining a political party was not important in order to be considered a good citizen; only 55% felt that knowing about the nation's history was important; only 50% regarded following issues in the media as important; and 66% regarded engaging in political discussion as unimportant. The relatively strong commitment to voting was downplayed in the report as merely echoing the compulsory status of voting in Australia (Mellor et al., 2001, p. 160). Yet what seemed equally clear in the IEA study is that the AC side of civic life is far more attractive to young Australians: 80% said it was important to engage in activities that benefit others, 74% wanted to protect the political environment, and 68% were concerned about human rights. The authors conclude that Australian students were inclined to look outside government for solutions to political problems.

What were the implications of this increasingly familiar young citizen profile for Australian civic education? The results of the IEA study became the basis of a report from the Australian Council of Educational Research on the goals for civic education in Australia. The recommendations of the ACER report included a sensible blend of the AC and DC sides of contemporary citizenship (Mellor, Kennedy, and Greenwood, 2001). I list their recommendations below, taking the liberty of noting that the first three seem to reflect DC goals, and the remainder AC goals.

- Knowledge of Australian political institutions and structures
- Values concerning democracy, the rule of law, social justice, equity and fairness
- Commitment to including all Australians in the political process
- An obligation to see citizenship in an international perspective
- Understanding the everyday lived experiences of young people and their apparent alienation
- Recognising schools and classrooms as democratic institutions
- Accepting that citizens are constructed by multiple identities rather than a single identity.

Where is Australia in crossing the AC/DC divide? The Ministerial Council on Education, Employment, Training and Youth of Australia (2002) surveyed national civic education policy, and analyzed all available documents from agencies promoting or conducting civics education programs. The first conclusion was that civics is not even among the 8 key learning areas established for all schools in Australia. Indeed, there is concern that civics has slipped from the required curriculum in many nations, reflecting the educational turn toward basic academic skills and, perhaps, reflecting underlying struggles to depoliticize the schools. The second conclusion of this national survey was that only three content areas were widespread throughout Australian civics curriculum documents: (1) Australian democratic heritage and operation of government and law; (2) Australian national identity and cultural diversity; and (3) the set of skills and values necessary for informed and active participation in civic life. These goals are very similar to the three DC goals identified in the recommendations from the IEA study. Still missing from the general civics learning picture in Australia were the goals that might engage the AC citizen.

BRIDGING THE AC/DC DIVIDE: A COMMUNICATION-BASED MODEL OF CIVIC EDUCATION

The case of Australia suggests that even when the challenges of addressing complex citizenship are recognized, the solutions are elusive. In part, this may be due to generational differences in the perceptions of citizenship that favor policies and curriculum designed by older citizens who do not experience public life from the standpoint of younger generations. This may be compounded by the false, but commonly heard, impression that approaches to civic education that include AC perspectives necessarily sacrifice DC virtues. The overriding problem may be the absence of a model for integrating both AC and DC elements of citizenship in a coherent curriculum.

In the remainder of this essay, I suggest various ways in which the logic of civic education from the policy level to the classroom may begin to address this issue of changing citizen roles without sacrificing the focus on DC skills and activities. In particular, I suggest a heuristic approach to engaging young citizens in their educational environments through four sequential steps toward civic engagement, each involving a communication process that enables the individual learner to define her own relationship to: (1) meaningful issues that enable personal identification; (2) relevant information that motivates rather than discourages linking the issue to government; (3) other (citizen) learners who may provide peer recognition and political support for initiatives involving the issue; and (4) and available citizen pathways to effective governmental action on the issue. The goal here is not to turn AC individuals into DC citizens, but to allow some appreciation for DC civic life to grow from personally meaningful AC origins.

These four communication/learning processes aimed at better integrating the AC and DC aspects of citizenship are defined in the following four sections of the paper. Taken as a set, these elements of civic learning show the importance of communication skills to contemporary citizenship, from face to face issue deliberation, to navigating the mass media, to using interactive digital channels to communicate with other citizens and engage with government.

A PLACE TO BEGIN: USING STANDPOINT ISSUES TO COMMUNICATE IDENTITY IN POLITICAL CONTEXT

A starting point for engaging AC learners who experience a distant and often disagreeable DC world is to allow them to define their own political standpoints—and avoid immediately requiring them to locate those standpoints in terms of conventional politics. This may be easier than it initially appears. Political standpoints for the AC emerge fairly easily around issues that matter in their daily lives. Moreover, exploring shared experiences with those issues enables a shift in the framing of those experiences from private to common concerns.

There is evidence that the DotNets are concerned about issues and problem solving, and even more inclined toward collective identification with their peers than predecessor generations. For example, the U.S. civic health of the nation survey found higher levels of generational identification (69%) among the DotNets (those born between 1977 and 1987) than among

GenX (42%), the Baby Boomers (50%), or the Matures (51%). However, in keeping with their AC citizenship bias, the DotNets were by far the least likely (38%, 48%, 60%, 59%) to say that good citizenship entails responsibility (Keeter et al., 2002). At the same time, the DotNets are as likely as any generation to have engaged directly in political consumerism in support of environmental and other causes, and they are nearly twice as likely as other citizens to have participated in protest politics. What can be done to channel these clear indications of political interest and potential for common identification in more conventional political directions?

A simple proposition about civic learning consistent with these trends is that conventional skills such as engagement and information-seeking begin with motivation—generally powered by interest in specific issues or problems (Neuman, Just, and Crigler, 1992). A promising beginning to any civic learning experience is to empower the learners to find issues in their immediate communities that seem important to the people with whom they live and associate. One model for this is the Student Voices project, a national civic learning program developed by the Annenberg Public Policy Center in the United States (Student Voices, 2004). Student Voices begins by training students to take simple surveys of their communities and bring the results (community concerns) back into the learning environment (usually a class-room) to explore through deliberations under the guidance of the learning facilitator (usually a teacher). The Student Voices model is interesting because learners introduce issues with which they identify personally, and they contribute through group deliberations to the development of a class issue agenda that results in a collectively constructed issue or problem that becomes the focus for subsequent civic learning (Student Voices, 2004). A similar model is offered by the Project Citizen curriculum developed by the Center for Civic Education in the U.S. (Project Citizen, 2004).

Once learners have identified with a personal issue and participated in constructing a collective framing for a common issue (which may or not end up resembling their initial issue), they have taken the first step in understanding how to construct a public discourse and negotiate interests in common with others with whom they identify. These elements of the civic learning process can be enhanced through a combination of conventional and technology-driven communication processes. For example, the results of deliberations can be posted on discussion boards for follow-up reactions from those involved in the deliberations, and for sharing with others engaged in similar experiences in the same school, across the city, or around the world. Sample discussions can be viewed at Seattle Student Voices (2004), a project housed at the Center for Communication and Civic Engagement (2004).

The mixture of face-to-face deliberation and subsequent individual-level input through on-line messages and chats can create a sense of personal ownership in the issue adopted by the learning community. The issues may cover a wide variety of topics, from crime, drugs, education, and teen recreation issues, to local or global environmental concerns. The actual issue is less important than its origins in individual and collective definition and mutual recognition processes, aided by the willingness of the facilitator not to impose too much definition from on high.

Once a motivating issue is constructed, the natural next questions involve: What is being done about this problem? Who is doing it? What works? What doesn't? Why? The next step at this point is to open up various kinds of access to information and to provide learners with perspectives on the biases and benefits of various communication channels in society.

A NEXT STEP: NAVIGATING THE POLITICAL INFORMATION ENVIRONMENT

Young citizens are immersed in what may be the richest, yet most fragmented information environment in human history. The channels that young citizens use to gather information and to communicate about their political issues are important considerations in creating engaged citizens. Tuning out is surely as useful a skill as knowing what and when to tune in. Media literacy training can create awareness of the dilemmas of incorporating DC information skills into the often discouraging real world media experiences of young citizens. This entails lessons aimed at more critical deconstruction and use of available information channels, and at finding channels that address the issue (defined above) at the center of the learning experience. These aims can be advanced by introducing civic learners to several different slices of the media environment in which they live. Some obvious candidates for attention include: *election communication, conventional news and entertainment*, and *the digital information sphere*.

Electoral communication is important to highlight in order to demystify the process through which campaigns seek votes, a process that often excludes substantial voter blocs such as young people. Opening the discussion of citizen communication with this focus addresses honestly the young citizen's questions of Why aren't politicians talking to me? Why don't they seem to care about my issues?

Painting today's democratic process with a broad brush finds parties and politicians scrambling for electoral support by placing their appeals in the hands of professional communication consultants who target narrow voter blocs to gain tactical electoral advantage (Blumler and Kavanagh, 1999). The near universal consensus among these consultants is that spending precious campaign budgets on messages aimed at young voters is a waste of time and money. Young people are deemed hard to reach through conventional media strategies, and even harder to convince that politicians are not all alike. The idea that campaign messages and candidate images are marketed to voters much the same way that that commercial products are sold may help young citizens to see that, in communication terms, they represent demographic market segments—highly prized for selling fashion and entertainment products, but less valued in electoral marketing strategies. A simple proposition about youth disengagement is that since they are not asked in meaningful terms to participate in the electoral process, they don't do so (Keeter et al., 2002; Bennett and Xenos, 2004).

This introduction to political communication offers learners an honest appraisal of their place in the political scheme of things in most countries, and may help them see why many of their peers reject a political system that implicitly ignores them. At the same time, it is important to show that electoral results do have consequences for various social groups, including young people. It is also important at this point to introduce citizen engagement options—both electoral and non-electoral—that provide both information and pathways to effective action concerning the issue defined in the last learning module. The general goal here is to begin moving away from the idea of the citizen as a passive spectator in the electoral arena, or more generally, in relation to government, and toward a model of active citizenship.

Understanding the political influence of news and entertainment media offers a next step for helping young citizens think about their political views. A major obstacle to active citizenship is the relationship that many young citizens establish with the mass (particularly commercial) media. The absence of citizens—particularly young citizens—playing central roles in conventional news and public affairs programming reinforces impressions that issues are too confusing or that there is nothing that ordinary people can do about them. In addition, the portrayal of scandal and unpleasant images of politics may further reinforce negativity toward politics, politicians and government. Whether these media trends actively produce or merely echo a late modern culture of antipolitics, the evidence is clear that most mass media content, particularly on commercial television, ranges from apolitical, at best, to overtly negative toward politics. And, what may be just as civically isolating, most youth programming aims at full immersion in a commercialized environment selling fashion, entertainment, and other consumer products as the core elements of social identities anchored in lifestyles (Bennett, 1998). Examining that media environment seems an appropriate next step in understanding the broad rejection of politics and the common experience of being lost when thinking about the problems and issues that do matter.

Case materials suitable for a politically focused media literacy curriculum abound in nearly every national context. Consider, for example, the market research materials produced by the German public service broadcaster ARD. The monthly reports called *Media Perspektiven* often publicize the network's market research with a focus on audience demographics and content comparisons between public service and commercial television outlets. These studies demonstrate common, cross-national audience trends such as the graying of the public service news audience, and the disproportionate

appeal of infotainment news on commercial channels to younger viewers.
The implications of these trends for politics and citizenship are dramatic.
For example, people who exclusively watch news on German public service
channels consistently demonstrate two to three times the levels of interest
in political affairs, depending on what is happening during the periods
when polls are taken (*Media Perspektiven*, 6/2002).

The explanation for this political interest gap is most likely a combination of what these audiences are offered by different media sources, and
what interests they bring to their viewing in the first place. For example,
an analysis of news content on the public and private channels shows that
political content fills 66% and 63% of news programming on the two leading German public channels, ARD and ZDF, compared to just 29% and
28% on the leading private channels RTL and Sat1 (*Media Perspektiven*
2/2002). Audience political tastes are considerably at odds as well, with
public service audiences preferring information about national politics,
state politics, social issues, and international affairs, and private channel
audiences ranking natural disasters, crime, and accidents as their favorite
news fare (*Media Perspektiven*, 5/2001).

The moral of this media literacy story is that media choices matter.
While it may be difficult to convince young learners to tune in public service news, there are other high quality and personalized news sources that
may appeal to them. In learning environments with school or home access
to the Internet, the most obvious direction for DotNets who have issues
that they want to understand is the rich sphere of discourse and information on the Web.

The digital information sphere offers a rich menu of interactive information options for individuals seeking information about issues that motivate learning and action. For example, the BBC has launched a prototype
experiment called *iCan*, which enables citizens to define and post their own
issues, link to broad networks of similarly concerned individuals, find information about public actions and government responses, and, ultimately,
push for BBC coverage of their concerns. There are also many dubious sites
that merit another round of communication literacy training in the digital
sphere. In general, however, the information habits of *netizens* suggest two
promising trends (based on research in the U.S.): (1) young people increasingly prefer their information in online, interactive environments, and (2)
veteran Internet users are among the most informed citizens (Pew, 2004).

A policy problem facing the incorporation of information technologies
in civic education is that nations vary greatly in the development and distribution of Internet access. For example, the United States leads in the
category of computer-based online access, while Germany and France have
been slower to introduce the levels of service competition and infrastructure
necessary to democratize this important communication medium. However, increasing numbers of schools are wired and next generation mobile

phones will have search and information features that may enable young people to do more than download the latest hit songs as ring tones.

Where access is available, young people follow. In the United States, the Internet now rivals regular news programming and comedy shows as the leading sources of information about politics for young people (Pew, 2004). More importantly, those who use the Internet are far better informed than those who rely on other sources of information, and these *netizens* are far more interested in politics (Hamilton, 2004). The universal attraction of young people to digital communication technologies can be important for motivating engagement with their chosen issues, and, as outlined in the next set of recommendations, for helping to establish collective identifications with those issues as well.

INTRODUCING CITIZENSHIP AS COMMUNICATION PRACTICE: INFORMATION AND COMMUNICATION TECHNOLOGIES AND CIVIC LEARNING

Personalizing the information process in the ways that many ICTs make possible may risk fragmenting publics and isolating individual citizens. Developing a highly individualized sense of politics may not be regarded as a problem in the AC world, but it is often seen as antithetical to the DC view of the democratic polity. In order to counter the perils of isolation through overly personalized digital media experiences, the learning environment for next generation citizens must be designed to appeal to the affinity for networks and communities of interest. Interactive communication technologies should be aimed at creating echoing online environments that enable others to engage with and contribute to emerging understandings of the public issues at the center of the learning experience. This sense of common engagement with one's own and with others' issues introduces the experience of being part of a public as a core element of the learning process.

Research on the learning environments preferred by DotNets suggests that there are a number of fundamental changes that can be introduced productively into the traditional learning environment. As part of a Microsoft effort to design educational technology, Peden (2003) has summarized an effort in the United States to create national classroom technology standards for teachers. According to this perspective, the key to the successful introduction of technology in the learning environment is not just delivering hardware or software applications, but reorganizing the social and psychological contexts in which they are used. Peden contrasts the new learning preferences with the traditional classroom learning environment as outlined in Table 2.

These norms for introducing technology into the learning environment are also happily aligned with a more democratic experience for the AC

Table 2 Emerging learning preferences that may be enabled by ICTs

New learning preferences	Traditional learning environment
Student/group centered	Teacher centered
Multimedia	Single media
Collaborative work	Isolated work
Critical thinking/informed decision making	Fact/knowledge-based learning

Source: Peden (2003); based on International Society for Technology in Education. See ISTE (2004) National Technology Standards for Teachers.

learners. Current DC approaches to civic education often seem lamentably at odds with the ideal AC experience of peer-to-peer, nonhierarchical, network participation. For example, conventional civics education often treats the subject matter as: (1) another academic subject; (2) with right and wrong responses arbitrated by the teacher as central authority; and (3) students competing in isolation for academic favor. For example, the results of the IEA survey of high school students in the United States suggests that the dominant learning experience in civics classrooms was the traditional learning model of isolated learners, receiving fact-based material from teachers. For example 89% of 9th graders reported reading from textbooks, and 88% reported filling out worksheets, compared to only 45% reporting debating and discussing ideas, 40% engaging in role play or mock trials, 31% receiving visits from leaders, and 27%writing letters to express their opinions (U.S. Department of Education, 1999).

Further analysis of the U.S. IEA data by Campbell (2004) indicates that favorable attitudes toward a whole range of political activities were associated with the degree to which classrooms were more open, interactive, and focused on participation. However, the dilemma in his findings is that these open participation conditions seemed less likely to occur in mixed race classrooms, suggesting that young people are less likely to engage with each other across racial lines. The potential for ICTs to promote less racially cued communication is worth exploring in this context.

In general, research indicates that not only do students prefer interactive learning environments, but that these environments matter for the translation of civics skills into civic practice. For example the U.S. "civic health of the nation" study found that those who participated in high school debate were far more active politically after they entered public life than those who had no debate experience. The debaters were nearly twice as likely to attend community meetings and sign petitions, and three times as likely as those who did not debate to participate in boycotts. Joining groups in high school also significantly boosted a range of adult civic activities including regular voting (Keeter et al. 2002).

The lesson seems clear: learning environments that emphasize old style, fact based, teacher-centered pedagogy may succeed in imparting abstract facts and skills of the sort that can be tested, but, to return to the findings from the Australian case, they do not help young citizens translate that knowledge into later civic practice. Perhaps the message here is that providing learners with tools to experience actual civic practice in the learning environment makes more sense. Communication environments that offer collective experiences and provide public displays of group projects may create a first semblance of public life. The Student Voices projects described earlier illustrate these principles, as learners are introduced to an interactive digital web environment that enables them to tailor information and communication to their group issue projects. In addition to having access to external media input for information purposes, this interactive web environment also enables learners to communicate among themselves about emerging understandings of issues, and about the ways in which government and larger publics might become engaged with their causes. This brings us to the next logical next step in our civic learning model: linking communities of civic learners meaningfully to the real world of politics and government.

A FINAL STEP: TRANSLATING COMMUNICATION SKILLS INTO PARTICIPATION IN CIVIC NETWORKS

It is important for this issue-driven civic learning process to link ultimately to the entry points of public life such as press, government, issue organizations and community networks. For nearly every problem or issue identified by young citizens-in-training, there is abundant public information available about it, and much of that information shows how citizen interest and advocacy networks are trying to win the attention of government. In addition, citizens in nations that have embraced e-government initiatives have increasing access to relevant government activities through online record archives, and through televised coverage of government proceedings that are often archived digitally and streamed on demand. Perhaps most importantly, civic activists and public officials are often available to address the concerns of young citizens, whether through personal visits or participation in computer chats. Using these and other channels, the interactive learning situation can ultimately connect citizen-learners to sources of information about their political concerns, and to networks of citizens and officials involved in making policy about them.

One model that illustrates this linkage to the larger political world is Student Voices (2004) in the United States. The website for the project (http://student-voices.org/) introduces a set of information resources, along with linkages to government and civic organizations. Once there is an active connection between a group's issue project and relevant spheres of politics and government, it is important to facilitate real contact with the various actors those spheres. It turns out that representatives of civic groups and public institutions are generally willing to meet with young people, and to have remarkably open exchanges about their political concerns. Various formats can be developed for bridging the learning environment and the policy arena. For example, Student Voices links into local elections by inviting candidates to talk with students in schools and preparing students to interrogate candidates in a press-debate format held in an open public forum that is televised on local public access television. In addition, class issue projects are often presented as public policy recommendations, and judged in a civics fair by community leaders. Students have even produced series of public affairs programs from their own perspectives that were aired on local public television and then archived and streamed on demand over the web (http://www2.ci.seattle.wa.us/Media/ram_sc.asp?ID=2167). Linking the classroom and the surrounding political environment is also a major goal of Project Citizen (Center for Civic Education, 2004).

Building bridges between the citizenship learning environment, the public sphere, and the policy process not only results in learning a set of civic skills, but, more generally, developing a higher regard for participating in the political world of civic activism, government and elections (Bennett et al., 2002). In some cases, students have become actively involved in the policy process they developed as part of their issue projects. The overall result of this integration of the civics learning environment with the real political world is a bridge between the AC and DC models of citizenship that offers next generation citizens a broader repertoire of civic action than they might acquire in conventional approaches that, no matter how well-intentioned, risk reproducing the same aversion to the DC model of citizenship that many young citizens bring to the learning situation in the first place.

CONCLUSIONS

Creating a civics environment that integrates the AC and DC worlds is not always easy, as the earlier case of Australia suggests. Even if we leave aside the digital divide questions of technology deployment and access, there are various policy hurdles that must be confronted in order to implement models of the sort outlined above. Among the most obvious policy obstacles are three: elevating the importance of civics in the curriculum; getting curriculum developers and the policy officials who monitor them to understand the evolving nature of citizenship; and encouraging schools and teachers to offer students a taste of democracy in the learning environment by bringing issues that matter into the core of the process, and helping young citizens make contact with real political processes.

Bringing civics back in. Strange as it may seem to those of us who are passionate about civic education, courses on citizenship and government are far from standard in many national education systems, and even rarer in settings outside the schools. In the United States, for example, far fewer civics courses are taught today than several decades ago, suggesting that part of the decline in political participation may well be attributed to a parallel decline in the prominence of civics in the schools. Public officials and educators talk a great deal about education today, but the focus is on basic job skills such as reading and math, and not such basic life skills as citizen participation. The problem here may run deeper than casual neglect (oops we forgot civics!). In recent years, for example, the schools in America have become political battlegrounds policed by conservative groups who detect liberal political bias in most programs that favor creative thinking over strict academic discipline. Rather than being regarded as a virtue, the creative teaching of civics is likely to be viewed with suspicion in many communities. The case needs to be made by education leaders and public officials that the crisis in civic engagement requires giving the same priority to civics education that has been given to teaching basic reading or math skills.

Recognizing changes in citizenship. Bringing civics back in will do little good if those who design and implement the curricula implicitly assume that "good citizenship" looks like the traditional DC model. Youthful skepticism about authorities who do not invite meaningful dialogue on their terms will kill engagement if civics education models reinforce those perceptions and introduce citizenship in terms laden with duty and obligation. Ample evidence now exists (thanks to studies such as the IEA surveys and the PEW civic health polls) about how young people respond to various kinds of learning environments. Reproducing environments that alienate young citizens serve neither the educational nor the public good.

Opening the learning environment to the world. Even if new directions of citizenship are acknowledged and incorporated in the civics curriculum, the models of implementation in the learning environment become the final gate that can open or close the learning experience. Those who facilitate the learning experience must encourage an element of democracy in the classroom, as manifested in guiding young citizens through the construction of a meaningful public problem, enabling them to create a community of interest and understanding about the problem, facilitating open communication, and then making contact with groups and officials in the public sphere who are engaged with it. This process must be structured, of course, but creating a sense of ownership in the process on the part of the learner is the key to understanding how to take responsibility as a citizen after the learning experience is over.

Developing and deploying information and communication technologies can bring this democratic experience to life for young civic learners. As with most uses of technology, however, the value added depends on the organization of the social context in which the technology operates. In the case of citizenship education, the design of the learning environment must pay careful theoretical attention to changing realities in the societies and political systems with which young citizens must engage.

REFERENCES

Bang, Henrik. 2003. "A New Ruler Meeting a New Citizen: Culture Governance and Everyday Making," in Henrik Bang, ed., *Governance as Social and Political Communication*. Manchester: Manchester University Press.

Beck, Ulrich. 1999. *World Risk Society*. London: Blackwell.

Beck, Ulrich. 2000. *What Is Globalization?* Cambridge, UK: Polity Press.

Bennett, W. Lance. 1998. "The UnCivic Culture: Communication, Identity and the Rise of Lifestyle Politics." *P.S.: Political Science and Politics*, 31 (December): 741–61.

Bennett, W. Lance, Adam Simon, and Mike Xenos. 2002. "Seattle Student Voices: Comprehensive Executive Summary," Center for Communication and Civic Engagement.   http://depts.washington.edu/ccce/assets/documents/pdf/SeattleStudentVoicesExecSummaryFINAL.pdf.

Bennett, W. Lance and Mike Xenos. 2004. "Young Voters and the Web of Politics: Pathways to Participation in the Youth Engagement and Electoral Campaign Web Spheres," Center for Information and Research on Civic Learning and Engagement. http://www.civicyouth.org/PopUps/WorkingPapers/WP20Bennett.pdf

Blumler, Jay and Denis Kavanagh. 1999. "The Third Age of Political Communication: Influences and Features." *Political Communication*, 16: 209–230.

Campbell, David E. 2004. "How an Open Classroom Environment Facilitates Adolescents' Civic Development." Paper prepared for CIRCLE advisory board meeting, December 3, Washington, D.C. http://www.civicyouth,org

Center for Civic Education. 2004. http://www.civiced.org/index.php.

Center for Communication and Civic Engagement. 2004. http://www.engagedcitizen.org.

Civics Education Research Group, Canberra University. 2004. http://www.canberra.edu.au/civics/links/links.html.

Crick, Bernard. 1998. *Education for Citizenship and the Teaching of Democracy in Schools: Final Report of the Advisory Group on Citizenship*. London: Qualifications and Curriculum Authority.

Deutshes Jugend Institut. 2003. "Bulletin: On the State of Young People and Youth Policy in Europe." http://cgi.dji.de. Accessed July 21, 2004.

Eliasoph, Nina. 1998. *Avoiding Politics: How Americans Produce Apathy in Everyday Life*. New York: Cambridge University Press.

Giddens, Anthony. 1991. *Modernity and Self-Identity: Self and Society in the Late Modern Age*. Stanford, CA: Stanford University Press.

Hamilton, James T. 2004. *All the News that's Fit to Sell: How the Market Transforms Information into News*. Princeton, NJ: Princeton University Press.

IDEA. Institute for Democracy and Electoral Assistance. 1999. *Youth Voter Participation: Involving Young People in Tomorrow's Democracies*. Stockholm. http://www.idea.int/99df/daniela-int2.html.

Inglehart, Ronald. 1997. *Modernization and Postmodernization. Cultural, Economic, and Political Change in 43 Societies*. Princeton, NJ: Princeton University Press.

International Society for Technology in Education. 2004. "National Educational Technology Standards for Teachers." http://www.iste.org/standards/.

Istituto di Ricerca, Milan. 2001. *Study on the State of Young People and Youth Policy in Europe*.

Keeter, Scott, Cliff Zukin, Molly Andoline, and Krista Jenkins. 2002. "The Civic and Political Health of the Nation: A Generational Portrait." Center for

Information and Research on Civic Learning and Engagement. http://www.civicyouth.org.

Media Perspektiven. 5/2001. ARD German Television. http://www.ard-werbung.de/mp/publikationen/.

Media Perspektiven. 2/2002. ARD German Television. http://www.ard-werbung.de/mp/publikationen/.

Media Perspektiven. 6/2002. ARD German Television. http://www.ard-werbung.de/mp/publikationen/.

Mellor, Susanne, Kerry Kennedy, and Lisa Greenwood. 2001. *Citizenship and Democracy: Students' Knowledge and Beliefs. Australian Fourteen Year Olds and the IEA Civic Education Study.* Report to the Department of Education, Training, and Youth Affairs by the Australian Council of Education Research. http://www.acer.edu.au/research/Research_reports/Civics_Citizenship.htm.

Ministerial Council on Education, Employment, Training, and Youth, Australia. 2002. http://online.curriculum.edu.au/anr2002/ch_11majordev.htm

Neuman, W. Russell, Marion R. Just, and Ann N. Crigler. 1992. *News and the Construction of Political Meaning.* Chicago: University of Chicago Press.

O'Toole, Therese. 2004. "Explaining Young People's Non-Participation: Towards a Fuller Understanding of the Political." Paper presented at the 2004 European Consortium of Political Research, Uppsala Sweden; e-mail: m.t.otoole@bham.ac.uk.

Peden, Craig. 2003. "Unlocking Human Potential through the Power of eLearning." Microsoft Corporation; e-mail: cpeden@microsoft.com.

Pew Internet and American Life Project. 2004. "Political Information Sources and the Campaign," January 11, 2004. http://www.pewInternet.org/reports/reports.asp?Report=110&Section=ReportLevel1&Field=Level1ID&ID=475

Pirie, Madsen and Robert Worcester. 1998. *The Millennial Generation.* London: Adam Smith Institute.

Pirie, Madsen, and Robert Worcester. 2000. *The Big Turnoff.* London: Adam Smith Institute/MORI. http://www.adamsmith.org/policy/publications/media-culture-sport-pub.html.

Project Citizen. 2004. http://www.judiciary/citc/special/project-citizen/2004.html.

Putnam, Robert D. 2000. *Bowling Alone: The Collapse and Revival of American Community.* New York: Simon and Schuster.

Rahn, Wendy M. 2004. "National Identities and the Future of Democracy, Part II: Globalization and the Decline of Civic Commitments." Paper presented at the Conference on Democracy in the Twenty-First Century. University of Illinois, October 24–26.

Schudson, Michael. 1998. *The Good Citizen: A History of American Civic Life.* New York: The Free Press.

Student Voices. 2004. http://student-voices.org/.

Torney-Purta, Judith, Rainer Lehman, Hans Oswald, and Wolfram Schulz. 2001. "Citizenship and Civic Education in Twenty-eight Countries: Civic Knowledge and Engagement at Age Fourteen." International Association for the Evaluation of Educational Achievement. http: www.wam.umd.edu/~iea/. Accessed July 19, 2004.

United States Department of Education. 1999. National Center for Education Statistics. Civic Education Study.

Part II

Situating young citizens' media use

5 Young people's identity construction and media use
Democratic participation in Germany and Austria

Uwe Hasebrink and Ingrid Paus-Hasebrink

This chapter aims first to provide an overview of empirical evidence regarding young people's attitudes towards political participation, and their use of old and new media in Germany and Austria. Second, starting with the concept of identity construction (Paus-Haase 2000a), it discusses recent theoretical and empirical approaches in youth and media research, and their limitations when it comes to the question of how young people make use of new media against the background of the challenges they meet in growing up in today's Western societies. One upshot of these limitations is that research has to overcome several theoretical and methodological obstacles to providing a comprehensive understanding of the meanings of different forms of civic engagement. As one step towards this goal, this contribution proposes the concept of 'practical meaning' as a theoretical basis for research and to practical approaches regarding democratic engagement.

YOUNG PEOPLE'S CIVIC PARTICIPATION AND PATTERNS OF MEDIA USE IN GERMANY AND AUSTRIA

We shall focus on two aspects of civic engagement and political participation: what is traditionally called a general interest in politics, and the likelihood of engaging in different kinds of activities which can be interpreted as civil engagement.

Civic participation and engagement

In order to analyse developments of civic participation in different countries, it was necessary to compare longitudinal data on an international level. However, there are no studies which incorporate both of these aspects. Therefore the following overview is based on a composite of relevant longitudinal studies at a national level in two countries. In addition, findings are reported from a very recent cross-sectional comparative study which allows for the comparison of Germany and Austria as well as some other European countries.

With regard to long term data on young people's attitudes, values, and views on the world, the most important study for Germany is the Shell Youth Survey which has been conducted since the fifties, the most recent of which is Deutsche Shell (2003). The 14th edition is based on standardised personal interviews, realised in March/April 2002 among a representative sample of 2,515 young people between 12 and 25 years. Similar surveys were carried out in 1984, 1991, 1996, and 1999; thus, for some indicators in this study it is possible to make long term comparisons.

A first approach to the analysis of civic participation is to look at the general interest in politics as measured by means of a single-item question (Schneekloth 2003).

- In 2002, 34 percent of young people between 12 and 25 years said they were (strongly) interested in politics. This figure has been decreasing since the early nineties: in 1991 (when political interest and engagement reached a local maximum as a consequence of German unification) 57 percent of this age group said they were interested. Since then figures have gone down steadily: 1996, 47 percent; 1999, 43; 2002, 34.
- As has been shown in many other studies, this general indicator is strongly linked to several sociodemographic indicators, including: the older the participant, the more interested (12–14 years: 11 percent; 22–25 years: 44 percent); more male (37 percent) than female (23 percent) participants reported being interested; the more interested the parents, the more interested their children (parents strongly interested: 56 percent; parents not interested: 11 percent).

Other indicators show a strong feeling of distance from formal aspects of politics and some dissatisfaction with current politics; however, these are combined with a fairly high acceptance of the political system and democratic procedures. Compared to earlier studies, the latest survey emphasises that ideology does not play an important role as a frame of reference anymore, as was the case in the eighties and early nineties. Overall, the authors of the Shell Survey do not interpret today's young people as politically non-interested or even apolitical. Instead, they point out that political engagement is not an aim in itself anymore and even less a strategy for personal emancipation.

In order to explore new forms of civic activities the Shell survey included a specific instrument measuring indicators for civic engagement in a very broad sense (Gensicke 2003). Accordingly, many young people are at least occasionally active in the following social areas: interests of young people (51 percent); meaningful leisure activities for young people (47 percent); elderly people (43 percent); protection of environment and/or animals (37 percent); socially disadvantaged people (34 percent); intercultural aspects/

immigrants (34 percent); local communities (29 percent); people in developing countries (28 percent); security and order in the neighbourhood (26 percent); support for disabled people (22 percent); German culture and tradition (22 percent); social and political change in Germany (17 percent); and other areas (31 percent).

The institutional context of social activities is mainly shaped by different kinds of organisations: clubs, such as those for sports, culture, and music (52 percent); schools/universities (52 percent); youth organisations (25 percent); and religious organisations (19 percent). In contrast, political organisations are far less important; political parties (3 percent) and trade unions (3 percent) are still behind non-governmental organisations like Greenpeace or Amnesty International (5 percent) and topic oriented civil initiatives (4 percent); and far behind self-initiated projects or project groups (17 percent). In addition, almost one half of the young people say they pursue social activities on their own, without any organisational framework.

The situation of Austrian youth was reported on in an Austrian government publication (BMSG 2003). The report includes the results of a representative survey amongst young people between 14 and 30 years of age (n = 1,549) that was conducted in February/March 2003. The general results regarding political participation are quite in line with the German data (Zentner 2003). As in Germany, the main indicator has been the question 'Are you interested in politics?'

- In 2003, 37 percent of young people between 14 and 30 years said they were (strongly) interested in politics. Compared to earlier studies, this figure has been stable over the last ten years (Zentner 2003: 209).
- Slightly more male (39 percent) than female participants (34 percent) reported interest; the older the participant, the more interested (14–19 years, 26 percent; 20–24 years, 38 percent).

Other indicators emphasise that young people's engagement and participation often takes place outside the established (political) institutions. Whereas young people are unlikely to trust the official political institutions (e.g. the European Commission, the national parliament, trade unions, or political parties), they often participate in grass-roots organisations, local initiatives, and self-initiated activities (Zentner 2001).

Comparative data on Germany and Austria and some other European countries have been recently provided by the EU funded project EUYOUP-ART,[1] which is organised by a consortium of research institutions from Austria and Germany as well as from Estonia, Finland, France, Italy, Slovakia, and the UK. The nationally representative samples cover the age group between 15 and 25 years; in each country around 1,000 young people were asked about their interest in politics at the end of 2004.

According to preliminary comparative results, young people in Germany are quite interested in politics: 51 percent claimed to be very/fairly interested (SORA 2005).[2] The other countries ranked as follows: Italy (43 percent), Austria (42 percent), France (36 percent), Finland (35 percent), UK (30 percent), Estonia (29 percent), and Slovakia (28 percent). In Austria, as well as in all countries where the respective question, was asked (in the German survey it was not asked), non-governmental organisations like Greenpeace or Amnesty International are the most trusted institutions. Moreover, European institutions like the Parliament and even the Commission are more trusted than national institutions in the respective countries, in particular national parties and politicians. Although young people's trust in parties is very low, a majority of them say they feel close to a certain party, though there are substantial differences between the countries involved, with Italy (71 percent) and Finland (68 percent) having the strongest party orientation and the UK the weakest (23 percent) (SORA 2005).

The preliminary comparative analyses of the EUYOUPART study also reveal interesting correlations between political participation and several other indicators. According to these results, using the opportunities for democratic engagement as provided by schools goes along with political engagement even outside school. Furthermore, young people who inform themselves via active-reception media (i.e., newspapers, Internet) tend to be more politically active, whereas those using passive-reception media (television and to some extent also radio) show a lesser level in political participation (SORA 2005). Finally, a strong correlation is found between young people's political participation and the political behaviour of their parents.

The EUYOUPART study also provides evidence of the kind of political activities in which young Germans and Austrians (15–25 years) have participated (see Table 1). Regarding the role of new media for political participation, it is interesting to note that every tenth respondent in Germany and Austria claimed to have contributed to a political discussion on the Internet. This result may be interpreted as the Internet being regarded as one option among many others, but for the time being it is not a particularly important form of political participation.[3]

Patterns of new media use

Young people belong to those groups in today's societies that have the highest proportion of online users. The following empirical evidence for Germany is based on the JIM (youth, information, media) study 2004 (Medienpädagogischer Forschungsverbund Südwest 2004). The 2004 study was the 7th edition of this series of annual surveys, with the sample including young people between 12 and 19 years. Results show that among Germans youths, 58 percent use the Internet on a daily basis or at least several times per week, while 85 percent use it at least occasionally. This latter

Table 1 **Participation in political activities in Germany and Austria 2004**

Young people who have ever...	*Germany*	*Austria*
... signed a petition	41	14
... attended a political public meeting	31	28
... participated in a legal demonstration	28	18
... bought products for political reasons	15	22
... boycotted products	14	18
... written/forwarded a political letter	13	12
... contributed to a political discussion on the Internet	11	11
... worn a political badge	10	11
... contacted a politician	10	11
... donated money to a political group	8	7
... collected signatures	8	8
... written an article	7	8
... participated in a strike	6	12
... distributed political leaflets	5	5
... participated in an event where there was a violent confrontation with police	3	3
... participated in an illegal demonstration	3	4
... held a political speech	3	3
... written political graffiti	2	4
... participated in an event where there was a violent confrontation with opponents	2	2
... blocked railways/streets	2	2
... participated in a political event where property was damaged	2	2
... occupied buildings	2	1

Percentages of young people between 15 and 25 years, n=1,000 per country.
Sources: Wächter 2005; Picker and Westphal 2005)

figure is far above that for the general population (55 percent in 2004, see van Eimeren and Frees 2005: 363). Thus, we may say that for young people today, the Internet is an almost omnipresent medium.

The most popular online activities are e-mailing (47 percent of the Internet users send or receive e-mails every day or several times per week); searching for information (35 percent); listening to music (27 percent); getting the latest news (27 percent); education or employment related information (25 percent); and many others. The comparison between young male and female users reveals different patterns of Internet use: girls are more likely to use the Internet as a means of communication (e-mail, chat) and for information on education and employment related questions; boys are more likely to use music related services and the latest news.

For Austria, the most recent Youth Report (see above) includes empirical evidence on the use of old and new media technologies (Großegger 2003). As in Germany, young people in Austria belong to those groups in the society with the highest proportion of online users. Around 65 percent of those between 14 and 19 years report '(very) often' using the Internet; this figure is lower for the older groups covered in this study (20–24 years, 55 percent; 25–30 years, 48 percent).

The questions used in the Austrian survey differ substantially from those in the JIM survey; therefore, direct comparisons are not possible for further details. In particular, on the basis of the existing data, no link can be constructed between the use of the Internet and political engagement. What can be said is that the evidence provided does not hint at substantial differences from the observations for Germany. As in Germany, even the Internet is mainly used for entertainment reasons (music, games) and for communciation; dedicated search for specific information and communicative activities related to social engagement do not belong to the most important purposes to use the new technology. Regarding the debate on digital divides, it is interesting to note that girls and young women have considerably less access to computers; 33 percent of the girls between 14 and 19 years have their own computer compared to 47 percent of the boys.

The JIM study for the German youth also includes evidence regarding the information needs and the relative importance of different media. Similar to the aforementioned results of the Shell study, Table 2 illustrates that 'politics' and 'economy' in general terms are not among the topics of interest for young people; less than one fifth of the respondents claimed to be interested in these topics. The most important areas of interest are related to social relationships, to popular culture, and to education/employment and school.

The findings regarding the relative importance of different media clearly point out the significance of the Internet—for many topics in question young people regarded the Internet as the most important medium. The respective areas of interest are closely linked to specific and individualized information and orientation with regard to concrete challenges of young people's everyday lives (e.g., education, employment, and school). Beyond that the Internet is the most important medium for information on new technologies—here magazines are the second most important source of information—and some aspects of popular culture (music, movies, computer games). The core competence of television is related to sports, world news, and (music and movie) stars, whereas magazines are the most important sources for orientation about social relationships.

Regarding the overall question of this book about the relationship between political participation and new technologies, the results on this level indicate a minor role for the Internet. Even the few young people

Table 2 Thematic competencies of different media

Topic (selection)	a. % interest	b. Most important medium for information:					
		TV	Radio	Internet	Newspaper	Magazines	Books
Friendship	96	8	2	21	6	28	10
Music	84	28	18	34	2	15	1
Education/employment	75	5	0	50	15	11	10
Love/partnership	71	11	2	24	5	32	7
Sports	69	36	3	19	19	18	3
Current news (what happens in the world)	59	38	6	16	33	7	1
Cinema, movies	56	23	3	31	19	21	1
Internet	54	8	1	59	6	17	5
School	54	5	1	55	8	5	18
Fashion	53	18	0	17	5	50	2
Music stars, bands	53	35	12	23	4	25	0
Computer & accessories	53	6	0	38	7	35	9
Health, medicine	51	17	2	24	12	18	20
Environment (protection)	41	19	2	30	24	12	9
Movie-/TV-Stars	37	46	4	22	3	22	1
Computer games	34	8	0	50	6	30	1
Arts, culture	20	12	2	20	19	15	27
Economy	18	14	2	20	38	11	10
Politics (federal level)	16	43	4	13	35	4	0

(a) Percent of respondents who are interested [top 2 boxes of a 6 point scale from 1=very interested to 6=not interested at all] in the respective topic;

(b) Percent of those who are interested who say the respective medium is the most important for the respective topic (Source: MPFS 2004)

Table 3 Main channel for political information in Germany and Austria 2004 (percentages of young people between 15 and 25 years, n=1,000 per country)

	Germany	Austria
Television	65	46
Radio	13	17
Newspapers	16	25
Internet	4	6
None of these	2	6

Sources: Wächter 2005; Picker and Westphal 2005)

who are interested in politics do not think the Internet plays a major role; instead television and the newspapers are clearly ahead regarding politics.

This finding is supported by the results of the EUYOUPART study. Table 3 shows that television is still by far the most important channel for political information and even newspapers and radio are more important than the Internet. Whereas the German and Austrian results are quite similar, the comparison with other countries leads to substantial differences. In Finland and Estonia it is the Internet that plays a substantial role as a source of political information, whereas in France, Italy, and Slovakia television is the main source by a long way for young people wishing to inform themselves on politics; moreover in the UK, a substantial number of young people do not make use of any mass media for political information (SORA 2005).

LINKS BETWEEN CIVIC PARTICIPATION AND MEDIA USE

After this overview of political engagement and the use of new media technologies, the following section deals with empirical evidence regarding the direct link between these two areas of young people's activities. Within the framework of the latest Shell Youth Survey, 20 qualitative case analyses have been conducted with young people who meet two criteria: (1) some kind of civic engagement; (2) engagement via the Internet (Picot and Willert 2003). One of the aims of this study was to gather more insight into what has been termed 'new forms of civic engagement'. In previous studies this notion has often suggested a change of paradigms—from the lament about young people's decreasing political interest to the more optimistic view of young people actively looking for new forms of engagement. However, so far, empirical surveys show that they do not seem to be that important in quantitative terms. As the quantitative survey of the most recent Shell study indicates, civic activities in a very broad sense are not sufficiently frequent to balance the decrease of political interest. The qualitative analyses emphasised the following aspects of 'new' forms of engagement:

- *Action instead of organisation:* One of the aspects of politics, which keep young people increasingly distant from classical political activities, is their hierarchical, static, and bureaucratic structures. Young people prefer action, self-initiative, spontaneity; they like working on projects, in ad hoc groups or initiatives. And while they like to take on responsibilities for concrete tasks, they do not like to take a 'post' for a longer period of time. These kinds of activities are supported by the characteristics of the Internet. The Internet structures do not make it necessary to take a long walk through the institutions; for example, a discussion forum like 'democracy today' (dol2day) makes it very easy to launch new specific initiatives. An important aspect is the low levels of obligation connected to Internet activities: they can be abandoned at any time. The Internet helps to organise flexible structures, non-hierarchical networks instead of vertically structured institutions. One of the most prominent examples is the Attac movement. As the authors of the Shell study point out, the motto 'action instead of organisation' does not mean that young people want spontaneous disorganisation. On the contrary, they simply prefer network structures and well organised strategies to realise their aims.
- *Global perspective:* In contrast to previous studies which showed that young people's civic engagement concentrates on the local level, on small concrete steps, the 2002 study emphasises that the global perspective plays an important role with regard to civic engagement. Young people are dealing with the 'future of the world', and believe that their lives are affected by global ecological, economical, and social influences. This is one of the reasons for the attractiveness of the Attac network. From this point of view the Internet obviously is a driving force. The possibility of global communication is fascinating and raises awareness of global developments.
- *Pragmatism instead of ideology:* Ideology does not seem to play an important role in young people's civic engagement. Former normative views, according to which civic engagement should be an altruistic complement to hedonistic activities, do not satisfy young people; their civic engagement is intrinsically motivated and dedicated to concrete aims. These aims as well as the respective activities are rather pragmatic than ideological; political attitudes seem to be constructed like patchworks, not according to comprehensive ideological systems. From these young people's views one of the advantages of the Internet is that it provides opportunities to meet people with different opinions, something which rarely happens in their regular social contexts.

- *Publicity orientation:* Possibly as one of the consequences of the specific group selected for this qualitative analysis, it can be observed that public relations are an important aspect of civic engagement. Publishing relevant information on the Internet, participating in Internet discussions, planning public relation strategies for a specific topic is an integral part of civic engagement. The publicity is sought in order to campaign for certain ideas, acquire new members, get financial support, and for political debate. For these young people, compared to the Internet, the other mass media are viewed suspiciously as providing biased selections of reality. They are aware of the vast amount of information available via the Internet and they have the ambition to know as much as possible about their field of interest.

Overall, with regard to the Internet in the context of civic engagement, three functions can be differentiated for Internet use: (1) for communication within the framework of an existing organisation; (2) as a means for networking different autonomous projects; (3) as a platform for non-organised individuals to participate in discussing topics of interest to them, and in planning joint actions or in getting information.

Independent of the specific function for their own civic engagement, there are several characteristics that make the Internet highly attractive for young people. Besides the general fascination with the medium and the communicative opportunities it provides, the right and the possibility of expressing one's own opinion play an important role. Young people also like the underlying democratic structure of the Internet, which provides an ideal model of participation for them. In this respect young people increasingly reflect on additional mechanisms of direct democracy regarding the German political system.

In regard to publicity, most of the young people in this study report that they were successful in raising public attention for their particular topic or initiative, although they realistically take into account that they do not reach mass audiences. There is quite a lot of scepticism regarding the effectiveness of discussions on the Internet. On the one hand, it is emphasised that these discussions generate several useful ideas, on the other hand, it seems extremely difficult to realise many of these ideas. Important aspects of successful discussions online are trust and increasingly reliable personal relationships, but there is some disagreement on the necessity and practice of rules and moderation. The effects of Internet activities on 'real politics' are regarded with ambivalence. Those aiming at broad publicity think that classical mass media would be more useful—if they could afford to use them. Others, particularly those participating in networking activities, point out that the Internet and its specific features are the necessary condition for their activity.

The empirical results on political engagement and media use in Germany and Austria, as quoted here, provide some key evidence on the core themes of this book. However, these results hover on a superficial level. In order to develop strategies to learn democratic engagement, we think it is necessary to probe the theoretical basis of these studies. As a starting point for this discussion we have selected the concept of identity construction in general, and more specifically, its relevance within current youth research.

THEORETICAL APPROACHES TO YOUNG PEOPLE'S IDENTITY CONSTRUCTION

The theoretical ambition should be to better understand the complexity and contextuality of media related action. In order to do so, modern research on socialisation can provide useful concepts (Hurrelmann and Ulich 1991a). Inspired by various conceptions from psychology (learning theory, psychoanalysis, developmental and ecological psychology) to sociology (system theory, action theory, social theory)[4] the relation between the individual and society is understood as an interactive process. The central focus is on the active, reality-addressing subject (Hurrelmann 1990; Vinken 2004). This model underscores mutual relationships between the subject's 'inner reality' and socially mediated 'external reality': it puts the human subject into a social and ecological context that is subjectively perceived and processed, yet is always influenced, changed, and created by the individual (Hurrelmann 1990, p. 64).

Young people's identity construction

The sociological dimensions of the concept of identity, originally stemming from the psychoanalytical theory proposed by Erik H. Erikson,[5] have been elaborated by Krappmann (1969), following premises of symbolic interactionism (Mead 1980). According to Krappmann, ego-identity means a successful balance between personal and social identity; in Cooley's words: 'Self and society are twinborn, an independent ego is illusion' (Cooley, quoted by Baacke 1973: 83). Further, Jürgen Belgrad (1992) critically raises the issue of the increasingly differentiated late modern subjectivity. In contrast to the identity concept of Habermas (1988), who sees stabilised identity as a normative objective, Belgrad offers a theoretic view that opens up the possibility of distancing the self from various constraints. In a late modern vein he proposes a turn towards 'the other side of reason'[6] and towards 'play'.[7] Finding one's self and growing up today means being able to create identities, to drop, to redraft, and to maintain them; that is, to play with them and to accept basic uncertainties in one's own anticipated biography.

These concepts of identity are to be set against the background of social change. In doing this, and following Dieter Baacke (1989), we have to take into account that the everyday worlds of young people can be described as media worlds. The young generation, often called 'generation @' switches through channels, uses cell phones and the Internet, downloads music onto their workstation. With regard to today's young people, Ferchhoff speaks of 'multi-media youth' (1999: 227–29). Different kinds of media, used in differentiated repertoires, serve in many respects to challenge and evaluate their identity; the media allow for a hedonistic, non-directive reflection of one's self, they offer characters and forums for the acquisition or rejection of different styles of life (Paus-Haase et al. 1999).

Concepts of current youth and media research

One important core of recent youth research is made up of the approach of self-socialisation (Müller et al. 2004). This approach emphasises the individual's own contribution to socialisation, his or her agency. More than ever before, today's young people face the challenge of organising their construction of identity from an expert's position. They meet this challenge not least by employing various different media. The Internet is particularly significant here because it provides many options for participation, be they politically or non-politically oriented. One important consequence of this development is the decreasing role of socially integrative control and filter mechanisms operative in today's culture (Niesyto 2004: 10).

What is important for the process of identity construction is that young people do not simply receive, store, and process what the relevant environmental offers, but that they themselves also appropriate from the environment. They actively select, interpret, and use what is offered on the basis of their specific forms and schemata of perception.[8] Only in this way do the media become influential in the socialisation process. The approach of self-socialisation with its emphasis on young people's autonomy and choice, clearly invokes the thesis of individualisation, with its emphasis on patch-work or fragmented identity.

In this regard, the specific way in which young people construct their identity has been described as 'bricolage'. This term, introduced by Lévi-Strauss, refers to the restructuring and recontextualisation of objects in order to communicate new meanings (Baacke 1992: 20). According to Baacke, bricolage of style and fashion implies that the surface becomes the valid signifier of personality (1992: 20),[9] it functions as a symbol of status and as such becomes an expression of lifestyles.

Following McDonald (1999), young people's cultural practices of all kinds can be understood as 'struggles for identity' acted out within conditions of social change, aimed at creating and maintaining the impression of subjective coherence and the capability for action (Scherr 2004: 231). In this view, young people living in a phase of eroding (political) institutions, try to reduce uncertainty and to make sense of their experiences in order to achieve an at least relatively coherent self-construction (231). Thus, the predominant model of current research is that young people's constructions of identity are interpreted as the tension between individualisation and integration (Beck and Sopp 1997).

However, some scepticism should nevertheless be expressed with regard to this theoretical position (see also Scherr 2004). Insofar as political participation is concerned, recent studies on youth cultures and young people's lifestyles in Germany (e.g. Eckert et al. 2000, Hitzler 1999, both quoted by Scherr 2004) mainly focus on atypical distinctions and specific aspects of scenes and styles (Scherr 2004: 232). Yet, the more pervasive patterns of everyday communication are often neglected. Indeed, the hypothesis of individualisation that has often been the focus of interest in youth research tends to emphasise the 'colourful cows'[10]—distinctive and as such easily identifiable phenomena on the edge of the field—whereas the many fine differences among shades of 'grey' (i.e., ways of living of the vast majority of young people), are usually neglected (Paus-Haase 2000b). Thus, how 'normal young people' live their lives, use the media, and communicate via the Internet, is rarely covered in these studies. Recent studies show that the capacity to actively make choices in regard to identity matters is closely linked to cultural and social resources—and these are unevenly distributed, even in modern and post-modern societies (Niesyto 2004: 10).

Looking more closely at general youth surveys like the German Shell study or the Austrian Youth study, it becomes evident that even here the respective methods employed have limitations as well. One example closely related to our topic, the political interest of young people (Kuhn and Schmid 2004) is that most studies that deal with the political interest of young people rely on the single item question 'Are you interested in politics?' However, this indicator is traditionally associated with traditional fields of politics like economy and taxes, foreign affairs, defence policy, and political parties. Thus, use of this indicator ignores the whole array of emerging new politics, not least areas in which women and girls particularly have manifested involvement, such as feminism, health, and ecology.

Also, youth research has tended to emphasise one of two perspectives: developmental psychology focusing on processes of maturation and 'personal individuation', or sociologically oriented integration of individuals into the societal structure (Mansel 1997: 9). Vinken refers to these approaches in terms of the over-socialised person of modernity versus the over-individualised person of post-modernity (2004: 258); the two perspectives remain polarised. Finally, the concrete processes by which new media function in socialisation of young people has been neglected. Youth research needs to rethink its approaches.

'PRACTICAL MEANING'—A BASIC CONCEPT FOR YOUTH AND MEDIA RESEARCH

Against the background of this unsatisfactory situation of youth research, we propose an elaborated approach to youth media research to develop new tools for thinking, new theoretical and methodological ways that move beyond the current dichotomies in youth research. The aim is to better understand young people in the context of their complex living conditions and the challenges of constructing identity.

Five key concepts

In brief, we make use of the following key five concepts: identity, social milieu, habitus, experience, and orientation (Paus-Hasebrink, 2005). A core theoretical starting point for a re-positioning of youth and media research can be found in the notion of social action, which encompasses the concept of *identity*. Referring to Bourdieu's theory of practice,[11] one can identify the social field (1979, 1997), in which social action takes place, certain aims are followed, and certain patterns of action are socially 'accepted' (Weiß 2000: 47). Within this perspective, the focus is directed towards the character of *social milieus*.

Looking at social milieus, and at habitus as their phenomenological manifestations, it is possible to reflect on basic life circumstances. In particular it is no longer necessary to focus on the extraordinary; on the contrary, we emphasise that community is lived and experienced in shared meanings and unquestioned biographical practices (Lash 1996: 269). Broadly shared and community-building frameworks of meanings are produced through common experiences and can be observed in common habits. The concept of habitus also includes the 'bodily inscribed' and 'non-cognitive' categories which can be described as common knowledge (Lash 1996: 268). These categories, which refer to the embeddedness of the self into a network of biographical practices, point to the necessity of common meaning production and interpretation. The respective processes are realised, for example, within peer groups that deal with different forms of 'youth culture', the Internet being one important ingredient.

Today, processes of identity construction of young people are closely linked to increasing commercialisation on the one hand, and to an ongoing process of intimisation and increasing expectations towards events and experience on the other hand. It seems as if for young people the most important approach to reality[12] is increasingly seen in gaining firsthand *experience*. In order to be capable of acting, to make sense of everyday experiences, to cope with everyday life, *orientation* is needed; this concept too derives from Bourdieu's notion of action. Young people in particular ask for a non-directive, attractive, and emotional means of orientation—one reason why they use media in general and the Internet in particular.

Patterns of orientation are culturally negotiated and traded, they refer to societal positions. Transformed into everyday knowledge, they monitor individual actions and help to develop social and personal identities (i.e., to find one's own position, to gain the capability to act). Here again, we meet the interplay of internal and external reality and the danger of the respective 'hiatus' between them. However, looking at the means of meaning making, at the ensemble of practices used to cope with everyday life, this conceptual approach does not allow the individual to tackle the question from either a subjective or an objective perspective. Instead, the question is dealt with from the perspective of 'practical meaning', of 'praxeology'. In doing so, the focus is put on the individual context of life, but at the same time goes beyond subjective representations and takes into account social milieus, or spheres that are—actually or symbolically—at the individual's disposal. The centre of practical meaning is made up of self-interest and the respective tactical behaviour. The question at hand is how to use opportunities for individual success in the following spheres of *practical actions in everyday life* (here we follow Habermas 1988: 473):

- Work life (work, income, capital),
- Politics and law (social order, law, morality), and
- Private sphere (love, personal relationships, happiness).

In doing so, metaphorically speaking, people individually invest their capital as efficiently as possible. In terms of practical actions, any individual, by means of his or her capital, tries to seize the opportunities offered by the particular social sphere. This wealth of subjective capital is of course distributed in a highly unequal manner, as the different social positions of young people clearly demonstrate.

Taking the perspective of practical meaning, the question now is how young people, despite their low capital, can succeed in being as competent as possible, in coping with their everyday life and, in the case of our topic, in participating also in political issues. The answer has to be found in the respective social milieus and their habitus; it has to do with the different opportunities to develop one's identity and to acquire capabilities to act.

The concept of practical meaning goes beyond the dualism that has characterised the Hurrelmann model of productive processing of reality. By considering the individual's everyday life, as well as the societal conditions of media use, the conceptual framework described above also allows for a more appropriate understanding of how people integrate media into their everyday lives.[13]

THE IMPORTANCE OF 'PRACTICAL MEANING' FOR YOUTH AND MEDIA RESEARCH

Media reception includes the transaction of meanings of industrially produced objects of mass culture with the self-interest of the individual acquisition against the background of everyday orientations (Weiß 2003: 25). By employing media, recipients—without the obligations and challenges of everyday life, without the pressure to act—can succeed in learning about orientations and enjoying them in the course of experience. Thus, media related actions as an integral part of everyday culture are able to link the orientations of practical meaning that are adapted to the structural conditions of everyday practice, with the creativity, self-directed purpose, and emphasis on cultural action (Weiß 2003: 25–26).

Thus, with regard to young people, media as a part of everyday culture and popular culture provide different opportunities to create meanings, to foster awareness of oneself, to reflect, to clarify, or to re-define one's own position. The Internet in particular is used as a means for exchange, Internet related activities can become an indicator for being 'in' or 'out' within a particular peer group. The Internet can serve as a specific means to participate in culture and political processes. As a popular form of participation, it offers the symbolic material that can help young people to live their lives. In the specific way that young people use it, the Internet might allow for easier access to political participation, particularly for those who, as a consequence of their (low) formal education, their specific milieu, do not regard themselves as targeted by high cultural products.

CONCLUSION

This chapter has aimed at providing a short overview of empirical data on political participation and media use of young people in Germany and Austria. As with other countries, the general finding is that politics and political engagement in the traditional sense are not at all the focus of young people's interests. Furthermore the extensive use of media does not seem to be a means to actively participate in processes of public communication and political information; rather, it is dominated by the entertainment function. Scholars have been arguing for several years that this—from a traditional, normative perspective—'bad news' should not be mis-interpreted as if young people were not at all interested in social and political engagement. They provide lots of evidence indicating that young people engage in many different activities that are socially and politically relevant but not linked to classical political institutions. Patterns of political engagement as well as patterns of media use have become more individualised, more volatile.

Thus, research on young people's political participation and the role of new media technologies has to meet different challenges. On the one hand, a conceptual and methodological approach is needed (e.g., by means of tri-angulation; see Flick 2003) which allows for grasping complex structures and for starting from the perspectives of young people themselves. On the other hand, it seems to be important that politics is no longer dealt with as a separate sphere, outside everyday culture, restricted to 'official politics' and traditional forms of political participation. Hence, research should start from the young people's perspective, from what they understand as politics, from what they actually do with the Internet. Up to now, political education often misses young people, their interests, their media practices, and their views on social participation. Young people are not keen on formal procedures, they develop their own forms of participation, many of them being rather event-oriented and aesthetically attractive[14] and many of them being realised via the Internet. Therefore, these kinds of engagements and participation should be supported even within the framework of political education.

NOTES

1. For details see http://www.sora.at/wahlen/EUYOUPART.
2. Compared to the low figures reported above, this result seems to be surprising; it reminds us of the difficulties linked with the comparison of data from different studies; beyond differences in the respective population, even simple indicators like the question 'Are you interested in politics?' heavily depend on the exact wording of the question and the categories provided for the answers.
3. Further evidence regarding this point will be provided below.
4. For this discussion see Hurrelmann (1990: 13ff). As a common characteristic of all conceptions, Hurrelmann works out the rejection of a linear unidimensional determination of personality development. 'They share the idea that the development of personality happens in the course of an interaction process between internal and external reality, in which each individual uses and develops capabilities of adapting, processing, coping and changing reality' (Hurrelmann 1990: 63; translation: UH/IPH).
5. According to Erikson (1970), childhood and youth are to be understood as phases of psychosocial crises, which have to be passed through in the process of building a stable personality.
6. In this context one might refer to the concept of 'reason', which, starting in the era of the Enlightenment, formed the basis for the project of modernity and the critical reflection of it in post-modernity (Fromme 1997: 39ff.). The focus of post-modernity lies in a re-evaluation of reason, which had already previously been judged as perverted by Horkheimer and Adorno; this re-evaluation led to the inclusion of the body and of sensuality as the other side of reason and as such is of outstanding importance, particularly for young people.
7. The concept of 'play' goes back to Wittgenstein's term 'play of language' (Fromme 1997). In referring to this concept two aspects shall be emphasised: On the one hand, the openness of languages which corresponds to the differently constructed youth cultures; on the other hand, the plurality being expressed in various symbolic forms and requiring bricolage (Fromme 1997: 337).
8. With regard to approaching the perspectives of children and young people, constructivism is often regarded as an epistemological basis (Lange 1999: 60). Numerous, sometimes quite diffuse constructivist ideas can be observed in research. In order to clarify our own position in this respect: In distinction from radical constructivism which, to put it simply, denies the existence of a world outside the subject, we emphasise the significance of the societal environment for the construction of identity.
9. As quoted by Baacke (1992: 20), Paul Valery said: 'The deepest about human beings is their skin'.

10. This is a literal translation of a German idiom which refers to shining but rather exotic examples.
11. This idea refers to a concept developed by Ralph Weiß for the use of television (see below), that has its starting point in the strategies of meaning construction. With reference to Habermas and Bourdieu, Weiß advanced the socio-psychological concept of the 'practical meaning' of media communication, that has to be regarded as highly useful, especially for the field of reception research (Weiß 2000).
12. In order to explain this phenomenon, Scott Lash points out that the importance of cultural structures increased in combination with the decline in social structures (Lash 1996). Only cultural experience and commonly shared meaning can foster the feeling of community. This is what Gerhard Schulze's lucid term 'society of experience' describes (e.g. through globalised forms of brand orientation—Nike, McDonalds, Disney—that nevertheless remain only on the surface).
13. Under the heading 'patterns of praxeology', Weiß developed a theoretically well grounded system of orientations, that organises the everyday actions of people as generative principles. He furthermore developed an overview of different forms of perception that illustrates the 'way in which the TV-viewer internalises the meaning of the perceived'. These include: watching, getting into the mood, imagining, feeling, deciphering, aesthetically enjoying, and understanding (Weiß 2001: 249, translation UH/IPH). As the visual perception of the user adapts to the communicative genre of, for example, the TV programme, or as in this case, the Internet, specific forms of access to the content are being established. 'Programme forms or genres are characterised by typical patterns, through which they deal with the commonly relevant material' (Weiß 2001: 250, translation UH/IPH). Therefore, Weiß concludes that genres represent specific 'traditions of discourse', so that the viewer's distinct experience with television leads to a specific knowledge of the genre. This in turn provides orientation and helps television viewers or Internet users to decide how to decipher the 'reading instructions' of the producers and in the end how to take the content (ibid.). Thus, through a combination of everyday meaning and the forms of perception mentioned above, TV and Internet turn into the activities—watching television and using the Internet.
14. It should be emphasised that in this context the notion of 'aesthetics' refers to perception in general and not to categories of 'the beautiful'; see Hentig's (1975) definition.

REFERENCES

Baacke, D. (1973) *Kommunikative Kompetenz. Grundlegung einer Didaktik der Kommunikation und ihrer Medien*, Munich: Juventa.

Baacke, D. (1989) 'Sozialökologie und Kommunikationsforschung', in D. Baacke and H.-D. Kübler (eds.) *Qualitative Medienforschung. Konzepte und Erprobungen*, Tübingen: Niemeyer.

Baacke, D. (1992) 'Zur Ambivalenz der neuen Unterhaltungsmedien oder vom Umgang mit schnellen Bildern und Oberflächen', in H.-U. Otto et al. (eds.) *Zeit-Zeichen sozialer Arbeit. Entwürfe einer neuen Praxis*, Neuwied et al.: Luchterhand.

Beck, U. and Sopp, P. (eds.) (1997) *Individualisierung und Integration. Neue Konfliktlinien und neuer Integrationsmodus*, Opladen: Leske and Budrich.

Belgrad, J. (1992) *Identität als Spiel. Eine Kritik des Identitätskonzepts von Jürgen Habermas*, Opladen: Westdeutscher.

BMSG [Bundesministerium für Soziale Sicherheit, Generationen und Konsumentenschutz] (2003) 4. Bericht zur Lage der Jugend in Österreich. Teil A: Jugendradar 2003, Wien: BMSG.

Bourdieu, P. (1979) *Entwurf einer Theorie der Praxis—auf der ethnologischen Grundlage der kabylischen Gesellschaft*, Frankfurt/Main: Suhrkamp.

Bourdieu, P. (1997) *Sozialer Sinn: Kritik der theoretischen Vernunft*, 2nd ed., Frankfurt/Main: Suhrkamp.

Deutsche Shell (ed.) (2003) Jugend 2002. *Zwischen pragmatischem Idealismus und robustem Materialismus*, Frankfurt: Fischer Taschenbuch.

Eimeren, B. and Frees, B. (2005) 'Nach dem Boom: Größter Zuwachs in internetfernen Gruppen. ARD/ZDF-Online-Studie 2005', *Media Perspektiven* 8/2005: 362–79.

Erikson, E. H. (1970) *Identität, Jugend und Krise. Die Psychodynamik im sozialen Wandel*, Stuttgart: Klett-Cotta.

Ferchhoff, W. (1999) *Jugend an der Wende vom 20. Zum 21. Jahrhundert. Lebensformen und Lebensstile*, 2nd ed., Opladen: Leske and Budrich.

Flick, U. (2003) 'Triangulation', in R. Bohnsack, W. Marotzki, and M. Meuser (eds.) *Hauptbegriffe Qualitativer Sozialforschung*, Opladen: Leske and Budrich UTB.

Fromme, J. (1997) *Pädagogik als Sprachspiel. Zur Pluralisierung der Wissensformen im Zeichen der Postmoderne*, Berlin: Luchterhand.

Gensicke, T. (2003) 'Individualität und Sicherheit in neuer Synthese? Wertorientierungen und gesellschaftliche Aktivität', in Deutsche Shell (ed.) *Jugend 2002. Zwischen pragmatischem Idealismus und robustem Materialismus*, Frankfurt: Fischer Taschenbuch.

Großegger, B. (2003) 'Medien und IK-Technologien im jugendlichen Alltag' in BMSG (ed.) 4. *Bericht zur Lage der Jugend in Österreich*. Teil A: Jugendradar 2003, Wien: BMSG.

Habermas, J. (1988) *Theorie des kommunikativen Handelns*, 4th ed., Frankfurt/Main: Suhrkamp.

Hentig, H. von (1975) 'Allgemeine Lernziele der Gesamtschule', in Deutscher Bildungsrat (ed.) *Gutachten und Studien der Bildungskommission*, vol 12., Lernziele der Gesamtschule, 4th ed., Stuttgart: Klett.

Hurrelmann, K. (1990) *Die Einführung in die Sozialisationstherorie. Über den Zusammenhang von Sozialstruktur und Persönlichkeit*, 3rd ed., Weinheim/Basel: Beltz.

Hurrelmann, K. and Ulich, D. (eds.) (1991a) *Neues Handbuch der Sozialisationsforschung*, 4th ed., Weinheim/Basel: Beltz.

Hurrelmann, K. and Ulich, D. (1991b) 'Gegenstands- und Methodenfragen der Sozialisationsforschung', in K. Hurrelmann and D. Ulich (eds.) *Neues Handbuch der Sozialisationsforschung*, 4th ed., Weinheim/Basel: Beltz.

Kuhn, H.-P. and Schmid, C. (2004) 'Politisches Interesse, Mediennutzung und Geschlechterdifferenz. Zwei Thesen zur Erklärung von Geschlechtsunterschieden im politischen Interesse von Jugendlichen', in D. Hoffmann and H. Merkens (eds.) *Jugendsoziologische Sozialisationstheorie. Impulse für die Jugendforschung*, Mannheim/Munich: Juventa.

Krappmann, L. (1969) *Soziologische Dimensionen der Identität. Strukturelle Bedingungen für die Teilnehme an Interaktionsprozessen*, Stuttgart: Klett.

Lange, A. (1999) 'Der Diskurs der neuen Kindheitsforschung: Argumentationstypen, Argumentationsfiguren und methodologische Implikationen', in M.-

S. Honig, A. Lange, and H. R. Leu (eds.) *Aus der Perspektive von Kindern? Zur Methodologie der Kindheitsforschung*, Weinheim/Munich: Juventa.

Lash, S. (1996) 'Reflexivität und ihre Doppelungen: Struktur, Ästhetik und Gemeinschaft', in U. Beck, A. Giddens, and S. Lash (eds.) *Reflexive Modernisierung. Eine Kontroverse*, Frankfurt/M.: Suhrkamp.

Mansel, J. (1997) 'Selbstsozialisation und Mediengebrauch', *Medien praktisch*, 21, No. 4: 9–11.

McDonald, K. (1999) *Struggles for Subjectivity*, Cambridge: Cambridge University Press.

Mead, G. H. (1980) *Geist, Identität und Gesellschaft*, 4th ed., Frankfurt/M.: Suhrkamp.

Meder, N. (1997) 'Wittgenstein oder die Poetik der Postmoderne', in N. Meder (ed.) *Der Sprachspieler*, Köln: Janus.

Medienpädagogischer Forschungsverbund Südwest (ed.) (2004) *JIM-Studie 2004. Jugend, Information, (Multi-)Media. Basisuntersuchung zum Medienumgang 12- bis 19-Jähriger*, Baden-Baden: Medienpädagogischer Forschungsverbund Südwest.

MPFS — Medienpädagogischer Forschungsverbund Südwest (ed.) (2004) *JIM-Studie 2004. Jugend, Information, (Multi-)Media*. Stuttgart.

Müller, R., Rhein, S., and Glogner, P. (2004) 'Das Konzept musikalischer und medialer Selbstsozialisation—widersprüchlich, trivial, überflüssig', in D. Hoffmann and H. Merkens (eds.) *Jugendsoziologische Sozialisationstheorie. Impulse für die Jugendforschung*, Mannheim/Munich: Juventa.

Niesyto, H. (2004) 'Kritische Anmerkungen zum Konzept "medialer Selbstsozialisation"', *Ludwigsburger Beiträge zur Medienpädagogik*, No. 5: 10–12.

Paus-Haase, I. (2000a) 'Identitätsgenese im Jugendalter. Zu den Koordinaten des Aufwachsens vor dem Hintergrund veränderter gesellschaftlicher Bedingungen—eine Herausforderung für die Jugendforschung', in H. Kleber (ed.) *Spannungsfeld Medien und Erziehung. Medienpädagogische Perspektiven*, Munich: KoPäd.

Paus-Haase, I. (2000b) 'Jugendforschung im Spannungsfeld polarer Perspektiven. Überlegungen zu interdisziplinären Wegen für theoretische und methodische Konzeptionierungen', unpublished lecture at the Faculty for Education of the University of Bielefeld, 12 Mai 2000.

Paus-Haase, I., Hasebrink, U., Mattusch, U., Keuneke, S., and Krotz, Friedrich (1999) *Daily Talks im Alltag von Jugendlichen. Der tägliche Balanceakt zwischen Orientierung, Amüsement und Ablehnung*, Opladen: Leske and Budrich.

Paus-Hasebrink, I. (2005) 'Grundsätzliche Überlegungen zu "neuen Denkwerkzeugen" in der Jugend(medien)forschung', in H. Kleber (ed.) *Perspektiven der Medienpädagogik in Wissenschaft und Bildungspraxis*, Munich: KoPäd.

Picker, R. and Westphal, S. (2005) Political participation of young people in Europe—Development of Indicators for comparative research in the European Union (EUYOUPART). WP8/D15—Working Paper on National Survey Results; National Report: Austria. Vienna: SORA (Institute for Social Research and Analysis). Online. Available HTTP: <http://www.sora.at/images/doku/D15AustrianNationalReport.pdf> (accessed 24 September 2005).

Picot, S. and Willert, M. (2003) 'Politik per Klick—Internet und Engagement Jugendlicher. 20 Porträts', in Deutsche Shell (ed.) *Jugend 2002. Zwischen pragmatischem Idealismus und robustem Materialismus*, Frankfurt: Fischer Taschenbuch.

Rosenmayr, L. (1985) 'Wege zum Ich vor bedrohter Zukunft. Jugend im Spiegel multidisziplinärer Forschung und Theorie', *Soziale Welt*, 36: 274–98.

Scherr, A. (2004) 'Selbstsozialisation in der polykontexturalen Gesellschaft. Primat des Objektiven oder Autopoiese psychischer Systeme?', in D. Hoffmann and H. Merkens (eds.) *Jugendsoziologische Sozialisationstheorie. Impulse für die Jugendforschung*, Mannheim/Munich: Juventa.

Schneekloth, U. (2003) 'Demokratie, ja—Politik, nein? Einstellungen Jugendlicher zur Politik', in Deutsche Shell (ed.) *Jugend 2002. Zwischen pragmatischem Idealismus und robustem Materialismus*, Frankfurt: Fischer Taschenbuch.

SORA (Institute for Social Research and Analysis) (2005) Political participation of young people in Europe—Development of Indicators for comparative research in the European Union (EUYOUPART). Summary of Results, Vienna: SORA. Online. Available HTTP: <http://www.sora.at/de/start.asp?ID=240&b=236/> (accessed 24 September 2005).

Vinken, H. (2004) 'Civic Socialization in Late Modernity. Perspectives on Young People's Alleged Withdrawal from Civil Society', in D. Hoffmann and H. Merkens (eds.) *Jugendsoziologische Sozialisationstheorie. Impulse für die Jugendforschung*, Mannheim/Munich: Juventa.

Wächter, F. (2005) Political participation of young people in Europe—Development of Indicators for comparative research in the European Union (EUYOUPART). WP8/D15—Working Paper on National Survey Results; National Report: Germany. Munich: German Youth Institute. Online. Available HTTP: <http://www.sora.at/images/doku/D15GermanReport.pdf > (accessed 24 September 2005).

Weiß, R. (2000) '"Praktischer Sinn", soziale Identität und Fern-Sehen. Ein Konzept für die Analyse der Einbettung kulturellen Handelns in die Alltagswelt', *Medien und Kommunikationswissenschaft*, 48: 42–62.

Weiß, R. (2001) *Fern-Sehen im Alltag. Zur Sozialpsychologie der Medienrezeption*, Wiesbaden: Westdeutscher.

Weiß, R. (2003) 'Alltagskultur', in H.-O. Hügel (ed.) *Handbuch populäre Kultur. Begriffe, Theorien und Diskussionen*, Stuttgart/Weimar: J. B. Metzler.

Zentner, M. (2001) 'Gesellschaftliche Beteiligung und politisches Bewusstsein', in C. Friesl (ed.) *Experiment Jung-Sein. Die Wertewelt österreichischer Jugendlicher*, Vienna: Czernin.

Zentner, M. (2003) 'Gesellschaftspolitisches Engagement Jugendlicher', in BMSG (ed.) 4. *Bericht zur Lage der Jugend in Österreich. Teil A: Jugendradar 2003*, Vienna: BMSG.

6 Interactivity and participation on the Internet

Young people's response to the civic sphere

Sonia Livingstone

FROM MASS TO INTERACTIVE MEDIA, FROM AUDIENCES TO PUBLICS

The question of whether the new media have the potential to overcome young people's low levels of participation in the political process contrasts strongly with more traditional framings of the relation between mass media and participation. Typically the media have been held partly responsible for low participation rather than being seen as offering a way forward. It is thus commonly claimed that 'media culture generally, with its emphasis on consumption and entertainment, has undercut the kind of public culture needed for a healthy democracy' (Dahlgren, 2003: 151; see also Putnam, 2000). This widespread suspicion of the mass media has a long history which is strongly if implicitly encoded in our present-day tendency to oppose mediated communication with face-to-face communication, judging the former as inferior by comparison. Cultural norms of authenticity, equality, trust, and accountability are all grounded primarily in face-to-face communication and so are routinely questioned in relation to the mass media.

Two significant changes result in our present research agenda—one concerns political culture, the second concerns the communication environment. First, a growing body of argument is seeking to re-frame the domain to be labelled 'political'. For, if we can 'see beyond the formal political system' (Dahlgren, 2003: 164), including not just matters of party politics, ideological belief systems, and voting, but also civic and community issues, life politics, and new social movements, then the view of the public as apathetic and ignorant about politics is challenged by evidence of a more lively, contested, and actively interested citizenry. Second, the communication environment is diversifying, specialising, globalising, and becoming more interactive. The Internet encompasses not simply one-to-many communication (characteristic of the mass media and, in turn, of mass society) or just one-to-one communication (as in telephony and in face-to-face communication), but also the communication from many to many characteristic of a network society (Castells, 2002), resulting in an expanded range of communicative possibilities (Morris and Ogan, 1996).

These two changes are strongly interlinked, with the Internet being widely hailed as the technology to bring new, more participatory forms of civic and political engagement to the masses (Bentivegna, 2002; Coleman, 1999; 2003; Livingstone, 2005a). For while the media have proved only partially effective in informing citizens about political issues, they have proved far more effective in shaping identities, lifestyles, and so, potentially, identity politics and lifestyle politics. Precisely because of the Internet's interactive mode of engagement and its heterarchical, even anarchic network structure, and the way it can reposition the audience of mass communications as the citizens of cyber democracy, many are asking whether—unlike previous media—the Internet may become less part of the problem than part of the solution. Can the Internet facilitate greater transparency and reflexivity in the political process, the disintermediation of elite/public communication by obviating the need for gatekeepers, virtual spaces for physically dispersed citizens to deliberate amongst themselves, so enhancing public connection within and across communities? Whether we call this political participation or, more loosely perhaps, participation in the civic sphere, continues to be debated (Bennett, 1998; Dahlgren, 2003). The preceding question is whether such public or civic connections are occurring at all to any significant degree (Couldry, in press; Livingstone, 2005b).

YOUNG PEOPLE AND PUBLIC PARTICIPATION— IS THE INTERNET THE ANSWER?

> We know the computer, we're the generation of computers. (Focus group with 14–16-year-olds, London, 2003)

The idea that, for democracy to work, 'there must exist channels of communication providing for a free flow of information both amongst citizens and between representatives and voters' (Coleman, 1999: 67), is driving Internet-related policy in many countries. The UK government has expressed as its goal not only a series of initiatives towards transparent government and civic participation but also the intention '...to enable all adults to have the ICT skills they need to learn effectively online, become active citizens in the information age and [...] contribute productively to the economy' (Office of the e-Envoy, 2004: 11). Intriguingly, there appears to be a promising match between the style of deliberation afforded by the Internet and that preferred by the very population segment—young people—who are most disengaged from traditional forms of political activity. The focus here on young people draws not only from the widespread concern that young people are indeed disengaged from the traditional political process but also from the growing optimism that quite the opposite holds for new forms of engagement and new forms of politics.[1]

The productive coincidence between young people's preferred style of political or civic engagement and the Internet is stimulated by the growing evidence that the Internet especially appeals to young people—it is 'their' medium, they are the early adopters, the most media-savvy, the pioneers in the cyber age, leading rather than being led for once, reversing the generation gap, and gaining confidence and expertise as a result. While this view is often overstated, for there is little solid evidence of a dramatic historical break from one generation to the next (notwithstanding the optimism of Kellner, 2002; Negroponte, 1995; Poster, 1997; Tapscott, 1997; Turkle, 1995), the evidence does support the view that young people are particularly skilled and motivated in relation to the Internet, making it a viable proposition to seek to encourage their participation through this means. Hence, it seems that the Internet supports, and young people prefer to engage with, new civic or life-political issues, whether on a local or a global scale. Particularly, they respond to project-focused, pragmatic, and low-obligation yet high profile activities, which are organised through forums characterised by open and spontaneous, ad hoc, low-commitment, self-reflexive, and strategic communications within a flexibly defined, peer-based network.

Three quarters of households with children in the UK now have domestic Internet access, and 98% of 9 to 19-year-olds have used the Internet—92% at school, 75% at home, and 64% elsewhere (Livingstone and Bober, 2004). The ways in which the Internet is becoming embedded in everyday life raises questions about access and inequalities, about the nature and quality of use, about the implications for young people's social and educational development, and, ultimately, about the balance between the risks and opportunities posed by the Internet for children and their families. On the one hand, children and young people are developing online competencies and literacies greater than their parents, proudly labelling themselves 'the Internet generation'; on the other hand, they are the most vulnerable and potentially at risk from the dangers of inappropriate content and contact online (Livingstone, 2003). Further, despite the rhetoric, young people (and their parents and teachers) vary in confidence and competence when faced with the twin challenges of getting the best from the Internet while also avoiding the problems it brings.

While families are investing resources in gaining access to and developing skills for using the Internet, considerable commercial interests seek to target and expand the child and youth market, inviting young people to take up the online contents and services being developed. In the public sector too, there are hopes that the development of informational, civic, and political contents and forums will stimulate young people's civic interests, political engagement, and community values. How much are children and young people taking up some of these online opportunities? Are they responding to the range of 'invitations on offer to participate online'? Many suspect that, though the opportunities are considerable, they are to a great extent still untapped at present. While, sometimes understandably, much media attention, and hence public concern, is directing policy attention towards the task of minimising the dangers, it would seem timely also to direct increased attention to the challenge of maximising opportunities.

The research project *UK Children Go Online* (UKCGO) has investigated 9–19-year-olds' use of the Internet in the UK, comparing girls and boys of different ages, backgrounds, etc., in order to ask how the Internet may be transforming—or may itself be shaped by—family life, peer networks, and learning, formal and informal. It combined qualitative interviews and observations with a major national face-to-face survey of children (N=1511, users and non-users) and their parents (N=906). The project charted the rapid increase in and diversity of forms and quality of access, and this diversity is also characteristic of emerging patterns of use (Livingstone and Bober, 2004). In this chapter, I draw out some of the project's findings as they relate to the broad issue of participation—social, civic, and political—in order to ask whether young people's interest and expertise in the Internet be harnessed so as to promote their participation. Or, are their various activities online not, after all, usefully characterised as peer, civic, or political participation? My strategy is to triangulate three sources of data—the perspective of those who produce participatory websites for young people, a series of 14 focus group discussions with young people (see also Livingstone and Bober, 2003), together with their online discussions on our project message board, and the national survey of the activities of 9- to 19-year-olds on the Internet (see also Livingstone and Bober, 2004; for methodological details, see http://www.children-go-online.net).

FROM THE PERSPECTIVE OF THE PRODUCERS—GROUNDS FOR OPTIMISM?

Giving youth 'their say'

> We want children and young people to feel that they can influence the services they receive. We want to see them contributing to and benefiting from their location communities. We want them to feel heard and valued and to be able to make a difference. (John Denham, Minister for Young People, in Children and Young People's Unit, 2001: 1)

This quotation accords with the spirit of Article 12 of the UN Convention on the Rights of the Child, promoting participation, consultation, and democratic opportunities for young people to learn about getting heard, having a voice, and becoming active citizens. Indeed, a variety of non-profit organisations, both major and small, are now initiating innovative and interesting opportunities for public or civic participation of one kind or another, with greater or more modest ambitions (e.g., the British Youth Council, Children's Express, Children's Rights Alliance for England, the United Kingdom Youth Parliament; see Children and Young People's Unit, 2001).

One result is 'an abundance of civic and political activity by and for youth', which 'invite[s] young people to participate in a wide range of issues, including voting, voluntarism, racism and tolerance, social activism and, most recently, patriotism, terrorism and military conflict' (Montgomery et al., 2004: 2; for a critique, see Sundin, 1999). In the course of our research, we visited several organisations committed to using the Internet to facilitate children and young people's participation in a range of ways by encouraging user-generated content, peer-to-peer communication, community-building, mediated public deliberation, and so forth.[2] In each case, we have met enthusiastic, dedicated, and energetic adults committed to improving opportunities for children and young people and delighted to show us the facilities they provide or are developing.

THE BENEFITS OF PARTICIPATION

Interestingly, 'participation' seems to mean several different things to these organisations. It seems widely anticipated that getting youth to participate on the Internet as an end in itself (i.e., actively contributing to the medium rather than using it passively, as a receiver of content only) will lead to participation on and offline as a means to an end (i.e., social participation, empowerment, and citizenship). In our interviews, we found that ideas of exactly how this might work were rather less clear. Indeed, the *Carnegie Young People Initiative* (Cutler and Taylor, 2003: 11) notes with some concern that:

> The benefits and impacts of children and young people's participation are not clearly identified.... There is a need for a programme of work that more clearly identifies and quantifies the range of personal, social and economic benefits of children and young people gaining greater influence over decision-making.

In a more positive vein, Montgomery et al. (2004: 13–14) draw implicitly on a public sphere model to identify a range of potential benefits for young people. Thus, they argue that such websites provide young people, with opportunities to hone a variety of civic skills, including the following:

- develop and articulate their thinking on issues of public concern
- share ideas with youth from different backgrounds, who may hold contrasting opinions

- build the habits of initiative, analysis, and independent thinking
- develop their own sense of being invested in civic issues and actively involved in the civic arena.

However, as they too note, with some chagrin, 'youth civic websites open doors to access and participation in civic projects, but which young people utilize these opportunities, how, and with what effects over time, are topics that call for more systematic research' (p. 13).

This lack of clarity about the success of such websites in achieving their goals is partly because budgets are generally tight, permitting little systematic market research. Hence, we found that organisations tend to rely on ad hoc contacts—what Montgomery et al. call 'glimpses', or online traces, of the activities of real users—such as, children who send in web material, those who visit on open days, phone calls from parents, hits to websites, queries to advisors. While it seems that some children are keen to participate, generous with their time, creative in their interests, and just waiting for the opportunity to participate in their peer and wider community, it is possible, even likely, that these are a highly self-selected, probably privileged minority. This seems confirmed by the picture that emerges from our focus groups with children and teens, conducted in schools with a broad cross-section of the population.

LISTENING TO YOUNG PEOPLE— A GLOOMY PROGNOSIS?

> At the end of the day, you're going to look at what you're interested in. And if you haven't got an interest in politics, you're not going to get one from having the Internet. (Lorie, 17, from Essex)

Despite the activities of the motivated minority, many children and young people rarely if ever find these interesting and creative websites. Rather, they stick to branded or commercial sites, following their favourite pop groups, football teams, or television programmes instead of checking out the Youth Parliament, the Childnet Academy, or even the civic/community options on the BBC site. The young people we interviewed in the focus groups were notably uninterested in or disillusioned by the possibility of political participation via the Internet.

'Politics is boring'

Over and again, the conversation flagged when we switched from communicating with friends to the idea of communicating online in order to connect to the world of politics. Consequently, these were not always easy discussions, even though we attempted to draw on examples that might be expected to concern young people. Several times we found we had to 'rescue' the conversational flow of an otherwise lively focus group. Here is a group of 14- to 15-year-old boys from Essex: [3]

Interviewer: And what about politics? Are any of you interested in politics?
Sean: No!
Ryan: Don't be silly!

They seem more interested in being in touch with celebrities, as one 15-year-old girl from London said:

Padma: Yeah. I get like a—sometimes, like, two weeks, every two weeks, I get personal mails from celebrities. My favourite celebrities. That's ok!
[....]
Interviewer: Ok, ok. But you don't get in touch with politicians, or...
[Laughter]
Padma: I'm not really interested in.... They all chat crap, so...

And perhaps their interests are primarily local, rather than national or international:

Why care about something going on miles away when you've got something going on in a hundred metres? (Steve, 17 years, Manchester).

'No-one listens to us'

When Oliver (17, a middle-class boy from Kent) commented with deliberate provocation on our message board, 'I'm not in the least bit interested in politics, and think it extremely boring, no amount of games can disguise the content', we had a chance to explore his reasons further. This revealed that young people (probably like adults) are not always internally consistent in their views. For him and others we talked to, the routine ways in which children are ignored in our society is a telling factor.

Interviewer: One of the things we were interested in was how kids got involved in the stop-the-war protest...
Oliver: Kids don't see that they have a choice in the matter, it's a 'Grown up' thing.... Ask almost any child and they will tell you 'War is bad'.... The net just gives them a way to tell everyone and to share their ideas with each other.

Having said, first, that kids should not vote, he goes on to imply that kids do hold political views (anti-war), that the Internet offers them a voice, but that no-one but other kids are listening, for the grown-ups have already decided. Young people not being listened to turns out to be a major theme in our focus groups also:

> I think the problem is how formal they are because they probably have a secretary typing it for them, if they're Prime Minister or something like that. With the e-mail, they won't read it anyway. (Mitch, 17 years, Essex)

We try to push beyond this, but their scepticism is strong, as stressed by this 17-year-old from Essex:

Interviewer: The other thing people say is that the Internet makes things more democratic. Because now you could e-mail your MP, or go on a political chat room...
   Hazel: Yeah, you can e-mail him, but is he going to listen?

A comment posted on our message board from 15-year-old Anne, also from Essex, again stresses the marginalisation of young people in society as a reason for their apparent political apathy:

Message no. 99

Posted by ANNE on Tuesday, November 11, 2003 5:55pm
Subject: Re: Email Tony Blair

Politics causes me to become frustrated because the Government has too much control over your lives, e.g. euthanasia being illegal. Anyway, I don't think young people are interested in politics due to the example set by the adults we are surrounded by, i.e. the poor turn out of voters and one of our teachers telling us they don't see the point in voting etc.

I have never written to, or emailed my local MP, or the PM [Prime Minister] because I do not think my letter/email will even be looked at. I am also put off by society's ageist attitude towards people of our age.... young people's opinions are not at all valued, especially not by politicians.

As a BBC report observes (BBC, 2002: 4), the public (here, aged 18–44) finds it difficult to relate 'politics' to their everyday lives precisely because they can see no means of two-way dialogue with politicians; hence 'news and political broadcasting lacks a tier of entry points to engage or re-engage people'.

'Uncool websites', uncool politics

The aesthetics (and economics) of websites matters to a generation imbued with the values of commercial media. Several young people compared civic sites unfavourably to the glossy production standards of commercial sites, such as this group of 14–15 year olds from Essex:

Interviewer: Do you ever go to any [name of their city] websites, any sites that are about what's happening in [city]?
Ryan: They're so boring!
Jim: Yeah, they're hyper-boring. You can tell they're so cheaply made as well.
Sean: Yeah.
Jim: Yeah, it's like the italic links with the boxes round them on cheap websites. It has things like that, it's just unbelievable.

There is a pervasive sense that politics itself is 'uncool', offending against peer group norms. It is difficult to guess the extent to which some individuals refrain from expressing political interests in group settings where such views are clearly disparaged.

Institutional structures matter

Not all are uninterested, in politics, raising the question of when and why some young people do get involved. We get a hint during this discussion, among inner-city teens (14–16-year-old boys from London), when they suggest that their school (rather than the Internet) played the key role in instigating action:

Interviewer: Because when they had all those stop-the-war protests, and lots of kids were involved weren't they? I don't know if there was anything here in school, or people protested or...
Elkan: All done in a non-uniform day.
Amir: We paid one pound.
Elkan: We all paid one pound, send money for...
Prince: For the children of Iraq. So we paid a pound to...
Elkan: Non-uniform.
Interviewer: And did the school organise that?
Prince: Yeah, the school did.

The other key institution in young people's lives, their family, also emerges as a key institution in encouraging participation. On our project message board, an individualised space, Milly (15, from Essex) expresses strong political interest, together with a frustration about her peers:

Message no. 77

Posted by MILLY on Wednesday, November 5, 2003 6:59pm
Subject: Re: Email Tony Blair

I really don't understand how people could have said that they aren't interested in politics! What about the 'Don't attack Iraq' rallies and marches. There was a massive under-18 turn out. What about the banning of live music without licensing! What about the massive probability that everyone in the UK will have ID cards within the next 5 years! What about national curfews for under 18s!

But when she expresses a similar interest in the focus group discussion, it becomes evident both that this interest stems from her father's expertise and that in the peer context her interest is expressed only with reluctance:

Interviewer: Tell me if you ever use the Internet for being part of something bigger than you and your friends. Um, doing something in the community or getting involved in politics?
[Silence here much longer than before]
Milly: Hmm, my Dad like teaches politics at University, so I get interested in it. And it's just like looking up to see different people's views? Like, did you hear about that guy who was writing for Iraq?
Interviewer: Yes.
Milly: I didn't know that stuff.

VARIETIES OF PARTICIPATION—WHO DOES WHAT AND WHY?

Are we right in surmising that Milly's background makes the difference? In turning to the findings from our survey of 9- to 19-year-olds in the UK, the question is how many young people take part in online activities and why?

In what follows, we examine young people's take-up of a range of activities that might be considered 'participation', whether with peers or experts, whether for civic, political or personal reasons. Each of these activities invites from the individual user an active or creative contribution that directs or modifies the flow of events online or directs the user towards a civic or social enterprise larger than that of individual reception or exchange. Being restricted by the measures employed in the survey, the findings are analysed in terms of comparisons by age, gender, and social class (here 'middle class' and 'working class' households are identified using the market research categories ABC1 and C2DE). The main survey findings are summarised in Table 1 (see also Livingstone, Bober, and Helsper, 2005).

Peer-to-peer

E-mail, chat, and instant messaging are popular forms of socially interactive media, primarily used peer-to-peer to communicate with known rather than unknown others, serving to co-construct and potentially reconfigure social networks and relationships. Social class, gender, and age all make a difference, with middle-class, older girls tending to take part the most, with the exception of chat rooms.

Other online activities also connect peers, with game-playing (often though not always online) more common among boys than girls and less among older teens, while boys and the older teens also download music more often. Only one in five visits websites of clubs they belong to and fewer still are interested in visiting other people's homepages, suggesting a preference for professional over amateur websites, notwithstanding the supposed incentive of 'user-generated content' online.

INTERACTIVITY

Websites invite their users to interact with them in a range of ways, each of which asks the user to contribute something and, often, promises a response. Among 9- to 19-year-olds, we found that 44% have completed a quiz online (more girls than boys); 25% have sent an e-mail or SMS to a website (more older teens); 22% have voted online (more middle-class and older teens); 17% have sent in pictures or stories (more younger children);17% have contributed to a message board (more middle class and older); 9% have offered advice to others (more older); 8% have filled in a form (more older); and 8% have signed a petition online (more middle class and older).

Overall, 70% report at least one form of interactive engagement with a website, suggesting a high level of interest and motivation. Yet, on average, young people have responded in just one or two ways out of the possible eight, suggesting that despite the many invitations to interact—to 'tell us what you think', 'e-mail us your views', 'join our community', 'have your say'—take-up remains low (Table 1). Again we find demographic differences: middle-class children interact with websites in more ways than do working-class children, as do teenagers compared with younger children, suggesting the existence of a digital divide not (only) in terms of access but in the quality and depth of use.

Table 1 **Varieties of participation online, by demographics**

	All	Boys	Girls	ABC1	C2DE	9–11 years	12–15 years	16–17 years	18–19 years
Peer-to-peer communication									
Send/ receive email	72%	**69%**	**75%**	**77%**	**65%**	**45%**	**71%**	**87%**	**92%**
Use instant messaging	55%	53%	57%	**59%**	**50%**	**18%**	**58%**	**72%**	**65%**
Use chat rooms	21%	23%	20%	**19%**	**24%**	**11%**	**23%**	**26%**	**26%**
Peer-to-peer connection									
Play online games	70%	**75%**	**64%**	68%	71%	**78%**	**78%**	**61%**	**42%**
Download music	45%	**50%**	**39%**	45%	45%	**23%**	**47%**	**54%**	**61%**
Visit sites of clubs you're a member of	19%	**21%**	**16%**	19%	19%	**14%**	**17%**	**26%**	22%
Visit personal homepages	14%	15%	15%	14%	14%	N/A	**12%**	**19%**	14%
Interactivity									
Breadth (0–8) of interaction with sites	1.49	1.44	1.56	**1.64**	**1.32**	**0.87**	**1.50**	**1.89**	**1.92**
Civic interests									
Seek information (not for school)	94%	94%	94%	95%	93%	**89%**	**94%**	**96%**	**97%**
Look for news online	26%	28%	22%	28%	22%	N/A	**17%**	**34%**	**41%**
Seek advice online	25%	26%	23%	26%	23%	N/A	**21%**	**29%**	**32%**
Breadth (0–5) of civic sites visited	1.0	0.90	1.11	1.17	0.79	N/A	0.78	1.24	1.34
Creativity									
Make a personal web page	34%	**42%**	**26%**	36%	32%	**18%**	**39%**	**44%**	**32%**

Base: 9–19 year olds who use the Internet at least once a week (*N*=1,257), with the exception of 'seek advice online', 'look for news online' and 'look at other people's personal homepages', where the base is 12–19-year-olds who use the Internet at least once a week (*N*=975). Note: Comparisons in bold are statistically significant at least at *p*<0.05.

CIVIC INTERESTS

While information uses of the Internet are near-universal, much of this is entertainment or leisure related. One in four 12- to 19-year-olds who go online at least once a week read the news online, with more boys, more middle-class children and older teenagers doing so, and a similar proportion, especially older teens, have used the Internet to get personal advice (e.g., for advice related to homework, health, sexual matters, drugs, or money).

Most sites aimed at young people, as for the wider population, are commercially produced as part of a business strategy of e-commerce, branding or cross-media promotion. How often do young people visit sites designed to appeal to their public or civic interests? Avoiding the term politics we asked 12- to 19-year-olds about a range of civic and political sites (see Figure 1). Over half (54%) of 12- to 19-year-olds who go online at least once a week have visited at least one such website. Again, the range of sites visited is lower than the overall reach: on average, only one of these kinds of sites (out of a possible five) is visited by each individual (Table 1). Girls and young middleclass teenagers tend to visit a broader range of civic sites, and the breadth of civic sites visited also increases steadily with age. If these levels of participation are to be increased, further efforts—in design, in visibility, in communicating relevance, and in educational/ social support—will be needed.

As Figure 1 also shows, it seems that for all but a minority, political and civic sites are mainly a source of information than an opportunity to become engaged, especially for younger children. When we asked e-mail, IM, and chat users if they discuss political or civic issues peer-to-peer on the Internet, more than half (56%) say they never talk about these issues with anyone by e-mail, IM, or chat, though 14% have done so once or twice, 24% sometimes, and 4% often. Looking at the reasons why many (42%) teens never visit civic/political sites, low levels of online political participation would appear to be due to a general lack of interest rather than to more specific problems, such as website design, trust, or searching skills. Yet, it remains plausible that better designed websites could more effectively draw young people into political participation.

CREATIVITY

Many hopes have been pinned on the new opportunities to become not only a receiver but also a producer of content. More than for any previous media, the Internet makes it possible for anyone with a certain level of skills and technical resources, now fairly accessible if far from universal, to create their own content, for whatever purpose, and make it widely available on a hitherto unprecedented, even global scale. As Table 1 shows, one third of 9- to 19-year-olds—more often boys and teens—have tried to set up their own webpage. Unlike for visiting civic sites, social grade makes little difference.

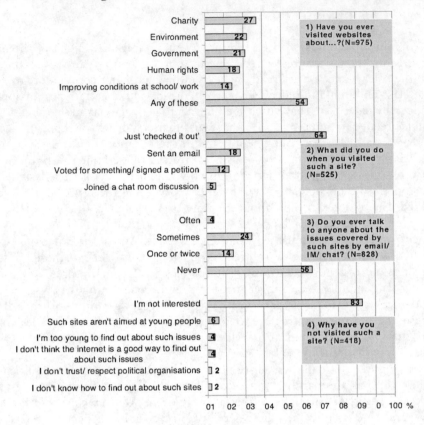

Figure 1 Visiting civic websites — what, how or why not?

Figure 2 suggests that making and maintaining a webpage is not easy, and commonly young people's sites are not either currently online or regularly updated. The skills or literacy required to maintain a webpage are, it seems, less widespread among young people than they would wish, given their initial interest in creating a webpage. While the reasons for making a webpage are varied, the most common reason is for a school project, pointing to the importance of institutional support in these (as in other) activities. As for the 65% of young people who don't have a webpage, the main reason given is that they do not know how to set one up, again suggesting a literacy gap.

VARIETIES OF PARTICIPATORS: TOWARDS A TYPOLOGY OF YOUNG PEOPLE ONLINE

Rather than simply dividing young people into those who participate more and those who participate less, a more complex explanation, based on

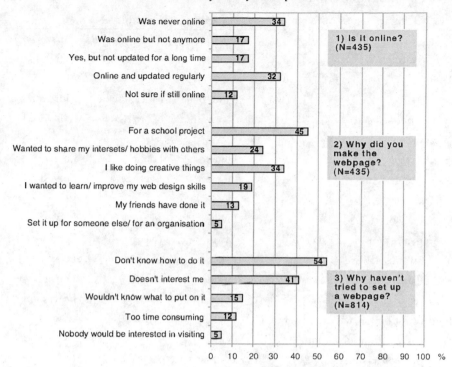

Figure 2 Making webpages — how, why or why not?

demographic and Internet use factors, is suggested if we are to understand what leads young people to take up opportunities to participate online in different ways. The 12–19 year olds who use the Internet at least weekly were grouped using cluster analysis, this suggesting distinct groups (or 'ideal types') of young Internet users in relation to activities of interaction and participation (see Table 2).

INTERACTORS

These young people engage the most interactively with websites, and they are the most likely to make their own webpages. More often boys, and middle class, they are the most privileged in terms of domestic access, and they use the Internet the most. Consequently, they have developed considerable online skills, permitting them to discover many advantages of the Internet and so use it in a wide range of ways, apparently ready to take up new opportunities as offered. Yet interestingly, this range and depth of online engagement does not lead them especially to pursue civic interests online.

Table 2 Characteristics of the three groups of online participators

	Interactors	Civic-minded	Disengaged
Demographics			
Age	Av. 16 yrs	Av. 16 yrs	Av. 15 yrs
Gender	More male	More female	More male
Socioeconomic status	More ABC1	More ABC1	Less ABC1
Access			
Home access	Higher	Higher	Lower
Broadband access	Highest	Average	Lowest
Internet use			
Frequency of use	Highest	Average	Lowest
Average time online per day	Most	Average	Least
Years of Internet use	Most	Average	Least
Self-efficacy/Internet expertise	Higher	Lower	Lower
Number of sites visited last week	Highest	Average	Lowest
Number of online activities (out of 10)	Highest	Average	Lowest
Peer-to-peer communication			
Frequency of using e-mail	Highest	Average	Lowest
Frequency of using Instant Messaging	Highest	Average	Lowest
Frequency of using chat	Highest	Lowest	Average
Peer-to-peer connection			
Play online games	Highest	Average	Lowest
Download music	Highest	Lowest	Average
Visit sites of clubs you're a member of	Average	Highest	Lowest
Visit others' personal homepages	Highest	Average	Lowest
Interactivity			
Breadth of interaction with web sites	Highest	Average	Lowest
Civic interests			
Seek information (not for school)	Average	Average	Average
Look for news online	Highest	Average	Lowest
Seek advice online	Most likely	Average	Least likely
Breadth of civic sites visited	Average	Highest	Lowest
Creativity			
Make a personal webpage	Highest	Average	Lowest

Base: 12- to 19-year-olds who use the Internet at least weekly (*N*=975). All group comparisons are statistically significant at least at *p*<0.05.

THE CIVIC-MINDED

While not especially likely to interact with websites generally or to make their own website, these young people visit a range of civic websites, especially charity and human rights-based sites. More often girls and middle class, these young people have adequate access to the Internet and they make only average use of it. Consistent with their civic interests, they visit websites for clubs they belong to and are least likely to chat or download music. It seems unlikely that new online opportunities on the Internet are drawing these young people into civic participation. Rather, having developed civic interests offline, they see the Internet as one way of pursuing them, even though they do not consider themselves especially skilled online.

THE DISENGAGED

These young people are the least active in online participation, however measured, being much less likely to interact with sites, visit civic sites, or make their own webpage. A little younger than the other groups, and from lower socio-economic status backgrounds, they are less likely to have home access or a broadband connection. The result is a less experienced, less expert group of Internet users who, though they do go online at least once per week, make average use of the Internet for information and music, visit few websites, communicate less online, and generally gain the least from the Internet, especially in relation to its potential for participation. Being disengaged in terms of both access and use, these young people, it seems, are on the wrong side of the digital divide.

CONCLUSIONS

Although the Internet is often used for rather aimless searches or chat with little consequence, this chapter has asked whether the Internet can also offer young people new and different opportunities to interact and participate in society, this contrasting with the receipt of ready-made, professionally produced, commercially profitable information and entertainment content. In triangulating three sources of data regarding young people's response to the invitation to participate, a somewhat conflicting story has emerged. According to the producers of civic websites for youth, many young people are eagerly contributing to the sites, creatively engaging with the online invitation to join in, to have their say, to represent themselves. But from the focus groups with ordinary young people, a more negative view emerges of a generation bored with politics, critical of the online offer, instead interested in celebrity and conforming to peer norms. Perhaps our questioning to these young people was unsubtle, leading them to take the opportunity to reject the adult world of politics, all too often framed rhetorically as 'not for them', rather than telling us of their commitments, their values, their concerns (and in more individual discussions, a less alienated picture does emerge). Yet the peer group matters. If privately explored interests cannot be expressed in public, among peers, and acted upon collectively, there is little hope for increasing youth participation (Eliasoph, 1998).

So, is youthful participation a majority or minority activity? The survey offers some resolution. Depending on which measure of participation one adopts (and this is far from settled since researchers continue to debate the very nature of 'participation'), anything between a small minority and a bare majority of children and young people can be said to respond positively to the invitation to participate on the Internet. The rest, by implication, do not, claiming a lack of interest and a lack of knowledge. How young people are distributed across these categories, or activities, is largely a matter of demographics—gender, age, and social class all play a strong, if not wholly determining, role, though as the cluster analysis suggests, access to and expertise in using the Internet further affect the breadth of use. Does this mean that little can be done to enhance young people's online participation?

If we listen closely to the producers and the young people, their stories begin to converge. The producers stress 'being heard', and this is also a common feature of the design characteristics and interface of youth civic websites. Young people, it is claimed, have a right to express themselves, for their voices to become visible, and the online community is keen for their contribution. Producers are less clear, however, about the benefits of participation, shifting the ground from political action to the question of skills. Through engaging with these sites, it is suggested, young people can develop the skills and competences for participation, even though such engagement may not lead to any political or civic consequences. Implicitly, it seems, young people are positioned by these sites not as citizens but as citizens-in-waiting: such online participation, like education, prepares young people for the life to come. But consider the protest running through the focus group discussions: 'being heard', or 'having your say' does not seem to mean 'being listened to', they complain. It seems that young people consider the online invitation to be false—no adult is listening or responding, and decisions are taken elsewhere. Perhaps in consequence, it also seems that while these sites offer young people their 'right' to be heard, they generate little sense of any accompanying responsibility to participate.

If young people are to be positioned merely as citizens-in-waiting, it seems that there are other things they prefer to do with their time. The survey findings add a further twist, for they suggest a generation that is, even though marginalised as non-adults (Qvortrup, 1995), not entirely cynical. Rather, they are initially interested and willing, ready to try things out. In sizeable numbers, they visit civic websites, attempt to create content, respond to online invitations to interact. But they visit only one or two civic sites, and they don't take it further. If they can't get their website online, they give up. They send in their e-mails and votes but get little in return. One is tempted to suggest that it is those making the invitation, not those responding to it that lack the motivation to participate. Further, since the online community remains less significant to young people than their offline community of peers, it is in that forum that the online offer is tested and rejected, as the dynamics of the focus group discussions reveal.

Only if the institutional structures (school, family, peers) that shape young people's daily lives support civic participation does it seem that young people feel enabled to engage with the civic or public sphere, on or offline. Historians of childhood argue not only that these institutional structures present a stratified array of opportunities and constraints that is, for the most part, beyond young people's control but also that traditional cues to participation and citizenship are becoming ever less in evidence (Kimberlee, 2002). It seems that, despite widespread optimism regarding online youth participation, we are led to agree that 'despite the recognition of children as persons in their own right, public policy and practice is marked by an intensification of control, regulation and surveillance around children, this impeding rather than facilitating the ability of organisations to encourage children's participation' (Prout, 2000: 304), not least because 'children's participation can threaten adult hegemony and established practice' (Hill and Tisdall, 1997: 36). But for those seeking a more optimistic conclusion, there is surely much more to be done that builds on young people's undoubted excitement over the Internet, their growing expertise, and their willingness to try things out, in terms of ensuring that opportunities for youth participation are more formally and structurally connected to adult spheres of political and civic decision making and action. In short, if children and young people do participate, who among those with power is going to listen?

ACKNOWLEDGEMENTS

This chapter reports research funded by an Economic and Social Research Council grant (RES-335-25-0008) as part of the 'e-Society' Programme, with co-funding from AOL, BSC, Childnet-International, Citizens Online, ITC, and Ofcom. Thanks are due also to the project's Advisory Panel and to its Children's Panel for informing the design and interpretation of the project (see http://www.children-go-online.net). Also thanks to Magdalena Bober for her work on the project, to BMRB for conducting the survey, to Ellen Helsper for valuable statistical analysis. An earlier version of this chapter was presented, 'Young Citizens and New Media: Strategies for Learning Democratic Engagement', Lund, September 2004, and the many constructive comments offered by seminar participants are gratefully acknowledged. Lastly, this work has been enabled by the author's participation in the European Science Foundation's *Changing Media, Changing Europe* Programme.

NOTES

1. See van Deth et al. (1999), Kimberlee (2002), Hill and Tisdall (1997), Norris (1999), Park et al. (2002), and Prout (2000) on youth participation in general. See Angeles-Bautista (1999), Coleman (1999), Hall and Newbury (1999), Montgomery et al. (2004), McNeill (1999), and Sundin (1999) on the civic potential of the Internet.
2. Such organisations include: Children's BBC (http://www.bbc.co.uk/cbbc), which encourages creating and disseminating material online and on television, sending feedback to television programmes, using story circles to engage disadvantaged and disengaged groups (e.g., disabled children), and so forth; Epal (http://www.epal.tv), a pilot Government project for 13- to 19-year-olds in Greater Manchester to use 'digital technology to develop an online community of young people, support youth participation in public life, and deliver public services to young people in new ways'; and the Childnet Academy (http://www.childnetacademy.org, part of Childnet-International), which runs an annual award competition for websites made by children and young people that benefit other children worldwide.
3. All children interviewed have been given pseudonyms (see the project's research ethics policy, http://www.children-go-online.net).
4. In a multiple regression analysis seeking to predict which young people interact with these sites (in terms of demographic and Internet use variables), only age was a significant predictor of interaction: older teens are more likely to interact with civic websites and not just visit them or look for information.
5. In a multiple regression analysis seeking to predict which young people discuss these issues on the Internet (in terms of demographic and Internet use variables), age and self-efficacy were significant predictors: older teens and those more confident of their online expertise are more likely to have discussed these issues with others on the Internet.
6. However, experience of and confidence in using the Internet does seem to encourage online content creation (Livingstone, Bober, and Helsper, 2004).
7. This was an especially common response among the 9- to 11-year-olds (69%), and interestingly, the youngest group was also the least likely to say that making a webpage does not interest them (28%, compared with 40–50% of the teens). These youngest children, then, have the biggest gap between motivation and skill, suggesting an 'unmet need' worthy of support.
8. A cluster analysis seeks to identify meaningfully homogenous subgroups of cases (here, individuals) in a population. The furthest neighbour technique was used (in SPSS 11.5); see Livingstone, Bober, and Helsper (in prep.) for details.

REFERENCES

Angeles-Bautista, F. de los. (1999). The Media and Our Children: The promise of participation. In C. von Feilitzen & U. Carlsson (Eds.), *Children and Media: Image, education, participation* (pp. 267–276). Sweden: The UNESCO

International Clearinghouse on Children and Violence on the Screen at Nordicom.

BBC (2002). *Beyond the Soundbite: BBC research into public disillusion with politics.* London: British Broadcasting Corporation. http://www.trbi.co.uk/trbi-politics.pdf

Bennett, L. (1998). 1998 Ithiel De Sola Pool lecture: The Uncivic Culture: Communication, identity, and the rise of lifestyle politics. *Political Science and Politics*, 31(4), 740–761.

Bentivegna, S. (2002). Politics and New Media. In L. Lievrouw & S. Livingstone (Eds.), *The Handbook of New Media: Social Shaping and Consequences of ICTs* (pp. 50–61). London: Sage.

Castells, M. (2002). *The Internet Galaxy: Reflections on the Internet, business, and society.* Oxford: Oxford University Press.

Children and Young People's Unit. (2001). *Learning to Listen: Core principles for the involvement of children and young people.* London: Department for Education and Skills.

Coleman, S. (1999). The new media and democratic politics. *New Media and Society*, 1(1), 67–73.

Coleman, S. (2003). *A Tale of Two Houses: The House of Commons, the Big Brother House and the people at home.* London: Hansard Society.

Couldry, N. (in press). Researching Digital (Dis)Connection in the Age of Personalised Media. In P. Golding & G. Murdock (Eds.), *Unpacking Digital Dynamics: Participation, control and exclusion.* London: Hampton Press.

Couldry, N., & McCarthy, A. (2004) (Eds.), *MediaSpace: Place, scale and culture in media age.* London: Routledge.

Cutler, D., & Taylor, A. (2003). *Expanding and Sustaining Involvement: A snapshot of participation infrastructure for young people living in England.* Dunfermline, Fife: Carnegie Young People Initiative.

Dahlgren, P. (2003). Reconfiguring Civic Culture in the New Media Milieu. In J. Corner and D. Pels (Eds.), *Media and the Restyling of Politics* (pp. 151–170). London: Sage.

Eliasoph, N. (1998). *Avoiding Politics: How Americans produce apathy in everyday life.* Cambridge: Cambridge University Press.

Hall, R., & Newbury, D. (1999). 'What Makes You Switch On?': Young people, the Internet and cultural participation. In J. Sefton-Green (Ed.), *Young People, Creativity and New Technologies.* London: Routledge.

Hill, M., & Tisdall, K. (1997). *Children and Society.* London and New York: Longman.

Kellner, D. (2002). New Media and New Literacies: Reconstructing education for the new millenium. In L. Lievrouw & S. Livingstone (Eds.), *The Handbook of New Media: Social shaping and consequences of ICTs* (pp. 90–104). London: Sage.

Kimberlee, R. H. (2002). Why Don't British Young People Vote at General Elections? *Journal of Youth Studies*, 5(1), 85–98.

Livingstone, S. (2003). Children's Use of the Internet: Reflections on the emerging research agenda. *New Media and Society*, 5(2), 147–166.

Livingstone, S. (2005a). Critical debates in Internet studies: Reflections on an emerging field. In J. Curran & M. Gurevitch, (Eds.), *Mass Media and Society*, 5th ed. London: Sage, pp. 9–28.

Livingstone, S. (2005b) (Ed.). *Audiences and Publics: When cultural engagement matters for the public sphere.* London: Intellect Press.

Livingstone, S., & Bober, M. (2003). *UK Children Go Online: Listening to young people's experiences.* London: London School of Economics and Political Science. http://www.children-go-online.net

Livingstone, S., & Bober, M. (2004). *UK Children Go Online: Surveying the experiences of young people and their parents*. London: London School of Economics and Political Science. http://www.children-go-online.net

Livingstone, S., Bober, M., & Helsper, E. (2004). *Active Participation or Just More Information? Young people's take up of opportunities to act and interact on the Internet*. London: London School of Economics and Political Science. http://www.children-go-online.net

Livingstone, S., Bober, M., & Helsper, E. (2005). Active participation or just more information? Young people's take up of opportunities to act and interact on the Internet. *Information, Communication and Society*, 8(3), 287–314.

Lunt, P., & Livingstone, S. (1996). The Focus Group in Media and Communications Research: The critical interpretation of public discussion. *Journal of Communication*, 46(2), 79–98.

McNeill, S. (1999). Moving towards Participation on the Internet: New radio initiatives for children and young people. In C. von Feilitzen & U. Carlsson (Eds.), *Children and Media: Image, education, participation* (pp. 347–353). Sweden: The UNESCO International Clearinghouse on Children and Violence on the Screen at Nordicom.

Montgomery, K., Gottlieb-Robles, B., & Larson, G. O. (2004). *Youth as E-Citizens: Engaging the digital generation*. Washington, D.C.: Center for Social Media, American University. http://www.centerforsocialmedia.org/ecitizens/youthreport.pdf

Morris, M., & Ogan, C. (1996). The Internet as Mass Medium. *Journal of Communication*, 46(1), 39–51.

Negroponte, N. (1995). *Being Digital*. New York: Vintage Books.

Norris, P. (1999) (Ed.). *Critical Citizens: Global support for democratic government*. New York: Oxford University Press.

Office of the e-Envoy (2004). *UK Online Annual Report 2003*. http://www.e-envoy.gov.uk

Park, A. et al. (2002). *British Social Attitudes: The 19th report*. London: Sage.

Poster, M. (1997). Cyberdemocracy: Internet and the public sphere. In D. Porter (Ed.), *Internet Culture* (pp. 210–218). New York: Routledge.

Prout, A. (2000). Children's Participation: Control and self-realisation in British late modernity. *Children & Society*, 14(4), 304–315.

Putnam, R. D. (2000). *Bowling Alone: The collapse and revival of American community*. New York: Simon & Schuster.

Qvortrup, J. (1995). Childhood and Modern Society: A paradoxical relationship. In J. Brannen & M. O'Brien (Eds.), *Childhood and Parenthood* (pp. 189–198). London: Institute of Education.

Sundin, E. (1999). The Online Kids: Children's participation on the Internet. In C. von Feilitzen & U. Carlsson (Eds.), *Children and Media: Image, education, participation* (pp. 355–368). Sweden: The UNESCO International Clearinghouse on Children and Violence on the Screen at Nordicom.

Tapscott, D. (1997). *Growing Up Digital: The rise of the net generation*. New York: Mc-Graw Hill.

Turkle, S. (1995). *Life on the Screen: Identity in the age of the Internet*. New York: Simon & Schuster.

van Deth, J., Maraffi, M., Newton, K., & Whiteley, P. (1999). (Eds.). *Social Capital and European Democracy*. London: Routledge.

7 Patterns of Internet use and political engagement among youth

Jo-Ann Amadeo

For many years, researchers, educators, and policy-makers from around the world have acknowledged the role the media play in the development of young people's social attitudes, political knowledge, and democratic engagement. In the United States, more than a decade ago, the president of a foundation dedicated to the advancement of teaching concluded:

> It is no longer enough simply to read and write. Students must also become literate in the understanding of visual images. Our children must learn how to spot a stereotype, isolate a social cliché, and distinguish facts from propaganda, analysis from banter, and important news from coverage. (Boyer as cited in Kubey & Baker, 1999, p. 1)

This cautionary note remains as true today as it did a decade ago. While there is wide variation both within and across countries, one thing seems quite clear: Most young people in industrialized countries are frequent consumers of the media. Notably in recent years, an online media culture has emerged for adolescents—one which exposes them to ideas, people, and information (both global and local) to an extent almost unimaginable a generation ago.

Furthermore, young people are turning to the media, especially the Internet, at a time in their lives when identity formation is their most compelling developmental task (Erikson, 1968). Adolescence and early adulthood are time periods during which many young people develop ideals for society and attach themselves to ideologies and social movements. The media have the potential to provide information and images that adolescents and young adults may use in the formation of beliefs, gender identity, occupational aspirations, as well as their expectations for the future.

This paper addresses the intersection of young people's expectations for the future and their Internet use by analyzing data from an international study of civic knowledge and attitudes. The first section of the paper presents a brief overview of media use—particularly Internet use—among young people, drawing largely on descriptive studies conducted in the

United States. The second section addresses the notion of civic engagement and civic identity development. These reviews on Internet use and civic engagement are not intended to be exhaustive reviews of previous research. Rather, they are intended to provide an overall context within which to view the empirical analyses which follow. The third section introduces the IEA Civic Education Study, including its theoretical framework. The remaining sections of the paper present exploratory analyses examining Internet use among 14-year-old students in Chile, Denmark, and England and correlates of Internet use. More specifically, the analyses describe patterns of Internet use to get political news and the relationship of that Internet use to civic engagement, attitudes, and knowledge. The paper concludes with thoughts about a theoretical framework through which Internet use might be viewed and directions for future research.

ATTENTION TO MEDIA

Adolescents and young adults use the media as sources of entertainment, coping strategies, youth culture identification, as well as connections to social networks. The media can transmit images, values, and social cues in a wide range of areas, including the civic and political world. In short, the media play an important role in the everyday lives of young people at a time in their developmental trajectories when identity formation is paramount.

The role the media play in the development of young people's civic knowledge and engagement can be examined from multiple perspectives. Media sources (in particular television, newspapers, and the Internet) have been used in school classrooms explicitly to engage students in the acquisition of civic and political knowledge. Immediate access to up-to-the minute information about current and political events is available over the Internet, and cable networks have brought television news into the classrooms of a significant number of students in the United States and elsewhere. Television viewing also has been used, in educational settings, to break down gender and racial stereotypes, and to complement classroom learning on issues ranging from elections and campaigns to violence reduction. On the other hand, there are also unintended consequences of media use which cannot be discounted when examining the media's role relating to the civic education and engagement of youth. While the media can provide opportunities for learning in this area, they can also present obstacles. Concern and public debate about the danger of online predators, the technology gap between the rich and the poor, and the effects of violent videogames is evident—and some argue has never been higher—in the United States and other parts of the world (Roberts, Foeher, Rideout, & Brodie, 1999).

This concern is likely because of the dramatic changes in the types and uses of the media. In the 21st century, children, adolescents, and young adults have numerous media choices, most of which are available to them

24 hours a day. Cellular telephones and personal computers have altered how many young people communicate with friends and form social networks, and the Internet has forever changed the manner in which information is disseminated (Nichols & Good, 2004). Furthermore, because they have grown up amidst these technological advances, many children and adolescents know more than their parents about computers, chat rooms, and the World Wide Web. Keeter and colleagues (2002) argue that people born after 1976 have grown up in an environment where information "has always been virtually costless and universally available; technology cheap and easily mastered; community as much a digital place of common interest as a shared physical space" (p. 5). And, as stated in a 1999 report disseminating the findings from a media usage study conducted in the United States:

> ...most of today's high school students cannot recall a time when the universe of television channels was fewer than three dozen...and their younger siblings have never known a world without interactive video games, personal computers, and the World Wide Web. (Roberts et al., 1999, p. 1)

These technological advances have made information and images from most parts of the world immediately available to adolescents and adults alike. The Pew Internet and American Life Project surveyed a random sample of Americans aged 18 years and older in 2004 and found that large numbers of the respondents were turning to the Internet for news, especially for images of events not covered by other news sources. Often those images reflected the political world in ways that could be considered both educational and disturbing. For example, the Pew researchers found that significant numbers of Americans (aged 18 and older) were turning to the Internet to view visual images from the war in Iraq which were considered to be too graphic or violent for the mainstream media. However, after accessing the images, there were differences in the viewers' levels of comfort regarding the availability of the most graphic war images online. Men and respondents aged 18 to 29 were more likely to approve of the display of violent war images than were women and respondents over the age of 30. More specifically, 52% of the people aged 18 to 29 who responded to the telephone survey approved of the display of images from the war in Iraq whereas only 37% of the respondents over the age of 30 expressed the same approval (Fallows & Rainie, 2004). This finding related to age is perhaps not surprising, since, as discussed above, adolescents and young adults have grown up in a culture dominated by instant access to information of all kinds.

In fact, in another recent survey conducted by the Pew Internet and the American Life Project, researchers found that 73% of youth 12 through 17 years of age use the Internet. Of those online adolescents, 76% indicated that they would miss the Internet if it were no longer available to them (Lenhart, Rainie, & Lewis, 2001). This is consistent with the findings from the Kaiser Foundation media usage study (1999): If forced to pick one form of media to have with them on a desert island, most children 8 years and older selected a computer with Internet access.

According to the Pew study, young people's reasons for accessing the Internet varied. Although most of the survey respondents indicated that they turn to the Internet to read or send e-mail, more than two-thirds (68%) reported that they have searched for news online (Lenhart et al., 2001). However, Keeter and his colleagues (2002) found in their study of generational attitudes, that American adolescents were no more likely than their elders to regularly use the Internet for news. There does seem, nevertheless, the potential to engage young people through the use of the medium with which they seem to be so comfortable. It could be argued that exposure to multiple images and diverse opinions could be associated with the development of tolerance. Here, Keeter et al. (2002) did find a generational difference: The young people (whom he calls the DotNet generation) appear to be more tolerant and appreciative of diversity than older generations. Clearly, there are many factors associated with this finding, but investigation of the relationship between the new media and tolerance may be an interesting line of future inquiry.

Internet use among youth is not by any means only an American phenomenon. Researchers from the UCLA World Internet Project found "remarkably consistent" online behaviors across more than a dozen countries in its study. The project, organized by the UCLA Center for Communication Policy, is one of the first to focus on international comparison of the effects of Internet use and non-use. Among the findings reported in January of 2004, survey data from the World Internet Project indicated that as Internet use increases, television viewing decreases in all countries participating in the study, especially in Chile and Hungary; that information found on the Internet is generally considered to be reliable by users in most countries, particularly in Korea; and that more men than women use the Internet in all of the surveyed countries, with the largest gender gap found in Italy (http://www.ccp.ucla.edu).

Finally, the Internet not only incidentally exposes young people to news and information, many sites geared to youth have explicit political or civic intentions. For example, MTV International in association with the Kaiser Family Foundation hosts a comprehensive sexual health website for youth including advocacy and grassroots opportunities (http://www.kff.entpartnerships/mtvinternational.cfm). A non-profit, non-partisan coalition of musicians, entertainers, and athletes called "Rock the Vote" seeks to mobilize youth with the goal of increasing youth voter turnout. Their website provides information on voter registration in both English and Spanish and in September 2004 (two months before the American presidential election) reported that it had registered 702, 199 new voters (http://www.rockthevote.com). Candidates for public office and political parties in the United States have launched websites, researchers have examined their content and messages, and made distinctions between "electoral" and "youth engagement" websites (Bennett & Xenos, 2004). Finally, less reverent sites with political perspectives are also easily found. In the United States, on the site http://www.jibjab.com a political parody of the presidential candidates set to the music of a classic American song was posted before the election. Also, rock bands sometimes use their websites to campaign through music and online videos against or for an issue or candidate (for example, http://www.nofxofficialwebsite.com).

In summary, the Internet has been available to young people for some time now, and its use seems pervasive in many parts of the world. It has changed the way young people interact with each other and collect information, and it is quite often an integral part of their everyday lives. The extent to which the Internet creates a social space and connects young people to both local and global communities may open many possibilities for democratic or civic engagement and community participation. What role does civic engagement play in the development of citizenship? How does participation contribute to an understanding of democracy or the development of attitudes or skills necessary for citizenship in democratic societies? There are multiple perspectives on these perspectives, some of which are described in the following section.

CIVIC ENGAGEMENT AND THE FORMATION OF CIVIC IDENTITY

Youniss, McLellan, and Yates (1997) employed a developmental approach to understanding the notion of civic identity and participation among youth and adults. They focused on the "construction of civic identity" and addressed the question of how youth become adults whose "civic engagement helps to sustain, reform or transform civil society" (p. 620). Based on a review of the literature in the United States, Youniss et al. contend that research supports the hypothesis that adolescents involved in school or community activities are likely to grow up to be involved adults. The authors argued that organized group participation has a lasting impact because it introduces adolescents to basic group roles and processes, and because it helps adolescents to incorporate civic involvement into their personal identities at a time when identity issues are particularly salient. Thus, the formation of civic identity—enhanced by participation—is the developmental link between active adolescents and involved adults. Seen from this perspective, the authors argued that researchers should draw the question away from how civil society disappeared, and focus more on how adults can enhance opportunities for youth to participate in a broad range of activities. Though not included in their review, it would seem that the

Internet could help to create or inform young citizens about opportunities for participation.

France (1998) also addressed the issue of young people's identities as citizens in his examination of perceptions and experiences of citizenship. Based on interviews with more than 50 individuals (aged 14 to 25 years) in a working-class community in England, France argued that community life is important to citizenship identity because community life can provide the young person with safety and familiarity at a time when "moving into the adult world" may seem risky. The extent to which the participants in the study developed these social relationships and felt they were accepted by the community seemed to influence their willingness to accept social responsibility. Thus, while Youniss and his colleagues took a developmental approach to understanding civic identity and participation, France emphasized the importance of social interaction as it relates to the development of citizen identity and responsibility. An interesting extension of this line of reasoning relates to the extent to which cyberspace can foster the kinds of social relationships that France argued are so essential.

Fuentealba (1998) also examined citizenship and citizenship identity from a social and economic perspective. Based on his survey of 3,200 families in two cities in Chile, he identified five types of political participation: protest, political parties, localities, trade unions, and elections. While formal participation in trade unions and political parties has diminished among the urban Chilean poor since the 1970s, Fuentealba argued that their local and neighborhood participation and protests have actually increased. This then broadens the more traditional view of democratic engagement.

Finally, Hahn (1998) explored from a comparative perspective how adolescents develop a sense of what it means to be a citizen. Her study, conducted in England, Denmark, Germany, the Netherlands, and the United States, took a look at the political beliefs, attitudes, and experiences of adolescents as well as the classroom climate in which citizenship education occurs. Hahn found clear country differences in adolescent political attitudes, experiences, and anticipated activities that are related to differences in each country's overall political culture. It remains to be seen, however, the extent to which (if at all) the Internet enhances or mitigates those cultural differences described by Hahn.

In conclusion, research suggests that the development of civic knowledge among young citizens, while quite important, is not sufficient. Tolerance, willingness to participate in democratic life, and developing an understanding of responsibilities as well as rights are important elements of citizenship in democratic societies (Torney-Purta et al., 2001; Amadeo et al., 2002). It is unlikely that there is a single approach that will enhance all facets of citizenship; peers, families, and other societal institutions, particularly the media, all play a role. It was within that perspective that the IEA Civic Education Study was framed.

THE IEA CIVIC EDUCATION STUDY

The International Association for the Evaluation of Educational Achievement (IEA), headquartered in Amsterdam, is a consortium of educational research organizations in approximately 60 countries, with a history of conducting cross-national research in education. In the mid-1990s, IEA initiated the Civic Education Study to examine the ways in which young people are prepared for their rights and responsibilities as citizens in democratic societies. The IEA Civic Education Study was designed and implemented in two phases, the first phase more qualitative and the second more quantitative. During the first phase, national researchers from more than 20 countries collected documentary evidence on the circumstances, content, and processes of civic education in their countries, including students' engagement and interest in the democratic process. These case studies provided insight into the political, social, economic, and educational context within which civic identity develops and civic education occurs (Torney-Purta, Schwille, & Amadeo, 1999). The data collected during the first phase also contributed to the design of a test of civic knowledge and skills and a survey of civic attitudes and behaviors administered to students during the second phase of the study.

During phase 2, approximately 90,000 14-year-old students from 28 countries were administered tests of civic knowledge and skills and surveys were made of civic attitudes, activities, and anticipated actions. These data were collected in 1999, findings were released in 2001, and reported in *Citizenship and Education in Twenty-eight Countries: Civic Knowledge and Engagement at Age Fourteen* (Torney-Purta, Lehmann, Oswald, & Schulz, 2001).

In the following year, over 50,000 upper secondary school students from 16 countries received a similar test of civic knowledge and skills (and also economic literacy items not given to the 14-year-olds) and the same survey of civic attitudes and behaviors (Amadeo et al., 2002). In sum, during the second phase of the study, quantitative data were collected from over 140,000 students to provide a series of snapshots of the civic knowledge and engagement of both younger and older adolescents across a diverse set of democratic societies.

The theoretical framework of the IEA Civic Education Study conceptualizes the ways in which "the everyday lives of young people in homes, with peers and at school serve as a 'nested' context for young people's thinking and action in the social and political world" (Torney-Purta et al., 2001, p. 20). This theoretical model has its roots in ecological theory (Bronfenbrenner, 1988) and situated cognition (Lave & Wenger, 1991; Wenger, 1998). In short, the model posits that adolescents' engagement in the community, and the development of an identity within the group, allows young people to learn about citizenship and democratic processes. Face-to-face interactions with families, teachers, peers, as well as the impact of broader society such as the media and other institutions influence the development of civic knowledge, attitudes, and democratic engagement (Torney-Purta & Amadeo, 2004).

The IEA dataset includes a substantial amount of information on young people's civic and democratic knowledge, engagement, and attitudes. The survey administered to the students included questions related to their media use (including the Internet for a subset of countries) and students' current and anticipated civic engagement. Engagement was conceptualized as both conventional activities such as voting or running for public office as well as a more social-movement kinds of actions such as working in the community or collecting money for a charity.

All 28 countries involved in the IEA Study of 14-year-olds asked students to report on the extent to which they view television news, read newspapers, and listen to news of the radio. Only seven countries, however, included as a national option a survey item related to the use of the Internet "to get news about politics." Fairly low percentages of students in these seven countries reported that they "often" used the Internet to get political news. This contrasts with the results from viewing television news—where on average, slightly more than half of the 90,000 students in the international sample reported that they "often" view television news broadcasts. Moreover, students reported not only that they view television news, but they also expressed trust in what they see and hear on television. To illustrate, close to 20% of the students in the international sample reported that the "always" trust television news, whereas only 8% of these students indicated that they "always" trust their national governments (Amadeo, Torney-Purta, & Barber, 2004).

Although television appeared to be the most frequent source of news for these young people, in three of the seven countries where use of the Internet was queried, about 20% of the students did report that they use the Internet "to get news about politics." Those three countries—Chile, Denmark, and England—are the focus of the analyses that follow. The data are from the IEA Civic Education Study of 14-year-olds and the analyses below offer three views. The first set of analyses describes the use of the Internet by 14-year-olds in Chile, Denmark, and England to get political news. Second, bivariate correlations exploring the relationship between various forms of media use and political engagement are presented. The third and final set of analyses are exploratory regression analyses examining multiple correlates of expected democratic engagement.

WHO IS ONLINE?

Table 1 reports the frequency with which students responded that they use the Internet to get news about politics. The response options available to

Table 1 Use the Internet to get news about politics, percent of 14-year-old students

	Country		
	Chile	*Denmark*	*England*
	(n=5556)	*(n=3017)*	*(n=2723)*
Often & sometimes	24%	18%	21%
Rarely	18%	22%	22%
Never	56%	58%	54%
Internet hosts/1000 people	2.0	56.3	24.6*

Notes: Internet hosts per 1000 people as of 1998; data collected from students 1999. *Figure for United Kingdom.
Sources: IEA Civic Education Study; Human Development Report, 2000.

the students were: "often, sometimes, rarely, and never" calculated on a four-point scale as were the other media items. About 20% of the students in all three countries indicated that they "often" or "sometimes" use the Internet to get news, whereas about the same percentage responded that they "rarely" did so. More than half of the 14-year-olds in all three countries stated that they "never" use the Internet to get political news. We do not know from these data, however, how many of these students use the Internet for entertainment, communication with friends, or to retrieve information they do not consider political in nature.

Students in Chile were most likely to say that the use the Internet for news—in fact, almost a quarter of the Chilean students indicated Internet use, six percentage points higher than in Denmark. This is somewhat surprising given that in the year before these data were collected, there were only 2 Internet hosts per 1000 people in Chile (Human Development Report, 2000). This distribution of Internet availability contrasts sharply with Denmark, where there were 56 Internet hosts per 1000 people in 1998 (Human Development Report, 2000).

CHARACTERISTICS OF THE ONLINE STUDENTS

Consistent with results reported by the World Internet Project (http://www. ccp.ucla.edu) and elsewhere, more males than females reported on the IEA Civic Education Study survey that they used the Internet. As illustrated in Figure 1, this gender gap was particularly high in Denmark where 24% of the male students reported Internet use as compared to 11% of the female students. The gender difference in Internet usage was smallest in England, with a 6 percentage point difference between male and female 14-year-olds. Finally, the difference among Chilean students was about the same as that found in England—a 7 percentage point difference between males and females. This difference could be interpreted as a difference in male

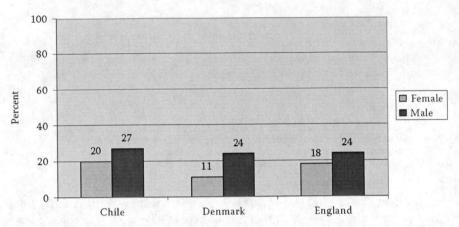

Figure 1

and female preferences for using the Internet or it could reflect gender differences in young people's interest in politics. (The question was phrased in the following manner: How often do you use the Internet to get information about politics?) In most of the 28 countries that participated in the IEA Study, more males than females expressed an interest in politics. This finding, however, did not hold true in Chile where equal percentages of male and female students expressed political interest (Torney-Purta et al., 2001).

While there was only a relatively small gap in Internet usage among Chilean males and females, the gap in use between Chilean students with many literacy resources in their home and those with few was more pronounced. Stated another way, students who indicated on the survey that they had few books in their home (1 to 10) were less likely to agree that they used the Internet than students who reported they had more than 200 books in their home. This difference was most evident in Chile and England (see Figure 2). In Denmark, the percentage of students with low home literacy resources who use the Internet (19%) was essentially the same as students with high home literacy resources (21%). In contrast, in Chile 18% of students with low resources reported Internet use whereas 33% with high resources did so and in England, 14% of the low resourced students indicated Internet use whereas 27% of students with high home resources reported Internet use.

Finally, and perhaps not surprisingly, those students in the sample who strongly agreed that they were interested in politics were most likely to report that they used the Internet to get news. As shown in Figure 3, in all

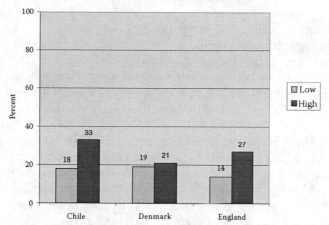

Figure 2

three countries about 40% of the students who strongly agreed that they were interested in politics reported using the Internet. In Denmark and England, only about 10% of the students who strongly disagreed that they were interested in politics responded that they often or sometimes use the Internet to get news. In Chile, 17% of the students who did not express in interest in politics indicated using the Internet.

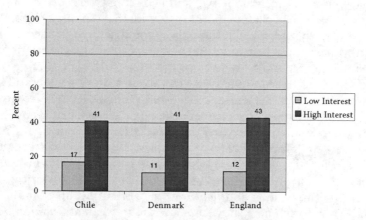

Figure 3

MEDIA USE AND CIVIC KNOWLEDGE, ATTITUDES, AND ENGAGEMENT

Bronfenbrenner (1988) and other ecological theorists posit that humans are constantly interacting with their environments, both shaping and being shaped by them. Developmental influences are both proximal and distal, and occur through daily interactions with those closest to us as well as through exposure to broad cultural norms and values. Thus, while parents, peers, and schools may provide information relevant to democratic engagement and knowledge, so too do societal institutions such as the media. How does exposure to the media in general, and Internet use in particular, relate to knowledge of democratic processes and institutions? Is there an association between media use and the development of civic attitudes such as tolerance and political interest? Finally, to what extent is a relationship evident between the use of the media and expectations for future civic or democratic engagement among young people?

These questions were addressed by again drawing on survey data collected from 14-year-old students during the IEA Civic Education Study. Specifically, a series of bivariate correlational analyses (Pearson Product-Moment) were used to explore the relationship between media use and civic knowledge, attitudes, and expectations for future participation. These relationships are descriptive and no causality between variables should be inferred.

Looking across the three countries—Chile, Denmark, and England—several trends are apparent (see appendix A for correlation tables by country). First, these data suggest, not surprisingly, positive relationships among different types of political media use, reading newspapers, viewing television news, listening to radio news, and using the Internet to get news (all items were measured on a four-point scale with the response options "often, sometimes, rarely and never"). In all three countries, the strongest relationship with Internet use is reading the newspaper; though the relationship is a moderate one, especially in England ($r=.18$, $p<.01$).

Secondly, it has been argued that the acquisition of democratic knowledge is an important element of citizenship though previous research suggests the relationship between media use and democratic knowledge to be somewhat weak compared to the association between media use and engagement (e.g., Torney-Purta & Amadeo, 2004). Knowledge was nevertheless included in these analyses because it can certainly be construed as a vital element to the formation of citizenship in democratic societies. Consistent with previous findings from the IEA study, an examination of the analyses reported here shows a moderate to weak association between the frequency with which students attend to news in the media and their scores on a test of civic knowledge administered during the IEA Civic Education Study. The relationship between Internet use and civic knowledge is statistically significant in all three countries but particularly weak in Chile ($r=.09$, $p<.01$).

The third trend that emerges from the responses of these young people is that the relationship between the frequency of media use and students' positive attitudes toward women and immigrants is either weak or not significant. These attitudinal measures of support for women and support for immigrants are both scales, with higher scores indicating more support for the political and economic rights of women and the political and social rights of immigrants (see appendix B for a list of the items included in each scale). The weakest association in all three countries was between Internet use and attitudes toward women and immigrants: In fact, in most cases no relationship was found.

The strongest association between Internet usage and students' attitudes was the positive relationship between the frequency with which students indicated using the Internet to get news and their agreement with the single statement: "I am interested in politics." As seen in the bar graphs in the preceding section, the more interest the students had in politics the more likely they were to turn to the Internet to get news about politics. This relationship was strongest in Denmark ($r=.30$, $p<.01$). As with all of the associations discussed here, the direction of this relationship between Internet use and political interest cannot be discerned. It could be that those young people most interested in politics turn to the Internet for news or that messages or images on the Internet spark interest in politics.

Finally, in looking at the adolescents' expectations for the future, there were positive relationships with the frequency with which students attend to news in the media and their plans to vote when they became adult citizens as well as to volunteer in their communities. (Both expectations of voting and of volunteering used in these correlational analyses were measured by single items on the survey asking students to indicate how likely they were to undertake those activities in the future.) For example, Internet use in Chile, Denmark, and England was related to students' expectations that as adult citizens they would vote in national elections ($r=.11$; $r=.13$; and $r=.12$ respectively, $p<.01$). The relationship between Internet use and plans to volunteer in the community was much weaker in Chile than the relationship between Internet use and plans to vote

($r=.04$, $p.<.01$) and about the same in Denmark and England ($r=11$ and $r=.11$ respectively, $p <.01$).

In summary, these bivariate analyses offer a descriptive snapshot of the relationship between 14-year-old students' media use and their knowledge of democratic institutions and processes; their attitudes; and their plans for future civic engagement. What emerges is a description of a series of relationships such as those found among different types of media use; between adolescents' interest in politics and their use of the Internet; and between Internet use and plans for future democratic engagement, especially voting.

STUDENTS' EXPECTED CIVIC PARTICIPATION
AND POLITICAL ACTIONS

In addition to being asked about their use of the media, the adolescents were also asked about political or civic-related actions they may undertake within the next few years or as adults. In general, these actions were conceptualized in two broad areas (though there is overlap)—activities one undertakes in proximal settings (such as the local community) and activities that have implications that may more distal (such as voting in national elections). Therefore, two scales were formed from the survey items to measure young people's expectations of participating in: (1) social-movement activities, and (2) conventional activities. The items on the social-movement activities scale include the extent to which students thought that they were likely to undertake the following actions in the next few years.

- Volunteer time to help poor elderly people in the community
- Collect money for a social cause
- Collect signatures for a petition
- Participate in a nonviolent protest march

There are also activities adults can undertake in democratic societies that are more political in nature. Students were asked to consider these actions and indicate whether they expected to participate in these activities when they reached adulthood. These items were combined to form the conventional activities scale and include the following items.

- Vote in national elections
- Get information about candidates before voting in an election
- Join a political party
- Write letters to a newspaper about social or political concerns
- Be a candidate for a local or city office

For each item on both scales, students were given response options ranging from "I will certainly do this" (4) to "I will certainly not do this" (1).

TABLE 2 *Students' expectations for future activities by country*

	Country		
Type of activity	*Chile*	*Denmark*	*England*
Social-movement	3.0	2.4	2.4
Conventional	2.4	2.3	2.3

Notes. Ratings were made on the following scale: 1=I will certainly not do this; 2=I will probably not do this; 3=I will probably do this; 4=I will certainly do this. Cronbach alpha: Conventional .70 for Chile; .71 for Denmark; and .73 for England. Social-movement: .64 for Chile; .73 for Denmark; and .75 for England.

Higher mean scores indicate greater expectations among the students that they will engage in those kinds of civic or democratic actions. The mean scores for each scale are reported by country in Table 2.

As illustrated in Table 2, 14-year-olds in Chile were most likely to indicate that they would participate in social-movement kinds of activities over the next few years. Plans for engagement of either kind were comparatively low in Denmark and England.

PREDICTORS OF FUTURE ENGAGEMENT

In order to examine correlates of students' expectations of future civic involvement or political activity, two sets of simultaneous regression analyses were run for each country. First, predictors of the students' expectations of participating in social-movement activities in the next few years were examined. Second, a regression model was run to examine the correlates of expected conventional citizenship activities during adulthood.

The five predictors used in the exploratory models were selected to examine: (1) personal characteristics of the adolescent, that is, gender; (2) the adolescents' level of trust in government-related institutions (such as the police, courts, and Parliament); (3) the adolescents' knowledge of democratic institutions and processes as measured by the students' scores on the IEA test of civic knowledge and skills; (4) school variables such as the extent to which the young people perceived that they learned in school about the importance of voting and solving problems in the community; and (5) the frequency with which adolescents reported using the Internet to get political news. In short, the model examines engagement by looking at the individual characteristics of the young citizen (gender, attitudes, and knowledge) as well as societal institutions (school and media).

In Chile and England, young people's opportunity to learn in school about working in the community and the importance of voting were the strongest predictors of the 14-year-olds' expectations for social-movement and conventional engagement respectively. In Denmark, these school variables were also positively related to engagement, although other variables in the models were more potent predictors of the Danish adolescents' plans for engagement. For example, in Denmark, use of the Internet to get news was the strongest predictor of conventional civic engagement and the second most powerful predictor (after gender) of social-movement engagement. Internet use was significant in Chile and England also. It was the third strongest predictor of both social-movement and conventional engagement in Chile and the third strongest predictor of plans for social-movement activities in England (see Tables 3 and 4).

It is interesting to note the differences in correlates between the social-movement and conventional activities. While knowledge of democratic processes and institutions was a strong predictor of plans for conventional

Table 3 Regression models for 14-year-old students' expectations of social-movement citizenship activities, by country

	Predictor variables		
	Chile	Denmark	England
Gender (female)	.08	.27	.20
Trust in government	.08	n.s.	.09
Civic knowledge	-.05	n.s.	.08
Internet use	.06	.21	.12
Learning in school about helping in community	.17	.18	.23
R^2	.06	.15	.15

Notes. Standardized beta coefficients were reported. Significant at 0.01 level. n.s.=Nonsignificant coefficients.

activities, it was either a weak or non-significant predictor of social-movement kinds of actions. In most cases, trust in government-related institutions also was more closely associated with conventional citizenship activities than with social movement. Finally, it appears from these data, that young women are more likely than young men to plan on social-movement activities.

In conclusion, many other factors not included in these models have the potential to enhance (or deter) engagement. However, these models begin to explore the relative association between engagement and attitudes, knowledge and Internet use. Clearly these variables vary in meaning based on the society's cultural context and are all related to each other in varying degrees. For example, Internet use, which is so closely associated with political interest among the adolescents in these three countries, may be the behavioral manifestation of political interest.

Table 4 Regression models for 14-year-old students' expectations of conventional citizenship activities, by country

	Predictor variables		
	Chile	Denmark	England
Gender (female)	n.s.	.07	.09
Trust in government	.18	.11	.17
Civic knowledge	.09	.21	.21
Internet use	.09	.22	.16
Learning in school about voting	.30	.21	.26
R^2	.16	.19	.20

Notes. Standardized beta coefficients were reported. Significant at 0.01 level. n.s.=Nonsignificant coefficients.

DISCUSSION

Ecological theorists view development and learning as a series of reciprocal interactions between the individual and societal institutions. Among
adolescents, societal institutions that are of particular relevance include the
family, school, peer groups, and most certainly the media. Young people
turn to the media to connect themselves to social networks, to be entertained, and to seek out information. In 1999, about 20% of 14-year-olds
in Chile, Denmark, and England indicated on a survey that they used the
Internet to get news about politics. One can imagine that if this same survey
were administered today, that percentage would be considerably greater.
Several trends ran across the countries, the Internet users were more likely
to be male, from homes with high literacy resources, and to indicate an
interest in politics. Further, while causality was not established, analysis
of the IEA data suggests some relationship between Internet use and civic
engagement. This line of inquiry, along with adolescents' notions of tolerance and Internet use, could be followed up and teased out in greater detail
in the future.

In addition, socio-cultural theorists, such as Lave and Wenger (1991)
speculate that the various groups to which young people belong "situate" their learning and cognition. These theorists use the term "legitimate
peripheral participation" to describe individuals' observations (or partial
participation) during an activity or in a setting to which they are newcomers or novices. Socio-cultural theorists further argue that through experience that is either intentionally or unintentionally shaped by older group
members, novice members move away from peripheral participation to
more central involvement in a "community of practice" (Lave & Wenger,
1991).

This notion of "legitimate peripheral participation" can be applied to
citizenship and democratic engagement. For example, it was this notion of
moving from the peripheral to more central engagement in various levels of
one's community and nation that shaped the ideas about the formation of
citizenship in the IEA Study. Although 14-year-olds are not old enough to
take part in many the adult-oriented aspects of citizenship such as voting,
running for office, or giving money to candidates, adolescents can and do
observe these actions. Attending to the media is one way through which
these observations are made possible. The Internet, in particular, has the
potential to bring this peripheral participation into the homes of young
people, through a medium with which most are quite comfortable. In
addition, because of the diverse nature of information on the World Wide
Web, young citizens can be exposed to communities that are both local and
global.

In recent formulations of socio-cultural theory, Wenger (1998, 2001)
detailed some ramifications of the notion of "communities of practice,"
defined as "people who share a concern, a set of problems, or passion about

a topic and deepen their knowledge and share their experience by interacting on an on-going basis." The groups Wenger discusses range from work teams to community organizations to classrooms, but the Internet could certainly be considered in the same light. Adolescents can seek out those Internet communities most consistent with their developing identities and world views.

In communities of practice individuals negotiate identities, acquire knowledge and skills that are meaningful as defined by the group, and are engaged in practice. "Community" can be thought of as helping to define the other elements. "Learning as belonging" is the way Wenger phrases it. These groups define what type of participation is worthwhile, valued, and competent for their members. One of the aims of citizenship education is that young people feel themselves members of a community of practice consisting both of other citizens and of public or private leaders. The Internet has the potential to be such a community, and can link individuals with similar interests, passions, and concerns.

Practice is also central to the socio-cultural model. It takes the focus from the passive to the active. "Learning as doing" is the way Wenger phrases it. This usually consists of a joint enterprise or activity of some sort, and once again one can see how the new media can facilitate this aspect of Wenger's model. Through exposure to new ideas, e-mailing and instant-messaging friends, and entering into chat rooms with people with similar interests, adolescents can "practice" their views. This, however, does not speak to the concern many have about the unregulated nature of information available on the Internet or the fear of online predators.

Finally, membership in a community of practice helps its members develop and negotiate *personal identities*. "Learning as becoming" is the way Wenger phrases it. Identities are personal histories or trajectories that link the individual's experience in families with broader communities. The media can provide these links.

In conclusion, the every-day lives of young people are vital aspects of the development of democratic beliefs and civic identity. Adolescents are exposed to ideas, world views, and experiences through multiple sources, both manifest and latent. The role of the new media falls within this conceptualization, and is emerging.

ACKNOWLEDGEMENT

The comments and contributions to this draft by Professor Judith Torney-Purta (University of Maryland, College Park) are gratefully acknowledged.

REFERENCES

Amadeo, J., Torney-Purta, J, & Barber, C.H. (2004). *Attention to media and trust in media sources: Analysis of data from the IEA civic education study.* College Park, MD: Center for Information and Research on Civic Learning and Engagement. http://www.civicyouth.org

Amadeo, J., Torney-Purta, J., Lehmann, R., Husfeldt, V., & Nikolova, R. (2002). *Civic knowledge and engagement. An IEA study of upper secondary students in sixteen countries.* Amsterdam: IEA. http://www.wam.umd.edu/~iea

Bennett, W.L., & Xenos, M. (2004). *Young voters and the web of politics. Pathways to participation in youth engagement and electoral campaign web spheres.* College Park, MD: Center for Information and Research on Civic Learning and Engagement. http://www.civicyouth.org.

Bronfenbrenner, U. (1988). Interacting systems in human development. In N. Bolger, C. Caspi, G. Downey, & M. Moorehouse (Eds.), *Persons in context: Developmental processes* Cambridge: Cambridge University Press, pp. 25–30.

Fallows, D., & Rainie, L. (2004). *The internet as a unique news source.* Washington, D.C.: Pew Internet and American Life Project. http://www.pewinternet.org

France, A. (1998). Why should we care? Young people, citizenship and questions of social responsibility. *Journal of Youth Studies, 1,* 97–111.

Fuentealba, J. (1998). Citizenship and participation: Limits and opportunities of political participation of the urban poor in Chile. *Estudios Latinoamericanos, 5*(10), 145–173.

Hahn, C. (1998). *Becoming political: Comparative perspectives on citizenship education.* Albany: State University of New York Press.

Hart, R. A. (1997). *Children's participation.* New York: UNICEF.

Kaiser Family Foundation (1999). *Kids and media at the new millennium.* http://www.kff.org/entmedia/loader

Keeter, S. Zukin, C., Andolina, M., & Jenkins, K. (2002). *The civic and political health of the nation: A generational portrait.* College Park, MD: CIRCLE.

Kubey, R., & Baker, F.(1999). Has media literacy found a curricular foothold? *Education Week, 56,* October 27.

Lave, L., & Wenger, E. (1991). *Situated learning: Legitimate peripheral participation.* Cambridge: Cambridge University Press.

Lenhart, A., Rainie, L., & Lewis, O. (2001*). Teenage life on line.* Washington, D.C.: Pew Internet and American Life Project available http://www.pewinternet.org.

Nichols, S.L., & Good, T. L. (2004). *America's teenagers—Myths and realities. Media images, schooling, and the social costs of careless indifference.* Mahwah, NJ/London: Lawrence Erlbaum.

MTV International (2004). *Staying alive* website. http://www.kff.org/entpartnerships/mtvinternational.cfm/

Roberts, D., Forhr, U.G., Rideout, V.J., & Brodie, M. (1999, November). *Kids and media @ the new millennium: A comprehensive analysis of children's media use.* Menlo Park, CA: Kaiser Family Foundation.

Torney-Purta, J., & Amadeo, J. (2004). *Strengthening democracy in the Americas through civic education: An empirical analysis highlighting the views of students and teachers.* Washington, D.C.: Organization of American States.

Torney-Purta, J., Lehmann, R., Oswald, H., & Schulz, W. (2001). *Citizenship and education in twenty- eight countries: Civic knowledge and engagement at age 14.* Amsterdam: IEA. http://www.wam.umd.edu/~iea

Torney-Purta, J., Schwille, J., & Amadeo, J. (Eds.), (1999). *Civic education across countries: Twenty-four national case studies from the IEA civic education project.* Amsterdam: IEA.

United Nations Development Programme. (2000). *Human development report 2001.* Oxford, New York: Oxford University Press.

Wenger, E. (1998). *Communities of practice: Learning, meaning, and identity.* Cambridge: Cambridge University Press.

UCLA Center for Communication Policy (2003). *The UCLA Internet report: Surveying the digital future year three.* http//www.ccp.ucla.edu

Youniss, J., McLellan, J.A., & Yates, M. (1997). What we know about engendering civic identity. *American Behavioral Scientist, 40*, 620–631.

APPENDIX A. BIVARIATE CORRELATIONS BY COUNTRY

Notes. All correlations significant at p < .01
n.s.=non-significant

Table A.1 **Chile**

	2.	3.	4.	5.	6.	7.	8.	9.	10.	11.
1. Read newspaper	.303	.247	.226	.203	.284	.144	.236	.138	.107	.073
2. TV news		.249	.127	.134	.178	.063	.157	.100	.062	n.s.
3. Radio news			.158	n.s.	.125	.117	.162	.079	n.s.	n.s.
4. Use Internet				.088	.112	.041	.183	.101	n.s.	.054
5. Civic knowledge					.230	-.166	.069	.036	.317	.123
6.Vote						.103	.363	.237	.143	.083
7. Volunteer							.057	.071	.125	.153
8. Political interest								.203	.041	.040
9.Trust									.042	.100
10. Support for women's rights										.327
11. Support for immigrants										

Table A.2 **Denmark**

	2.	3.	4.	5.	6.	7.	8.	9.	10.	11.
1. Read newspaper	.353	.216	.224	.127	.126	.193	.233	.111	.092	.100
2. TV news		.299	.233	.181	.120	.064	.309	.066	.097	.102
3. Radio news			.121	.115	.088	.107	.178	.086	.085	n.s.
4. Use Internet				.109	.149	.114	.304	n.s.	n.s.	.061
5. Civic knowledge					.059	-.112	.285	.109	.268	.210
6. Vote						.079	.290	.180	.274	.181
7. Volunteer							.093	.116	.172	.273
8. Political interest								.081	n.s.	.100
9. Trust									.184	.156
10. Support for women's rights										.361
11. Support for immigrants										

Table A.3 **England**

	2.	3.	4.	5.	6.	7.	8.	9.	10.	11.
1. Read newspaper	.432	.281	.180	.207	.063	.221	.159	.135	.175	n.s.
2. TV news		.430	.169	.223	.102	.242	.175	.124	.151	.089
3. Radio news			.109	.179	.065	.194	.185	.082	.108	n.s.
4. Use internet				.104	.129	.107	.277	.104	n.s.	n.s.
5. Civic knowledge					-.060	.094	.137	n.s.	.284	n.s.
6. Vote						.251	.172	.177	.267	.102
7. Volunteer							.181	.166	.223	.153
8. Political interest								.145	n.s.	n.s.
9. Trust									.060	n.s.
10. Support for women's rights										.278
11. Support for immigrants										

APPENDIX B IRT SCALES: SUPPORT FOR WOMEN'S RIGHTS AND SUPPORT FOR IMMIGRANTS

Support for women's rights

Items in scale:
- Women should run for public office and take part in the government just as men do.
- Women should have the same rights as men in every way.
- Women should stay out of politics. (negative)
- When jobs are scarce, men have more right to a job than women. (negative)
- Men and women should get equal pay when they are in the same jobs.
- Men are better qualified to be political leaders than women. (negative)

Support for immigrants' rights

- Immigrants should have the opportunity to keep their own language.
- Immigrants' children should have the same opportunities for education that other children in the country have.
- Immigrants who live in a country for several years should have the opportunity to vote in elections.
- Immigrants should have the opportunity to keep their own customs and lifestyle.
- Immigrants should have all the same rights that everyone else in a country has.

Response options: Strongly agree; agree; disagree; strongly disagree.

8 Finding a global voice?
Migrant children, new media, and the limits of empowerment

David Buckingham and Liesbeth de Block

New media are frequently seen to offer considerable potential for regenerating democratic participation. Digital technology, it is argued, can 'give citizens a voice', enabling them to contribute positively and autonomously to public debates, and to play a more active part in the political process. This is seen to be particularly relevant for the 'socially excluded', who have effectively been left behind by mainstream forms of political discourse. And these arguments are most frequently applied to the so-called 'digital generation', young people who are apparently developing new forms of global political consciousness and activity through their relationships with new media (Tapscott, 1998). These aspirations continue to exercise considerable fascination, not merely for over-excited cyber-gurus, but also for government policy-makers.

Academic researchers have increasingly challenged the 'technological determinism' of such claims. At best, it is suggested, they are based on unrepresentative instances, and fail to provide evidence for more generalised assertions about the liberating and empowering potential of new media (Buckingham, 2000: chapter 3). Yet even if we accept that technology does not automatically bring about gains of the kind its more enthusiastic proponents suggest, the question remains about how its potential benefits might be maximised. While dismissing technological determinism, we also need to avoid the pitfall of what Raymond Williams (1974) called 'determined technology'—an argument whereby any impact that technology might have is seen as merely a manifestation of other social and economic processes. If technology does make some kind of difference—in Williams's terms, if it creates possibilities and imposes constraints—then we need to explore the social and institutional conditions under which this difference might be made.

This paper presents some experiences from a cross-European project that sought to explore these possibilities in a highly practical way. The project was an experiment (in the everyday, rather than the scientific sense!)—and while it succeeded in some respects, it clearly failed in others. The difficulties we encountered might partly be traced to an excess of ambition, and an inability to foresee all the likely obstacles. But they also raise some interesting questions about the *pedagogic* dimensions of young people's engagement with new media technology that are worthy of further reflection. In particular, we want to question the idea of 'voice' that is often central to theories of radical pedagogy (cf. Orner, 1992). To what extent do new media *give* children a voice—or at least enable them to find one? What are the power-relationships that are inherent in the notion of 'giving voice'? In what contexts, and in what ways, are the 'voices' available to children defined, and in what ways might they actually be heard? And is possessing a voice straightforwardly 'empowering', or can it not also be seen as a potential burden?

THE PROJECT

'Children in Communication about Migration' (CHICAM) was a three-year project (2001–2004) funded by the European Commission (Framework V), involving partners from six European countries.[1] CHICAM aimed to explore how media production and Internet communication might allow refugee and migrant children to represent and to share their experiences of migration. The more political objective was to explore how the content and processes of this communication could inform policy initiatives in the areas of migration and childhood, by making children's voices heard in the wider public arena. Indeed, three of the specific research themes were closely connected to relevant social policy areas: friendship and peer relations, school/work and family. The fourth theme—which will form the main focus of this paper—was concerned with the media themselves: how do children use the 'languages' of digital media, both to create their own audio-visual 'statements' and to communicate with each other and with adults across cultural boundaries? This theme is particularly important considering the number of different languages represented in the project—both the European languages of the partnership but also the languages of origin for the children (which together amounted to more than twenty).

The idea for CHICAM grew out of a doctoral research project conducted with refugee and migrant children in one primary school in inner London (de Block, 2002). As part of the data collection, the researcher decided to involve the children in making videotapes about their lives. The children filmed in their local area, at home and at school, and made cut-out animations of their journeys to the UK. This participatory use of media is increasingly popular in research with children (Gauntlett, 1996; Bloustein, 1998; Goldman-Segal, 1998); and visual methods are also used in therapeutic work with refugee children; for example, by organisations such as the Medical Foundation for the Care of Victims of Torture. This approach offers a different means of access to children's experiences, and in this case allowed the children to talk about potentially difficult subjects in a more distanced way.

Another research project, 'VideoCulture', which was running concurrently at our research centre, involved an exchange of youth video productions between Germany, the UK, the Czech Republic, and the USA (Buckingham, 2001; Niesyto, 2003). Our aim here was to explore the potential of using visual (or at least non-verbal) means of communication, particularly for the purpose of intercultural communication across language barriers. Our analysis focused on the forms of visual symbolism and representation the young people were drawing upon in their productions, and how these were received and understood by youth audiences in the partner countries.

A significant new element in CHICAM, however, was the use of the Internet to facilitate a greater sharing of the young people's productions, both between the young people involved in the project and (eventually) among a wider audience. This partly reflected our awareness that many of these children were becoming increasingly familiar with global communications through family e-mail connections, satellite television, chat rooms, and so on (CHICAM, 2002). Yet we were also seeking to test out some of the claims made for new media described above, by using digital technology to convey these children's voices and perspectives into the wider public sphere.

The practical media work was based in six 'clubs', which met weekly. Most of these were after-school clubs based in schools and community centres (in Greece, for example, the club met in the offices of the Council for Refugees). All the children attending the clubs were recently arrived refugees or migrants between the ages of 10 and 14 years. In some cases the children already knew each other, although in others it was the first time they had met. They came from a wide range of countries. The club in the UK, for example, was comprised of children from Angola, Kenya, Somalia, Sierra Leone/Guinea, Sri Lanka, Pakistan, Lithuania, Russia, and Colombia. The children therefore all had very different experiences of migration, and motivations for migrating (Brah, 1996).

Each club was run by a researcher and a media educator, although in several cases a community worker or teacher who knew many of the children outside the club also participated. The clubs used exclusively digital technology for filming, editing, and disseminating material. Although there were some still images, most of the material produced was in the form of short videotapes, often only a couple of minutes in length. The projects were linked through a project website (http://www.chicam.net), which is designed on three levels. A public site holds the project details and finished research papers, as well as compilations of the media productions from the clubs, organised on thematic lines. A second level, entered by password, was for the children in the clubs to view the productions from the clubs and to post and exchange comments about them. There was also a general bulletin board for topics not directly related to the media work. A third level was for the researchers, and provided a space to discuss research concerns and ideas as they arose and to enter brief weekly notes on the fieldwork.

PROBLEMS, PROBLEMS

Even from this brief description, some of the logistical difficulties faced by the project should be readily apparent. Some of these were familiar from our past experience of such projects—the difficulty of gaining access, finding appropriate spaces in which to work, recruiting and retaining participants, and so on. Others were perhaps a function of our excessive ambitions—particularly the number of partners, and hence the number of languages involved. Still others resulted from the gap between rhetoric and reality that typically characterises discussions of the Internet. For example, all the partners assured us that they would have access to the Internet in their clubs, although in practice this was often quite uneven. Furthermore, although we were using state-of-the-art video streaming, it was impossible to run full-screen moving images. And difficulties to do with incompatible formats, lost files, and unreadable protocols bedevilled our project in ways that will probably be all too familiar.

Some of these issues will be considered in more detail below, but the main focus in this paper is on the social and pedagogic dimensions of the project. To what extent did access to these technologies provide the children with new opportunities for self-expression and communication? What and how did they learn about the use of new media, and what obstacles did they have to overcome in doing so? And to what extent did their use of these media reflect or represent their social position, both as migrants or refugees and as children? Our main aim here is to illustrate some of the complexities and difficulties that inevitably characterise attempts to use new media in this way—and hence to suggest that any potential they may have for 'empowering' young people is highly contingent on the ways in which they are used. In the process, we also seek to focus attention on some broader methodological and political issues at stake in this kind of work, which are drawn together in our conclusion.

WHAT WORKED

Until quite recently, it has been rare for young people's media productions, whether they derive from schools or from more informal settings, to find a wider audience (Harvey, Skinner, and Parker, 2002). At least in principle, the Internet should make this much more possible: there is a growing number of websites that feature youth-produced media, at least some of which are specifically political in focus (Montgomery et al., 2004). 'Finding an audience' could be seen as at least one aspect of wider civic participation; but it is also a process that should, at least theoretically, have an important impact on the process of production itself. Earlier studies in media education (Buckingham, Grahame, and Sefton-Green, 1995: chapter 4; Buckingham and Harvey, 2001) have suggested that the awareness of a 'real' audience can significantly help young people to conceptualise their finished product, and evaluate their own work—although they also suggest that this awareness is not easy to achieve.

As we have noted, the children's productions were placed on the CHI-CAM website, and the children were encouraged to provide feedback to each other by means of a bulletin board. In practice, however, communication between the clubs was limited and sporadic. Before exploring some of the reasons for this, we would like to discuss some examples of the communication that did occur, and what they tell us.

At an early stage in the project, each club made a 'hello' video, introducing themselves and their location to the other clubs. Even though these were group productions, the children were often nervous and wary of revealing themselves. Many of them focused—often in a rather formal way—on where they came from, using a map, rather than giving any details about their present environment. Initial reactions to these productions were mixed. The children noticed details about each other: age differences, who was good looking, who they thought they might like to be friends with. For some clubs, the videos did present important challenges to stereotypes. The Swedish club remarked on the dark skin of one of the UK girls. In Italy, the children thought that the German film came from Morocco because some of the girls were wearing the hijab (head scarf)—although in the UK, this only raised suspicion about whether the video was indeed from Germany at all. The Dutch club asked where the mountains and snow were in the Swedish film (it was filmed in a seaside town in the south of the country). Comments about locations were also important. The children compared the fabric of their respective school buildings, the Swedish and UK schools comparing favourably against the Greek and Italian.

There was then some rather polite exchange of questions and answers between the clubs, checking ages, who had done what in making the films, and so on. A level of competition also began to emerge here—about which production looked more professional, which had used the best music, which children were better looking. At least in the UK club, the children appeared to be judging the other children in order to assess whether they were 'cool' enough to consider at all. Members of several clubs were clearly impressed by the style and looks of particular children. Interestingly, the children in clubs in more 'stylish' countries such as Italy were deemed more 'attractive', fulfilling another form of national stereotyping. Nevertheless, these early attempts at communication were largely adult-led, and the children often had to be encouraged to respond at all.

Even at this stage, and certainly in subsequent exchanges, music proved to be particularly important in provoking response and dialogue. An early Italian production used a track by Eminem that was recognised by many of the other children: although the lyrics were in English and they did not really understand them, the music served as a powerful symbol of an international youth culture.

Another video that generated a strong response was a rap entitled 'The Place To Be', made by David, a boy of Angolan origin who was a member of the UK club. David's hero was the US rapper Tupac Shakur; and at the same time as his video appeared on the site, he posted a message asking other project members whether they thought Tupac was still alive or dead. The video generated some very positive responses from several of the other clubs; and boys in the Dutch and Swedish clubs quickly went on to make their own rap videos in response. In the case of Mohammed, an Albanian boy in the Swedish club, the rap begins with a pastiche of the American star 50 Cent, but then moves on, satirically employing the researcher's car as a 'limo' and concluding with a euphoric improvisation displaying influences from both Arabic and Albanian culture.

However, while David was pleased with the flattering responses, he was quite offended by the other clubs' attempts at being cool and enthusiastic, and refused to reply to most of them. This was compounded by the lack of response to his query about Tupac—a query that is, in a sense, more about mythical belief than reality. In effect, the other clubs had failed the test. They had latched onto the form but ignored the message of his video, which was actually about the importance of schooling—rather than more subversive intentions that seemed to have been read into it by some members of his audience. When David did reply to the Dutch rap, he was careful to retain his expert status, and to make the most of the subcultural capital he had demonstrated: he gave them faint praise (5 marks out of 10), complaining that the rap was too fast and the movements were wrong. His friend also chimed in with criticisms of the rap, and as a level of competition entered the exchange, communication effectively ceased.

There is an interesting contrast between 'The Place To Be' and another video production that provoked some communication between the clubs. 'Tragoudi' was produced by Elcin, a Turkish Kurdish boy in the Greek club, and is a rendering of a Turkish poem in Greek. The poem is by Nazim Hikmet, a poet who has been 'adopted' by the Kurdish liberation movement in Turkey (and it was probably introduced to Elcin by his parents, who are active members of that movement). Elcin plays a traditional musical instrument, the saz, and sings, while Rengin speaks the poem. The film met with a very positive response, particularly by children from Turkish and Turkish/Kurdish backgrounds. Even though the poem itself was (ironically) sung in Greek, the video created a shared platform for these children to communicate in their own language, Turkish, and take some control of the communication. Although the children could not understand the language, the direct emotional appeal of the voice and of the music was clearly very significant.

Despite the differences between these two musical forms—which might to some extent be seen as 'traditional' and 'global'—music in itself seemed to have created greater motivation for the children to communicate than the more 'politically correct', adult-oriented productions with which the exchange had begun. However, there is an interesting contrast in the responses to the two productions. The reaction to 'Tragoudi' was effectively about aesthetic recognition, at the level of cultural identity, rather than about content. Even if the content was important to Elcin and his family, it was not the focus of attention in the subsequent discussion at all. By contrast, when this kind of aesthetic response emerged in relation to David's rap, it was clearly seen (by him at least) as superficial and misleading, not least because it detracted from the content he was intending to communicate.

Beyond this, the genre that probably generated the most communication between the clubs was that of animation. Several clubs used animations, particularly claymations, to tell simple stories, often with just a minimum of verbal language. Animation seemed to offer the possibility of telling personal stories at a distance, with less danger of exposure for the children. By contrast, live action narratives were harder for the children to follow, both because they involved greater use of verbal language and also because they were seen by the children to compare unfavourably with more professional productions they were familiar with on television.

Finally, it is worth mentioning a couple of other aspects that appeared to motivate exchanges and dialogue among the participants—again, equally unsurprising ones. Like music, football was part of a global culture that provided a common ground for communication. Symptomatically, many of the children here chose to emphasise their support for the major European teams that they knew from the Champions League such as Real Madrid and Manchester United instead of the less well-known teams that they supported in their country of residence. And finally, another provoker of communication was sex. The children noticed others they were attracted to and wanted to initiate boyfriend/girlfriend contacts with. One boy in particular, from the German club, approached several girls in this way; but others also commented about the attractiveness of other club members and wanted more individual contact. Some even 'published' their mobile telephone numbers on the bulletin board in the hope of receiving more private communication from the objects of their desire.

Most of these more personal and playful elements were not related to any particular video. They were scattered among other discussion lines related specifically to video productions. It was difficult for the children, given the design of the site, to find a suitable place for them and to be able to follow them up. The children felt a little at a loss as to how their desire for more personal contacts fitted into the plan of the project and the research themes. They requested more concrete contacts, and so the clubs began to exchange hard copies of photos of club members and locations, bags of sweets, and football posters. In some clubs these gifts were a success, while in others the contact still felt too dislocated.

WHAT DIDN'T WORK, AND WHY

The instances we have just described were—although by no means unproblematic—relatively successful instances of intercultural communication. For
much of the time, our efforts to encourage this communication were much
less fruitful. There were several reasons for this, at least some of which hold
important lessons for future projects and initiatives of this kind.

Some of these were ultimately to do with access—which, as we have
noted, was not always as effective as we had initially hoped. In some cases,
using the site required the children to relocate to another building, while in
others (without broadband) it was frustratingly slow. This, combined with
the fact that the clubs were not all meeting at the same time, meant that
there was often a long gap between initiating a communication and receiving a response.

This was to some degree compounded by our own concerns about safety.
In the UK, as in some other European countries, anxieties about the use of
images of children in the media have recently taken on the proportions of
a moral panic: in one recent case, a local education authority banned the
filming of school Christmas plays on the grounds that the material might
fall into the hands of paedophiles. Despite our own reservations about such
arguments, we also needed to consider the particular position of the refugee children involved in our project, some of whom had fled war or violence
in their home countries. Partly for these reasons, we decided to monitor the
site and upload material centrally; although this inevitably led to delays in
distributing the children's productions.

As we have noted, the children involved in the clubs spoke a wide range
of languages, although not all of them were completely fluent in the language of their adopted country. The productions themselves used several
languages, and responses were also posted in Turkish and Spanish as well
as the languages of the adopted countries. However, English was the lin-
gua franca of the project, and the online dialogue was either conducted in
English or translated into English by the adults in the clubs. In addition,
of course, all the messages had to be typed in, and not all the children
possessed a sufficient degree of literacy (even in their home languages) or
indeed sufficient keyboard skills to do this easily. Here again, this meant
that communication between the clubs was highly mediated by adults:
unlike (for example) a chat room in their first language, it was clear that
the site was not 'owned' by the children themselves.

In fact, relatively few of the children involved in CHICAM had much
prior experience of the Internet; but even those who did not had quite high
expectations of what it would offer. They knew about chat rooms, and
they expected that kind of immediate synchronous communication; they
expected to be able to access and download material instantly; and they
probably expected to see full-screen, high-quality video images. These
were things we were unable to provide. Neither could we offer the level

of playful interactivity and child-oriented design that some of them might have encountered on commercial sites aimed at children.

In finding ways around these problems, it is interesting to note that both we and the children sometimes reverted to 'older' modes of communication. Our videos were sent to the webmaster by mail, put up on the site, and then (at least in some cases) downloaded so that they could be shown on a large screen. Meanwhile, as we have noted, the children exchanged telephone numbers and addresses (in the hope of finding 'pen pals'), and sent each other packets of sweets and other small gifts.

It may well have been that our own expectations in this respect were in advance of what was technically possible; but even if some of these problems had been resolved, the key issue is whether the use of the Internet in this way really engaged with the children's own motivations to communicate. Although the other clubs did represent a 'real' audience, the extent to which they were perceived as 'real'—and indeed the children's own interest in communicating with them—remained decidedly limited. Several children discussed the possibility of giving access to other friends who were not club members, but for the reasons we have explained we were reluctant to do this.

This was compounded by the fact that their membership of the club had already effectively positioned the children as refugees and/or migrants. What they appeared to have in common with the children in the other clubs—at least initially—was precisely this categorisation. Yet, as we shall see in more detail below, this was a position from which not all of the children were willing to speak.

The children were less than willing to fulfil our aspirations towards global communication: The reasons for this were complex. Their communications via the Internet—whether in the form of videos or in written language—were primarily with other people in the locality (such as their friends from school) or with friends and family in their home countries. There was no profound motivation for them to communicate with unknown others many thousands of miles away in countries they had never visited. Beyond maintaining contact with their families, their overriding concern was to make connections in the place where they were now living—both with children in their own diasporic communities but also with those from other, including majority, communities. While the prospect of making contact with children in other countries was initially interesting and had some curiosity value, it seemed remote from their everyday 'real' lives. Rather than imagining themselves as citizens of a global virtual diaspora, they wanted to be citizens in the here and now.

THE BURDEN OF REPRESENTATION

Many of the observations we have made above would obviously apply to all children, whether or not they are migrants. However, there are certain aspects that need to be taken into account when considering the specific experiences of the participants in the CHICAM project.

To some extent, the children's position as migrants offered them a wider diversity of cultural experiences and forms on which to draw. Their experience of relocation and change had given them a wide range of contrasting experiences, not least of institutions such as schools; and many of them had also been thrust into 'adult' roles and situations at a relatively early age. They were also, to a greater or lesser extent, 'global' media consumers, who were familiar with a broad range of local media cultures. This may have made them more willing to experiment and to play with media, and to use different forms and symbols.

In several of the clubs, as part of the discussions of the research themes, the children were given opportunities to draw. These drawings were often very revealing of the children's migration experiences. In the Netherlands, children did drawings of the refugee reception centres in which they had lived, and talked about the difficulties and emotional upsets of this experience. In Greece, making family trees and doing drawings related to family in preparation for the media productions were an opportunity for different formations of family to be discussed. Again, in the Greek club children initiated a session in which they drew their experiences of war. In the UK, children drew their previous schools and talked about their experiences of moving schools. In these cases, drawing also played a therapeutic role, allowing the children to speak of memories and experiences at a distance. Talking about these drawings with each other was often the starting point for the video productions.

In some of their video productions, the children set out to express their positions as migrants very forcefully; and in others they selected themes that express their everyday negotiations of inclusion and exclusion. For example, the children in Greece made an animation very early on that featured 'begging' as part of the narrative. This was at a time when there had been an intense media campaign against so-called 'economic' migrants who had been accused of street begging in many major Western European cities. A child who was living in the UK made a video about objects that she had at home that were important to her, many of which were connected in different ways with her country of origin. Others depicted, almost poetically, a sense of travel, of loss, and of wandering, as in the case of a video made by a boy in Greece which pans almost wistfully across the rooftops of Athens.

In other cases, however, the children clearly wished to avoid depicting the migrant experience—although of course this can tell its own story of exclusion or attempted inclusion. Many of the children in our study had good reason to want to preserve their own privacy, and that of their families. Some of these were perhaps typical of children of their age; but others were quite specifically to do with their status as refugees or migrants. Several of the children's families had left their country of origin under threat of violence, and their permission to remain in the host country had only been granted temporarily or was still in the process of being granted. Others had overstayed their visas, and were effectively illegal immigrants. This precarious status made them—and their families—justifiably suspicious of public visibility. As we have noted, this was a particularly important concern when it came to 'publishing' the children's productions on the Internet. On the one hand, we wanted to make the children's productions available to a wider audience; and we also wanted the children themselves to enjoy the self-esteem that this could provide. But we did not wish to do so at the cost of undermining or jeopardising their safety and their right to privacy.

More broadly, the children's position as migrants—as members of minority groups who were often stigmatised or abused by members of the host society—created a more general form of insecurity. From what position was it possible for them to speak? The constitution of our clubs—which were generally only open to those who were defined as 'migrants'—in some ways compounded this marginal position; and, of course, part of our interest as researchers was precisely in encouraging the children to offer us perspectives and representations that were specific to their position as migrants. In a sense, we could not avoid constructing the children as *representatives* of the broader category of 'migrant'—even though this was only one facet of their identities. The danger here was of 'othering'—and, in the process, of 'exoticising' or merely patronising—some essentialised 'migrant' experience.

However, the children did not necessarily want to be seen primarily as migrants, nor did they want to speak from that position—and some attempted quite strongly to disavow it. Several researchers in the team noted the children's growing impatience with endless discussions about the experience of migration, and the pressure to create more and more representations of themselves as migrants or refugees. Likewise, their interest in communicating with the children in the other clubs was not (as we had hoped) primarily to do with sharing their own past experiences of migration, but in finding similarities in the here and now. They did not want to focus on their immigration 'status' and how they might be perceived as 'other'.

Indeed, for some of the children, it was precisely the migrant identity that was 'other'. The children in the Italian club spoke pityingly of 'those poor refugees' in the other clubs, clearly dissociating themselves from such a label. A boy in the UK club suddenly decided to leave because he belatedly realised the club was 'for refugees', although he himself was a refugee and he had been told at the start about the aims and membership criteria of the club. After one of the sessions, another girl had a long discussion with her mother about what a refugee was, and why people needed to move from one country to another—although she reported this to the researcher as having nothing to do with her. It was clear that some of the children at least had internalised the generally pejorative view of migrants (and more specifically of asylum seekers) that was prevalent within the wider society. 'Speaking as a migrant' was therefore the very last thing many of them would have wanted to do. For these reasons, our aim of enabling the children to represent and express perspectives that were specific to the migrant experience was, to say the least, quite problematic.

ADAPTING THE APPROACH

With CHICAM, as with any educational project, there are things we would have done differently if we had had a second attempt. Indeed, at least some of the problems we encountered would have been resolved if we had simply had more time: if the fieldwork phase had lasted two years rather than a little more than one, the communication between the clubs would undoubtedly have developed and improved. In educational terms, we learnt a great deal from our mistakes as well as from what succeeded—and much of what we learnt is now accessible to educators in one of our reports (CHICAM, 2004). Broadly speaking, we remain committed to the idea that new media can indeed have empowering consequences for young people; but that this depends very much on the institutional, social, and pedagogic relationships in which the use of such technology is situated.

We would now be inclined to begin with simpler media, such as digital still cameras, and to allow a greater space for playful engagement with the technology. We would be less concerned, at least in the early stages, that the children should make (what we regarded as) meaningful 'statements' about their social position or about their experiences. We would also be inclined to focus more directly on the communication element from the very start of the project. We would make the project website more child-oriented, perhaps including a website design phase in which the children could experiment with their own designs and then incorporate these into the final version. Children could also have their own pages, and material could be uploaded from local sites rather than only centrally. We would also use more direct forms of communication; for example, audio messaging using voice and music, and organising real-time chat rooms (perhaps with webcams), depending on the schedule of the club meetings. Nevertheless, security remains a difficult issue here, particularly for migrant children, and compromises would have to be found.

More broadly, there is the question of the institutional context in which this kind of 'informal' media work is typically located. As we have noted, our clubs mostly took place in schools, albeit after the end of the formal school day. The children had left behind their school work and were now entering a liminal space in which they wanted the chance to enjoy themselves, and even to play. The extent to which the children continued to observe the rules for behaviour at school (for example, by attempting to please the 'teacher') or were able to establish a new and independent relationship with the staff depended very much on the specific educational approach that was adopted. However, the continued use of the school as a location and the presence of the adult educators and researchers meant that the club still remained an essentially educational context, and the children remained 'pupils' or at least 'students'. And, to say the least, democratic engagement on the part of students is not a noted characteristic of most formal educational settings.

For many reasons, it would be unrealistic to simply do away with all forms of adult mediation. The children needed access to adult expertise, not just to enable them to use the technology, but also to help them to make meaningful statements, to communicate, and to organise their own work. Even so, in a different context, it might have been worthwhile to involve others (both adults and children) from outside the clubs, rather than having such a clear differentiation between 'teachers' and 'students' (however 'informal' our relationships may have been). Wider local participation in the clubs could also have addressed some of the children's concerns about being labelled, as well as their need to build local relationships. This would have been difficult within the terms of this project; and it might also be problematic given the priorities of likely funding sources for such work. However, incorporating different forms of local participation might also have added useful dimensions to the inter-club communications and offered a more differentiated view of the processes of integration and cross-cultural communication.

THE LIMITS OF EMPOWERMENT

Beyond these more specific points, there are several broader issues that can be drawn out from this brief account of the project. These are not so much recommendations as unresolved dilemmas; and they are partly methodological and partly political. On one level, CHICAM could probably best be described as an educational 'action-research' project. Rather than research what was already happening, we had to make things happen in order to be able to research them. While this enabled us to explore issues that might otherwise have remained hypothetical, it also inevitably gave rise to tensions and contradictions that are widely recognised in the literature on action research (Hammersley, 1999).

In this instance, we were using media production both as a research tool and as a focus of research in its own right. Getting kids to make their own media would, we hoped, provide us with insights into aspects of their lives—our first three research themes—that might have proven more difficult to explore through more conventional methods such as interviews or observations. At the same time, we were interested—as educational researchers—in how they learned to use these media, in the forms their productions took, and how they used media in order to communicate.

These two motivations were not necessarily incompatible, but they occasionally resulted in a tension over different media genres (or models) and ways of working. In seeking to enable the children to represent aspects of their lives, we were implicitly drawn to favour particular media genres, such as documentary, reportage, or 'realist' drama. At least initially, we wanted the children to make more or less explicit 'statements' about their lives—not least because these could more easily conveyed to a (possibly impatient) public audience than material that was less direct, more difficult to interpret, or more inclined towards fantasy and play. Perhaps more fundamentally, the research inevitably positioned the children in particular ways. Although it was participatory in intent (in the sense that the participants would be representing themselves, rather than being represented by us), we nevertheless implicitly positioned the children as objects of our research—as 'children' and as 'migrants'—and expected them to speak in this capacity.

This tension was to some extent exacerbated by the context of our funding. The project was funded by the European Commission, and needed to be seen to respond to current imperatives in European policy. Like any research proposal, ours sought to press several important buttons. The rhetoric around the empowering potential of new media was certainly one, as was the contemporary debate about migration; but we also discussed the need for children—and for migrant/refugee children in particular—to be more involved in policy-making. Giving such children a voice in the debate would, we argued, help to counteract the tendency for them to be ignored or silenced, or treated as mere objects of well-meaning adult concern. And 'policy-makers', whoever they might be, would be somehow compelled to listen to them.

This is not to imply that we were naïve in any of these aspirations, or indeed that we were cynically jumping on the bandwagon. Our original proposal is appropriately cautious and critical about such claims. However, the imperative to 'make children's voices heard'—which is part of the rhetoric of a great deal of participatory research in Childhood Studies (Christensen and James, 1999)—was not unproblematic. In this case, it led to a tension between 'process' and 'product' which continues to haunt us as we prepare the final reports of the project and the video material that accompanies them.

Thus, as we have noted, the media educators often perceived there to be a pressure to create more or less finished 'productions', that could be put up on the project website, albeit initially only for the children in the other clubs to view and (if they wished) to comment upon. It was frequently agreed that a 'production' did not, in fact, have to be a fully polished final product, and that it would be useful for the children to have feedback on 'draft' material as they developed or re-edited their work. Yet even as the partners got to know each other, there was still a reluctance to 'publish' material that was seen to be unfinished.

While this may partly have been to do with the professional self-confidence of the media educators, it was also to do with the children's perceptions of the process of sharing productions. For example, in the UK club, Saieed stated that the piece he was editing was not finished because it was 'too short'. When the UK club was viewing their 'hello' production aimed at introducing themselves to the other clubs, one child stated that it couldn't be sent because it didn't give enough 'information'. From another angle, Peter in the UK club became very frustrated when his 'spy movie' didn't look slick enough and didn't match the speed of the films he watches on TV or the games he plays on the computer. As this implies, the children themselves did not necessarily want all their work to be available to a wider (and partly unknown) audience—although neither did they express much interest in 'redrafting' it in the light of others' feedback.

This tension between process and product is a very familiar issue in media education, not least when it comes to the process of evaluating students' production work (see Buckingham, Grahame, and Sefton-Green, 1995). In the context of educational research, it can also pose particular dilemmas: activities that 'fail' educationally—in the sense that students do not learn anything from them, or where students fail to achieve what they set out to achieve—may in fact prove to be more interesting for the purpose of gathering research data than those that 'succeed'. And in this context, this tension took on an additional dimension, partly because of the presence of a 'real' audience but also because of the wider political ambitions of the project.

Thus, when it comes to packaging the material for our imagined audience of policy-makers—a process that continues at the time of writing—the compromises are very apparent, and probably inevitable. The twelve-minute video 'advertisement' for the project that serves as one of the main public outputs necessarily speaks on behalf of the children: it is very difficult to avoid silencing the children whose voices we have claimed to be putting out into the public sphere. We hope that some of the policy-makers who see the video will also see some of the 'uncooked' productions made by the children themselves, which are now available on our public website; but we recognise that this is probably optimistic—and we also fear that what they see will not necessarily be self-evidently meaningful. Clearly, there is a broader issue here about how we conceive of the policy-making process, and the relations between research and policy. As academics, we are frequently told (not least by funding bodies) that policy-makers need 'bullet points' and 'sound bites'; although it is debatable whether apparently authoritative one-sentence 'research findings' are in fact any more influential in this respect than illuminating anecdotes or immediate personal testimony.

On one level, these dilemmas reflect the broader power-relations of the research process. Our research purported to be participatory—in the sense that it gave the participants a degree of control over their own self-representation. Nevertheless, 'we' were still researching 'them'; and our participatory methods were to some extent merely a more inventive means of extracting our data from the objects of our research. At this final stage, now the fieldwork is complete, we retain control, not just of the dissemination and packaging of the data, but also of defining the frameworks through which we would prefer it to be read and interpreted.

These issues were compounded by the broader political ambitions of the project—and it is in this respect that the research raises some more far-reaching questions about young people's political engagement. In positioning our participants as representatives of the categories 'child' and 'migrant', and in expecting them to speak as such to a wider public audience (albeit a partly imagined audience) of 'policy-makers', we inevitably constructed them as subjects in particular ways. We imagined them (in Habermasian terms, perhaps) as rational citizens, capable of making statements and offering testimony to their experiences, of speaking on behalf of the group they represent, of competently engaging in some form of transparent public communication. There is a very demanding and broad-ranging ethical imperative here, which is implicit in many arguments about children's rights, about children and citizenship, and (not least) about young people's political participation (see Archard, 1993; Buckingham, 2000, chapters 9 and 10). And it is this imperative that we hope readers of this book might wish to question and debate.

NOTE

1. Seven main partners were involved in the project: the co-ordinators, The Centre for the Study of Children, Youth and Media (CSCYM), Institute of Education, London, UK; WAC Performing Arts and Media College, London, UK; Fondazione Centro Studi Investimenti Sociali (CENSIS), Rome, Italy; Centre for Research in International Migration and Ethnic relations (CEIFO), Stockholm University, Sweden; Department of Media Education and Media Centre, University of Ludwigsburg, Germany; FORUM Institute of Multicultural Development and the University of Utrecht, Utrecht, The Netherlands; and The Greek Council for Refugees (GCR), Athens, Greece. The composition of the team reflects the project's cross-disciplinary approach, drawing on the areas of migration and refugee studies, media and cultural studies, sociology and policy studies. On the media production side we also involved media educators and media artists with experience of working with children, as well as people with an interest in and knowledge of Internet communication and the arts. We would particularly like to thank Horst Niesyto and Peter Holzwarth of the University of Ludwigsburg for their contribution to the analysis presented in this paper; and, of course, the European Commission for their funding of the project.

REFERENCES

Archard, D. (1993) *Children: Rights and Childhood* London: Routledge.

de Block , L. (2002) *Television as a Shared Space in the Intercultural Lives of Primary Aged Children* PhD Thesis, Institute of Education, University of London.

Bloustein, G. (1998) '"It's different to a mirror 'cos it talks to you": Teenage girls, video cameras and identity', in Howard, S. (ed.) *Wired-Up: Young People and the Electronic Media* London: UCL Press.

Brah, A. (1996) *Cartographies of Diaspora: Contesting Identities* London: Routledge.

Buckingham, D. (2000) *After the Death of Childhood: Growing Up in the Age of Electronic Media* Cambridge: Polity.

Buckingham, D. (2001) (ed.) *Journal of Educational Media,* 26 (3): Special Issue on Video Culture.

Buckingham, D., Grahame, J., and Sefton-Green, J. (1995) *Making Media: Practical Production in Media Education* London: English and Media Centre.

Buckingham, D. and Harvey, I. (2001) 'Imagining the audience: Language, creativity and communication in youth media production', *Journal of Educational Media* 26(3): 173–184.

CHICAM (2002) *Global Kids, Global Media: A Review of Research Relating to Children, Media and Migration in Europe* Report to the European Commission, http://www.chicam.net

CHICAM (2004) *Picture Me In: Digital Media Making With Socially Excluded Children* Report to the European Commission, http://www.chicam.net

Christensen, P. and James, A. (eds.) (1999) *Research with Children: Perspectives and Practices* London: Routledge Falmer.

Gauntlett, D. (1996) *Video Critical; Children, the Environment and Media Power* Luton: John Libbey.

Goldman-Segal, R. (1998) *Points of Viewing Children's Thinking: A Digital Ethnographer's Journey* Mahwah, NJ: Lawrence Erlbaum.

Hammersley, M. (1999) *Taking Sides in Social Research: Essays on Partisanship and Bias in Social Enquiry* London: Routledge Falmer.

Harvey, I., Skinner, M., and Parker, D. (2002) *Being Seen, Being Heard: Young People and Moving Image Production* London: British Film Institute.

Montgomery, K., Gottlieb-Robles, B., and Larson, G.O. (2004) *Youth as E-Citizens: Engaging the Digital Generation*. Washington, D.C.: Center for Social Media, American University, http://www.centerforsocialmedia.org/ecitizens/youthreport.pdf

Niesyto, H. (ed.) (2003) *Videoculture: Video und Interculturelle Kommunikation* Munich: Co-Paed.

Orner, M. (1992) 'Interrupting the calls for student voice in liberatory education: A feminist poststructuralist perspective', in Luke, C. and Gore, J. (eds.) *Feminisms and Critical Pedagogy* New York: Routledge.

Tapscott, D. (1998) *Growing Up Digital: The Rise of the Net Generation* New York: McGraw-Hill.

Williams, R. (1974) *Television, Technology and Cultural Form* Glasgow: Fontana.

Part III

Media, engagement, and daily practices

9 Democratic familyship and the negotiated practices of ICT users

Maren Hartmann, Nico Carpentier, and Bart Cammaerts

This chapter will focus on processes of democratic learning within changing and ever more complex family contexts. It is thereby assumed that democracy cannot be reduced to a formal legalistic system of ordering society, but that it also has a strong cultural component and is learned through discourses, everyday practices and performances. The family as a micro-system or social sphere is one of the places where learning about democracy and democratic practices can or—from a normative perspective—should take place. A distinction is therefore made between the family as a social system that can take very different forms—from very authoritarian to radically democratic—and the inherently normative concept of *democratic familyship*. The latter can be understood as an ideal-typical concept to describe situations where conflicts are negotiated and resolved through dialogue embedded in semi-egalitarian power relations between all actors within the family. Within the notion of democratic familyship, learning about democracy, dialogue and negotiation keeps the dialectics of control, as well as the power relations that drive them, in balance.

To illustrate these processes, we present the case of ICT user practices by (North Belgian) young adults. The focus is here on how these young adults deal with the conflicts that arise from those ICT usage practices and how they negotiate satisfactory outcomes. The emphasis is on the actual *practices* as the learning sites for democratic principles. As such, the *domestication* approach will be instrumental in providing a dynamic framework to contextualise these practices. The domestication approach is crucial to understanding media usage practices as it, amongst others, specifically deals with household power-relations that refer to media technologies. For the purpose of this chapter data that had originally been gathered for the EMTEL2 project dealing with ICT user practices of North Belgian youngsters (Hartmann 2003, 2004) was re-analysed. Our analysis aims to illustrate the (potentially) democratic workings of these Belgian families in the very specific situation of being confronted with ICTs. By looking at the way the family members deal with the conflicts related to the acquisition of, expertise of and use of ICTs, partially negotiated usages of ICTs are shown to be present.

THE FAMILY AS A SITE FOR DEMOCRATIC LEARNING

As most ideologically (over)loaded concepts, democracy carries the burden of manifold definitions and meanings, and is frequently the subject of a *politics of definition* (Fierlbeck 1998: 177). Despite this diversity, democracy nevertheless remains a major form of societal organisation that attempts to resolve basic social conflicts caused by the scarcity of resources and their unequal distribution. The ever-uneasy balance between the collective and the individual and between the universal and the particular is kept in check by a specific formalised system of power delegation (or representation), whilst maintaining a degree of popular participation and being supported by the presence of a democratic culture. Following Mouffe (1992), democracy is seen here as a project that can never be totally achieved, because new social conflicts and antagonisms will each time prevent its complete closure, rendering democracy a process and not a state. Moreover, the necessary presence of a democratic culture will require the support of processes of socialisation or enculturalisation, in order to construct citizens' democratic identities. In other words, from this culturalistic perspective, citizenship is seen as a dimension of the individual's subjectivity, and needs to be learned, developed, and protected.

Democracy: A learning experience?

Democratic learning can be highly formalised and oriented towards the introduction of citizens-to-be in the polis. Kelly (1995: 101), for instance, argues that one of the major tasks of the educational system 'is the proper preparation of young citizens for the roles and responsibilities they must be ready to take on when they reach maturity'. Gutmann (1987: 287) even calls this the prime task of the educational system: '"political education"—the cultivation of the virtues, knowledge and skills necessary for political participation—has moral primacy over other purposes of public education in a democratic society'.

Yet democratic learning goes well beyond the traditional educational system. Political participation as such can also be seen as an important part of this learning process. The pre-condition is of course that participation is sufficiently enabled within the political system, and thus that the inequalities embedded in the power relations are not too demotivating. One of the early authors who focussed on the educational role of participation in the political system is Jean-Jacques Rousseau. According to Pateman's (1970: 25) interpretation of Rousseau, the participation of 'the people' will have educational, legitimising, and integrative effects. The participatory process allows individuals to become responsible citizens that are sensitive to the general interest. As Verba and Nie (1987: 5) put it: 'Through participation, one learns responsibility'. In a more contemporary formulation, citizenship is thus seen as constructed through a wide series of discourses, practices, performances, and rituals.

This line of reasoning also brings the work of de Certeau (1988) into the picture, as he explicitly emphasises the importance of everyday practices (in contrast to textual representations or discourses). He stresses the importance of seeing everyday practices as non-discursive and unconscious forms of (illusionary) compliance and resistance—or in his words, strategies and tactics. Applied to the present discussion, this means that citizenship is also practised (or not) at the level of the pre-linguistic or pre-symbolic. This position resonates with the idea that democracy exists not just in thought, but also in practices and performances. Disregarding or underestimating the importance of civic practices would rather impoverish any type of analysis aimed at the educational aspects of civic behaviour. At the same time the Spivakian problem of the subaltern (1985) arises: being able to be heard in a context of hegemonic discourses often creates a very difficult threshold to overcome. In other words, discursive frameworks that can translate these civic practices into discourses of citizenship remain an important requirement: such discourses are able to structure and (re)direct these practices as tools for further learning.

The above discussion readily illustrates that democratic learning is not limited to the sphere that Thomas (1994) calls macro-participation. This expansion presupposes a definition of the political in the broad sense, not being restricted to a specific sphere or system, but as a dimension that is 'inherent to every human society and that determines our very ontological condition' (Mouffe 1997: 3). According to Thomas, the school, family, workplace, church, and community remain equally valid spheres for potential democratic learning through (micro-) participation. Although not completely overlapping, Thomas's conceptualisation of micro-participation clearly includes civil society. From his perspective civil society and other localised spheres such as the family can form vital democratic learning sites—or 'educational devices' as Pateman (1970: 35) calls them—for individuals to be acculturated into citizenship.

The pre-condition is of course the presence of democratic practices within civil society and other micro-systems. More specifically this implies the presence of dialogical forms of communication, negotiated conflict resolution, and (semi-)egalitarian power relations that keep the dialectics of control—as Giddens (1979) phrased it[1]—in check. In this context it is vital to stress that these micro-systems are not by definition democratic, participatory and just, but can sometimes be authoritarian, elitist and unjust. As Tonkiss (1998: 256) remarks: 'The limits of the state [...] do not in any case represent the limits of power. Within civil society networks of [...] 'experts' trace diverse patterns of regulation and control'. Fierlbeck (1998: 149) makes this point even more clearly by referring to 'less virtuous' civil society organisations: 'the mafia, it has frequently been observed, meets the prerequisites of numerous definitions of civil society quite well'. For this reason the process-related notion of democratisation is of vital importance because it underscores the need to achieve more just relations and more equal power balances within civil society and other micro-systems, in order to achieve a democratic learning experience.

However, the importance of civic participation in these micro-spheres should not be restricted to their potential educational roles. Democratising these spheres serves a purpose on its own; namely, to gain control over one's life in localised and everyday structures is seen as an important realisation. Focussing on the workplace, Pateman writes:

> Apart from its importance as an educative device, participation in the workplace—a political system—can be regarded as political participation in its own right. Thus industry and other spheres provide alternative areas where the individual can participate in decision making in matters of which he [or she] has first hand, everyday experience. (Pateman 1970: 35)

THE FAMILY AND DEMOCRATIC LEARNING

When we now turn to one of these 'other' spheres, namely the family, a similar line of argument can be made, especially since the family is today often seen as an integral part of civil society, in contrast to the older Hegelian and Marxist approaches to civil society. Cohen and Arrato (1992: ix), for instance, explicitly include the family as part of civil society:

> [...] it is precisely because the family is a core institution in and of civil society [...] that egalitarian principles can be applied to it to a far greater extent than to a firm or a bureaucracy. (Cohen and Arrato 1992: 724)

Not surprisingly, feminist theory in particular has focussed on the importance of the family as a democratic institution—or more specifically, its lack of democracy. The unequal domestic power balance, which had (and still has) an important impact on the family's division of labour in a household (Gerson 1985; Okin 1989), and which has led in some cases to domestic (sexual) violence, prompted second-wave feminism to identify the family as a site of oppression. Their demand was for a more democratic family and for the democratisation of everyday life, based on the assertion that the power imbalances in the private sphere needed to be politicised. Millett (1970) for instance coined the term 'sexual politics', thus expanding the notion of the political into the sphere of the private. In her chapter on the theory of sexual politics, she introduces the sociological approach with the simple sentence: 'Patriarchy's chief institution is the family' (Millett 1970: 33); in her view, the family, via child-rearing and by example socialise the young to reproduce sexist relations.

Yet authors conceptualise the family as a potentially democratic institution. Giddens expresses a warm plea for the 'radical democratisation of the personal' (Giddens 1992: 182). Although being knowledgeable about the difference 'between ideals and reality' (188), he argues that a symmetry exists between 'the democratising of personal life and democratic possibilities in the global political order at the most extensive level' (195–196). Again, participatory principles remain both the pre-condition for and result of democratic learning.[2] Interestingly, he does not exclude children from the democratic family. When he raises the question whether the relationship between a parent and a young child can be democratic, Giddens refers to James and Prout (1990) and kindly provides the following answer:

> It can, and should be, in exactly the same sense as is true of a democratic political order. It is a right of the child, in other words, to be treated as a putative equal of the adult. Actions which cannot be negotiated directly with a child, because he or she is too young to grasp what is entailed, should be capable of counterfactual justification. (Giddens 1992: 191–192)

These trajectories have provoked criticisms and resistance, also within feminist theory. For instance, Fraser (1989: 76) has protested against the expansion of the political: 'when everything is political, the sense and specificity of the political recedes'. Phillips (1991: 85) has stated clearly that there are limits to the democratisation of daily life. Although we do not share these critiques, Phillips's point that the signifier citizenship should be reserved for theorising the specific relationship between individual and nation-state, is well taken, and so we prefer to introduce the notion of *democratic familyship*.

Paraphrasing Held (1991),[3] this notion connects the political and social with the individual aspects of family life, as it highlights the democratic elements of this specific societal setting. As a micro-system the family can be governed by a diversity of regulatory systems (a diversity which is similar to the diversity of possibilities for regulating the polis). Governance within the family can be built upon unevenly distributed (often patriarchal) power relations, instrumental communication, and the suppression of conflict. In contrast, democratic families are governed by dialogical forms of communication, negotiated conflict resolution, and (semi-)egalitarian power relations. Democratic familyship then refers to the practices, attitudes, and ideologies that position individual family members within the family as a democratic system. In parallel to the different defining components of citizenship,[4] the importance of the protection of the rights[5] of the family members, their participation in the (often implicit) family decision-making structures, their welfare, and even the respect within the family for internal cultural differences, can be stressed. It should be added that the notion of the family should not be restricted to the nuclear family, because single parent families, gay and lesbian families, co-parenting, blended families, and other family types cannot be excluded (Silva and Smart 1999).

THE FAMILY AND THE POWER STRUGGLE FOR TECHNOLOGY

The ideal-typical notion of democratic familyship can of course not remain completely detached from localised and situated practices. In this section we explicitly focus on the introduction of ICTs in the family context, using the concept of democratic familyship as an analytical sensitising concept and a normative criterion for the evaluation of the actual family practices. In order to situate the power struggle of usages of technology within the family and the potential of democratic familyship, we will first turn to a theory of appropriation of technologies in a wider sense, and the reframing of the domestication approach. Second, we will look at a research project on ICT use to provide us with a number of examples of conflicts and power struggles within a family context and how these conflicts are (sometimes) resolved through negotiation.

Domestication of ICTs

Families are confronted with technologies, especially media technologies, every day. These technologies are only one of many issues they face, but they often do play an important role in families' lives and are central to the question of democratic familyship. How families deal with the introduction and use of technologies, and whether democratic preconditions are met, are crucial questions in the analysis of media use in everyday life. One approach that has focussed on the family and their struggles with technologies has been the domestication approach (for important formulations in the UK context, see, e.g., Morley and Silverstone 1990; Silverstone and Hirsch 1992; Silverstone and Haddon 1996).[6] The newness of the approach at the time of its first formulation (mid- to late 1980s) was the concentration on media *usage practices* and *context* rather than media *texts* (e.g., Morley 1995). The work of these authors was clearly influenced by an article by Hermann Bausinger, who had earlier formulated six general points concerning media use research. Amongst those were: 'The media are an integral part of the way the everyday is conducted' and 'It is not a question of an isolated, individual process, but of a collective process' (Bausinger 1984: 349–350).

The domestication approach emphasises that media are both symbolic and material objects and should be analysed as such. They are objects of consumption both in a wider and in a narrow sense of the word. The domestication approach provides a detailed analysis of power relationships within different household structures (mostly families) as they are expressed in relation to media technologies. They also hint at the interrelationship of these internal power relationships with the wider set of external relationships beyond the immediate family sphere and underline how families are embedded in these other structures, partly via their use of information and communication technologies.

Silverstone and Haddon (1996) concentrated on the general processes of media adoption into households. A model was developed showing a number of 'stages' that media go through.[7] The different parts describe the move from the creation of the media object by industry and marketing experts to its appropriation into diverse household routines.[8] Another aspect of the concept is the idea of a 'moral economy of the household', in which the adoption process is framed in terms of the values and attitudes that are affected by the introduction of new media technologies into the households. The technologies clearly help to negotiate the relationship between public and private spheres and are thus crucial for every household. All of these briefly mentioned processes are discourses and practices that have consequences for the learning of democracy within the family.

The early domestication research used ethnographic research methodologies (e.g., Silverstone 1990). In their research practice, this primarily meant qualitative interviews, coupled with such material as drawings of the homes and time-use diaries. The ethnographic approach has been a crucial factor in the analyses, but also eventually underlined the limitations of the questions that could be answered through such research. These questions become more pertinent in the context of new media technologies—and have not yet been entirely answered. When the times, places, and contexts of media use shift to more diversity and complexity, many of these research methods—and also some other assumptions made in the approach—cannot adequately map the emerging usage patterns.[9] Thus it is not surprising that the concentration within much of the older research has been on television—despite all claims to be researching media use in context.

One reason for this was the dominant role of the television set(s) in many households at the time. Morley, for example, managed to uncover the 'politics of the sitting room' (Cubitt in Morley 1995: 178) in which many forms of communication and especially negotiation about family and other matters take place via the interactions with and about the television set.[10] Yet dealing with other media can be more problematic. While television is often used as a medium that 'is simply on' without necessarily being watched, the computer affords a different engagement and therefore requires additional forms of research and interpretation (e.g., Bakardjieva and Smith 2000).[11] This becomes even clearer when we consider the role of the mobile phone and other interpersonal media, which do not at all provide the same emphasis on 'media consumption'. Another problematic issue, relevant to this chapter, is the concentration on family units living within one home.[12]

Families today are increasingly fragmented, in terms of both their living spaces and their relationships. Thus some aspects of the original domestication concept are not easily transferable to new media environments. The negotiations, however, remain crucial aspects of the relationships between families and ICTs and part of the democratic learning process.

NORTH-BELGIAN YOUNGSTERS NEGOTIATE ICT USE

The emphasis in the original research project was not actually on families, but on young adults. The youngsters were interviewed about their use and especially their understanding of the role of information and communication technologies in their lives. The interviewees were between 18 and 25 years of age, were mostly living in the Northern (Flemish) part of Belgium, and were interviewed by their 'peers' (i.e., by people of their own age).[13] These interviews were later analysed in terms of the characteristics of media uses by these youngsters and these characteristics were set in relation to discourses about the possible emergence of a 'web generation' (Hartmann 2003, 2004).

Re-analysing the data, it soon became clear that family contexts had been important in laying the foundations for later ICT uses and were crucial factors in the negotiation of uses of, as well as attitudes towards, ICTs. On a more general level, the overall impression concerning parent–child relationships in many of the interviews was rather positive. Many interviewees describe their parents as important people in their lives, very useful for support and guidance (not forgetting financial support). Overall, the generational distance is not perceived as highly important. Most visibly this distance occurred in the negotiations concerning ICT expertise, as will be discussed below. A cultural specificity of Belgium is the 'closeness' of families in terms of the frequency of contact (within this age group, but not only within this age group). Children often live with their parents until well into their mid-twenties. Others, mostly students, live in the place where they are studying during the week and at their parents' home on weekends and during holidays. The parents' house remains 'home'. The geographical proximity within Belgium easily allows for this kind of closeness.

During the interviews the youngsters did explicitly talk about the (dis)integrative role of ICTs, but much less about its connection to democracy in society and in the family. Moreover, Livingstone and Bober (2004: 7) point to the problems of discussing issues related to domestic regulation, 'for they concern the private, often unnoticed, sometimes secret or illicit practices of everyday life'. In our analysis, we start with those parts of the interviews that explicitly deal with the perceived role of ICTs in society. This is the question of *what* is taught at home (and elsewhere) about this relationship between ICTs and democracy. We then address a number of (power) conflicts in the family, where contested elements of democratic practices come to the surface. This part concentrates on *how* democratic familyship is put into practice and *how* it is taught.

DEMOCRACY?

Many families and youngsters suggest that participation in new media technology use can be seen as a learning process for participation in society overall:

> ...the citizens have to be computer-literate. It is obvious that society is changing. I also think this changes democracy, as many have said, Internet is a mass medium...and you can say whatever you need to say on the Internet.... But I think there will be long-term consequences and that it will become more democratic, because more people have the right to speak. (A2, female, 20, student)

The same attitude leads many parents to acquire the technologies for their children; without the skills or opportunity for access, chances (for a successful career) are seen to decrease. This is reflected in the frequent reference to 'must go with the flow' ideas in the interviews: 'And yes, well, in a certain sense you have to go along with it. Because society also develops and if you don't develop with it, then you will fall behind anyway' (WD5, female, 20, administrative work). This is a major driving force behind families' adoption of ICTs in the first place and thus important. The underlying belief in the logic of progress could be interpreted as problematic, but is not predominantly seen in this light, neither by the families nor by the young adults. Instead, the dominant tone amongst the interviewees claims that social (as well as economic) participation will only be possible if one learns to use the technologies. This is often framed not as an opportunity, but as a necessary requirement:

> Yes, I say it, I've always said it. Technology is progress and you have to go with our progress. And not go back, because we will not go back anymore, only idiots pretend that we live in the times of the apes. No, we have the technologies. Use them. (WM1, male, 21, tram driver)

One could see an underlying assumption that the relationship between ICTs and democracy is straightforward and unproblematic. Amongst the students, the danger of an increasing gap between the information-haves and the information have-nots was regularly expressed:

> How should people get information otherwise? If it continues like this, then the citizen really has to become an active citizen. People have to search for information themselves rather than that information comes to them.... (F1, female, 22, student)

UNIVERSITY OF WINCHESTER LIBRARY

Democratic practices within families seem fairly widespread, with an emphasis on general negotiations about resources, as well as about content, because content and different practices are differently valued and prioritised:

> Five [people used the computer], so quite a few...we had to agree 'now I'm on for an hour, then you're on for an hour'. That was necessary. And whenever my sisters had to use it for school, our games obviously had to stop. (V1, female, 18, student at school)

Games and playful uses are not valued in the same way as are educational or work uses. This is reflected in many of the interviews. This distinction, often stated by parents and youngsters alike, is mostly expressed in the allocation of resources and implicitly appears in the way computer applications are described.[14]

Besides this, as indicated above, dealing with the conflicts surrounding ICTs that were hinted at in the last quote and negotiating an outcome that satisfies most actors involved, is inherently part of democracy and of democratic familyship. Especially these moments when frictions within the family take place are relevant to us, as they are the rare occasions when the mechanisms for negotiation and resolution come to the forefront. These moments allow us to see how democracy is performed and thus sustained (or not) in very concrete family settings. It also allows us to see how the ideal-typical notion of democratic familyship is enacted by family members and at the same time how it is transformed by the specificity of their actions.

Conflict and negotiation: expertise and dialogue

Within the interviews relating to the use of ICTs by Belgian youngsters, as well as their views regarding ICTs, a number of conflicts within the context of the family were expressed. One of the more documented sets of conflicts (see Livingstone and Bober 2004), which related to (avoiding) exposure to unwanted content or contacts, is not present in this case study. This can be explained by the more mature age of the respondents. Beyond the conflicts about the acquisition and especially general use of ICTs, are those concerning the necessary expertise for using these particular media technologies.

More often than not, a change of power relations becomes visible because of shifts in expertise. Rather than parents teaching children, these (older) children begin to teach their parents. While not necessarily seeing themselves as the 'web generation' type of users of technologies (fluid, easy-going, without fear—see Hartmann 2004), many of the young people hint at the fact that they are more knowledgeable than their parents when it comes to new media:

Q.: Your parents.... How do they use technologies? Are they open-minded?

A.: They're open-minded, but they don't really participate in it.... My mother is quite interested in it all, but not my dad, and I think it is for that reason that they don't buy many new technologies. I think. Thus I assume, if I was still living at home, then I would bring new technologies into the house and then my mother would be very interested and ask questions about them, and in the long run she would sit and use the Internet. But since I'm not there now, they will never get it. (WP5, female, 24, unemployed)

Many parents not only feel that they are lagging behind in terms of user capabilities in relation to their children, but also sense that the power relationship is undermined through their lack of expertise:

Well, I see it now with me personally when my parents come to ask 'can you help me with this?' Then I always say...well, I say yes, but actually I think, 'Oh no, not again'. It is so easy for us and so difficult for them, and sometimes this is impossible to understand and can therefore lead to conflicts. (F1, female, 22, student)

Q.: Who taught her [the mother] to work with the computer and the Internet?

A.: I think it was mostly a friend of hers and me when I'm home, my brother when he's home. We tell her how to do things.... But we're not very patient all the time [laughs]. (WP6, female, 22, intern at the European Commission)

While this difference in expertise does not of course apply to all families, it often plays a major role in the way the relationship between parents, (grown-up) children, and ICTs develop. The power relations are not egalitarian in this respect, but become reversed. There is rarely an acknowledgement of a 'give and take' philosophy; that is, that expertise in other areas could be substituted for lack of expertise in this area. This shift in expertise is part of a general shift that takes place because of the child's transition from childhood to adulthood, but seems to be enhanced by the new technologies and their role in negotiations about expertise.

Use, time and space

The first conflict that emerges in most families relates to the initial acquisition of ICTs. In regard to conflict over use-time, this is often negotiated between siblings.

...but there are lots of conflicts amongst us kids, me with my brother and my sister, because we always all want to go online at the same time to e-mail and chat and so forth. (S2, female, 21, student)

Yes, here at home, I have to share technologies. Sometimes that's a problem, because our computer is being used quite a lot and we only have one. That's why there's often a bit of conflict about using it, you have to share it. In the 'kot',[15] I have a laptop and sometimes my friend uses that one, too. (D13, female, 21, student)

This kind of conflict is usually presented as solvable. The general recognition that the computer is an important resource, which needs to be shared, is an important aspect of the solution. Another important aspect is the acceptance of certain content-related values that also have to be shared: the distinction between education and entertainment needs to be accepted in order to manage the conflicts:

The computer downstairs is the best one, there is sometimes a conflict about who is allowed to use it, with my sister and my brother.... If you have something to do on the computer, school comes first.... And then you have to agree who goes first and how long. Then it usually works out. In the beginning it was a problem, because the computer was then still new. And also the Internet.... (D2, female, 20, student)[16]

The distinction between education, work, and entertainment ignores the potential that playing offers for the general acquisition of skills and competence:

At home, we had computers ever since we were small. Simple things, such as games, they're not difficult, you just learn it. I have three older sisters and I learned it from them. People in my family are busy with computers, they teach you things....When you're small, it's all great and 'cool', now I use it only for school. (V1, female, 18, student at school)

The distinction between education and entertainment can thus be useful when it comes to sharing resources. Overall, ICT use within families is usually not based on the children's individual needs and desires. Instead, patterns of use are prescribed. As in many other cases, a lack of resources is the reason for conflicts.[17] Therefore an important shift in ICT use can occur when the level of independence changes:

I now use it [the Internet] more than before, because now I have the possibility to buy things for myself, as, for example, having the Internet. I paid for it myself and therefore I use it more. (WD5, female, 20, administrative worker)

In this regard it also has to be noted that some of the respondents have started to lead their lives spatially or financially independent of their parents. This limits or liberates them from the control that parents, or indeed brothers and sisters, can exercise with regard to their (new) media usage.

Acquisition, expertise, and negotiation

However, parents do not just regulate their children's behaviour; they also enable their children's ICT use. Parents often play a crucial role with regard to the introduction of new media technologies into their children's lives. The interviewees did not necessarily grow up with widespread computer use in their early school years.[18] Computer use is therefore often more problematic than mobile phone use, since mobile phones were definitely common in the early years of these young people. Not all parents can afford to buy computers, or even see the need to buy them, and they certainly are not always in a position to buy individual computers for each child. Access, as has been shown above, has to be negotiated and can be a reason for conflict. Mobile phones, however, are personalised communication technologies.[19] They also have a conflict potential, but this is primarily due to costs (rather than access as such or content or knowledge), especially when parents pay the bills (often the case for students in our study). In terms of the acquisition, parents and other family members are clearly portrayed as important.[20]

A.:   Since I study, I think, I have a mobile phone. My mother bought it for me, and for my sister, via the Coca-Cola-quiz, which was really cheap. Since then I got a new one for Christmas. (D1, male, 21, student)

Q.:   How did you get this? [In reference to the Internet]
A.:   Well, actually through my brother. He studied at the time and sort of needed it, therefore we got it. (WD10, female, 21, hairdresser)

The role of these support networks obviously extends beyond the material realm. Siblings and friends play an especially important role in providing the necessary *expertise* rather than only the technologies as such:

I also have an 11-year-old sister, who I try to introduce to the Internet...I made an e-mail address for her so she can mail with her friend. She is getting quite independent in it lately.... Oh, I think that they [the friends] play an important role in this, because in the end you see them with it, you get to know the technologies through them. Apart from my mobile phone—that came entirely through my parents. My father had one for a long time, but I didn't think much about them at the time. As for the rest there are also my friends who teach me how to use them. (D10, male, 22, student)

Overall, it becomes clear that family and friends are often role models in terms of the way they acquire and use the technologies:

I wouldn't mind having a computer again now that mine lags behind the newest models by one or two years—or maybe five—at least if I didn't need new software for some time. This is just like my dad and others in my family—all of them clever people [laughs], who think before they go along with the hype and a fashion that does not serve them at all. [You have to ask:] What do you really need to do with a computer? (WV3, male, 25, cyber-café owner)

My mother, on the other hand, she is, well, one can actually probably say that she is addicted to computers, yes, so actually we all three have a computer: I have my own, my mother has her own computer and my father has his laptop, which my mother or I use whenever we need it. (W1, male, 24, student)

However, as the quote below suggests, negative role models get inherited as well:

Yes, a computer, that was always my opinion, a computer is for clever people, I believe. At home there is no one who understands much about them, only my dad a bit. I also know a tiny bit, but I think that, well, you have to be really clever for them. To understand what's going on. I find that difficult. (WD4, male, 20, works in supermarket)

Although still young, this interviewee does not suspect that many changes will occur in his ICT use in the future. Nor does he actually recognise that his successful use of the mobile phone (only bought after a longer period of resistance) or his participation in gaming could be perceived as ICT expertise. This case underlines the importance for a shift in public new media discourses (cf. education-entertainment divide discussion). More specifically, computer use is clearly related here to general issues of self-image—and the family's role is in this case unfortunately not a helpful one. Computer use is perceived to be part of skills and knowledge that are not generally available for all.

Another significant aspect has to do with the resistance towards the family's way of evaluating and using (or not using) technologies. Such developments can be seen as threats to the existing moral economy. This moral economy is an important aspect of the domestication concept. It underlines that the introduction of ICTs into specific contexts (such as families' home lives) threatens or challenges existing power balances boundaries and balances of values and beliefs. The moral economy thus helps to negotiate the introduction of ICTs into families' everyday lives, and thereby also the boundaries between the public and the private lives of families.

DEALING WITH CONFLICTS

All in all, each family finds its own way of introducing and using technologies. In terms of discourses surrounding such adoption procedures, many families follow the general assumption that adoption is useful and necessary. This process is easier if the parents themselves are somewhat involved in using the technologies, as this increases the likelihood of consensus within the family.

If this consensus is lacking, differences in opinion or in knowledge arise. Being taught by their children is usually a problematic but interesting process. It shows that within families the knowledge balance can be quite flexible and change over time. On the one hand, educating the other is not necessarily the prerogative of the parent; even the child might become an instructor. On the other hand, the issue underlines the conflictual nature of such power shifts. Where it goes wrong, it shows that democratic familyship requires conscious efforts. With peers and siblings, these exchanges tend to be much easier, since a more or less egalitarian stance is taken for granted.

The need for 'counterfactual justification' remains, as we noted earlier when discussing Giddens's (1992) work on democracy and the family. In these circumstances, parents rely on educational discourse. They assume that only acquisitions and uses that are directly linked to education are really useful in a utilitarian sense of the word and therefore have priority over other uses. Similar discourses can be observed with regard to the use of ICTs other than computers, such as mobile technology or game consoles. Only certain media—the computer—and only certain applications or services—educational—are seen as relevant for successful participation in society (see also Buckingham 2002; Livingstone and Bovill 2001; Livingstone and Bober 2004; Turow and Nir 2000). This preference is also often made in academia (and society overall): only the educational new media applications are labelled as useful while the entertainment aspects are often regarded as a threat (Buckingham 2002: 77–78). The interviews seem to suggest that both early exposure to new media and especially the playful experience of it leads to a much more comfortable use in later life (playful is obviously not per se entertainment, but it can be). Parental discursive strategies allow parents to partially regulate and justify acquisition and usage. The moral economy is temporally challenged and then potentially reinforced. At the same time, once the material is made available, children still have the opportunity to introduce new (non-educational) usages, again showing the flexibility of the power relations in the family and the complexities of domestication processes.

CONCLUSION

Limiting the floating signifier[21] 'democracy' to the realm of politics is wrongfully built on the assumption that 'democracy' is a stable concept with a fixed signification. This way, not only the distinction between the narrow political system ('politics') and the broad political dimension of the social (the 'political') is conflated, but three other essential elements are ignored: the variety of democratic manifestations and variants at all levels of the social; the distinction between formal democracy and democratic cultures and practices; and the constant socialisation or enculturation of members through democratic learning.

Focusing on the family allows us to see democracy at work in one of those realms of the social, and allows us at the same time to focus on democratic practices and democratic learning in an everyday life context. At this micro-level, democracy is constantly being practised and performed, as this highly accepted form of human co-habitation unavoidably requires constant negotiation between the different members of the family, however difficult this sometimes gets. This setting for social learning[22] potentially strengthens our much-valued democratic culture and offers family members an acceptable living context.

However, it cannot be presupposed that this negotiation will be based on dialogical forms of communication and (semi-)egalitarian power relations. In parallel to the discussions on citizenship, the presence of democratic familyship becomes the key condition to assure that this ideal-typical situation is embedded and materialised in family practices. As on all levels, this specific approach to conflict-resolution remains extremely demanding for all members involved and requires constant care. Feminist theorists such as Millett (1970) have made us attentive towards the innumerable derailments and inequalities within the private sphere that often remain implicitly accepted but might erupt at any time, when the apparent stability is ruptured by internal conflict.

Our data imply that conflicts in the family with regard to ICTs are indeed at least partially resolved through negotiation, dialogue, consensus-seeking, and counterfactual justification, although this situation is not always clear-cut. Domestication shows us that power relations within the family are also articulated through the acquisition, use, and learning of (media) technologies. Performing democratically within the intimate sphere as an ongoing learning process then also becomes a way to deal with conflicts that arise out of the negotiation processes that surround the acquisition, use, and learning of ICTs. Interestingly, the circulation of ICT knowledges within the family context reverses the traditional educational process, and increases youngsters' power base'. The acquisition and use remains the (budgetary) responsibility of the parents, although these decisions also become part of rather complex family negotiations. Quite often parents here refer to educational discourses to justify their decisions on acquisition and usage, without having the (ICT) expertise to implement or control them. This leaves the parents quite vulnerable to their children's resistance, as it is their ambition to combine educational and entertainment-related usages.

The family remains one of the areas of the social and the political where the presence and importance of performing, sustaining, and learning democracy is highly under-theorised and where empirical research is lacking. The family spaces also illustrate how (in a very de Certeauan sense) democratic practices are performed without necessarily being translated into democratic discourses, rendering them 'under-discussed', under-used, and under-valued as both normative guidelines and tools for learning. This modest study of ICT opens extremely interesting perspectives on democratic learning in the family (in the family's many different forms and stages), and raises more questions on the long-term effects than can be answered at this point. Nevertheless, it clearly shows that we tend to under-estimate the presence of highly sophisticated negotiation processes and the need for them to be embedded in and translated through the notion of democratic familyship.

NOTES

1. Giddens (1979: 91–92) discerns in the dialectics of control two components: on the one hand the transformative capacity of power—which analyses power in terms of agency and on the other hand dominance—which views power as a structural characteristic.
2. Giddens (1992: 194) explicitly mentions a similar circular process: 'On this point we come round full circle. Self-autonomy, the break with compulsiveness, is the condition of open dialogue with the other. Such dialogue, in turn, is the medium of expression of individual needs, as well as the means whereby the relationship is reflexively organised.'
3. According to Held (1991: 21) citizenship 'connects in rather unusual ways the public and social with the individual aspects of political life.'
4. Marshall's threefold distinction (1950/1992), expanded by the cultural studies emphasis on cultural citizenship (Hermes 1998).
5. This is partially supported by legislative frameworks at the macro-level.
6. In parallel to these early British formulations, Norwegian researchers also developed a domestication concept. They do not focus primarily on the domestic sphere, however, nor do they concentrate on media technologies only. Therefore their approach will not be used here.
7. The six (non-linear) stages are: (a) commodification, (b) imagination, (c) appropriation, (d) objectification, (e) incorporation, and (f) conversion.
8. This move can also be a rejection of the technology and adoption patterns can change radically over time.
9. One question that can be asked is whether the ethnographic roots have been taken far enough.
10. Morley (1986), for example, showed that television viewing in the home is (or was at that moment in time) extremely gendered—at least in the lower middle-class homes that he focussed on in his research. In these cases, the television was seen as an extension of existing domestic involvement for most women and thus did not provide the same 'relaxation' connotation as for the

men. The reference is not to biological determinism, but to historical formation of such behaviours (Morley 1995: 174–175).

11. The computer was actually one of four media (TV, VCR, computer, and telephone) that was meant to be researched in the original HICT study that formed the basis for the early formulation of what was later labelled 'domestication' approach.

12. One criticism has been that existing research has focused too much on the nuclear family. This, however, is not entirely true. Haddon and Silverstone (1995) at least have also interviewed single parents and stressed the particularities of their media use; for example, for childcare purposes.

13. The interviews were conducted by communication studies students from the Free University Brussels (VUB). The interviews formed part of a research project on young people and new media conducted by Maren Hartmann, which again was one project within the EMTEL research network (http://www.emtel2.org). All quotes were translated from Dutch to English by Maren Hartmann.

14. One question implied here is whether any use of new media should be interpreted as a form of participation in important social spheres. If we went along with this, overall use, rather than specific Internet applications would be seen as a form of participation. If this were the case, most young adults engage in the emerging cultural sphere. While use as such is important (especially in terms of skills and confidence), it leaves out possibly important distinctions between entertainment, education, information, communication, and similar categories or genres of media use. However, for normative aspects of citizenship—and therefore also democratic familyship—these distinctions remain relevant.

15. 'Kot' is a Dutch slang word used in North Belgium to refer to a student residence, typically a room in a shared student flat.

16. More explicitly, the content of use has been a major concern in relation to younger children (see Livingstone 2002: 3–8).

17. Resource-related conflicts also emerge in terms of (mobile) phone and other technology usage.

18. This has considerably changed in recent years and is still in the process of changing.

19. Other new technologies, such as Playstations or CD-writers, were also mentioned in the study, but they play a less important role in the question of information and communication. These and other new technologies should, however, not be underestimated in their role as communication topics and as signifiers for belonging to specific consumption groups.

20. But this begins to change as well—and not only when the children begin to earn their own money (see discussion above): some begin to buy technologies for their parents so that they, too, can participate (e.g., WV4, male, 23, unemployed).

21. Based on Laclau and Mouffe (1985: 112–113).

22. Here referring to Bandura's (1986) theory of social learning.

BIBLIOGRAPHY

Bakardjieva, M. and Smith, R. (2000) 'The Internet in everyday life: Computer networking from the standpoint of the domestic user', *New Media & Society*, 3(2): 67–83.

Bandura, A. (1986) *Social foundations of thought and action: A social cognitive theory*, Englewood Cliffs, NJ: Prentice-Hall.

Bausinger, H. (1984) 'Media, technology and everyday life', *Media, Culture and Society*, 6: 343–351.

Buckingham, D. (2002) 'The electronic generation? Children and new media', in L. Lievrouw and S. Livingstone (eds.) *The handbook of new media: Social shaping and consequences of ICTs*, pp. 77–89, London: Sage.

Cohen, J.L. and Arrato, A. (1992) *Civil society and political theory*, Cambridge, MA: MIT Press.

de Certeau, M. (1988) *The practice of everyday life*, Berkeley: University of California Press.

Fierlbeck, K. (1998) *Globalizing democracy: Power, legitimacy and the interpretation of democratic ideas*, Manchester: Manchester University Press.

Fraser, N. (1989) *Unruly Practices: Power, discourse, and gender in contemporary social theory*, Cambridge: Polity Press.

Gerson, K. (1985) *Hard choices*, Berkeley: University of California Press.

Giddens, A. (1979) *Central problems in social theory: Action, structure and contradiction in social analysis*, London: Macmillan Press.

Giddens, A. (1992) *The transformation of intimacy: Sexuality, love, and eroticism in modern societies*, Stanford, CA: Stanford University Press.

Gutmann, A. (1987) *Democratic education*, Princeton, NJ: Princeton University Press.

Haddon, L. and Silverstone, R. (1995): *Lone parents and their information and communication technologies*. SPRU/CRICT Report Series, No.12, University of Sussex, January.

Hartley, J. (1999) *Uses of television*, London & New York: Routledge.

Hartmann, M. (2003) 'The web generation? The (de)construction of users, morals and consumption', EMTEL2—Final Report, Brussels: SMIT, see URL: http://www.lse.ac.uk/collections/EMTEL/reports/hartmann_2003_emtel.pdf (accessed 01/08/05).

—— (2004) 'Young people='young' uses? Questioning the key generation', in N. Carpentier, C. Pauwels, and O. Van Oost (eds.) *Het on(be)grijpbare publiek/The ungraspable audience. Een communicatiewetenschappelijke verkenning van het publiek*, pp. 355–375, Brussels: VUBPress.

—— (2005) 'And where is the content? Media as technology', in T. Berker et al. (eds.) *Domestication: Revisiting media and technology in everyday life*, Milton Keynes: Open University Press.

Held, D. (1991) 'Between state and civil society: Citizenship', in G. Andrews (ed.) *Citizenship*, pp. 19–25. London: Lawrence & Wishart.

Hermes, J. (1998) 'Cultural citizenship and popular culture', in K. Brants, J. Hermes, and L. Van Zoonen (eds.) *The media in question. Popular cultures and public interests*, pp. 157–168. London: Sage.

James, A. and Prout, A. (1990) *Constructing and reconstructing childhood*, Basingstoke: Falmer.

Kelly, A.V. (1995) *Education and democracy: Principles and practices*, London: Paul Chapman.

Laclau, E. and Mouffe, C. (1985) *Hegemony and socialist strategy: Towards a radical democratic politics*, London: Verso.

Livingstone, S. (2002): *Young people and new media. Childhood and the changing media environment*, London: Sage.

Livingstone, S. and Bober, M. (2004) 'Regulating the Internet at home: Contrasting the perspectives of children and parents', paper presented at Digital Generations: Children, Young People and New Media, London, 26–29 July.

Livingstone, S. and Bovill, M. (2001) 'Families and the Internet: An observational study of children and young people's Internet use'. Final report to BT. http://

www.lse.ac.uk/collections/medi@lse/pdf/btreport_familiesinternet.pdf (accessed 01/08/05).

Marshall, T.H. (1992/1950) 'Citizenship and social class', in T.H. Marshall and T. Bottomore (eds.), *Citizenship and social class*, pp. 1–27, London: Pluto Press.

Millett, K. (1970) *Sexual politics*, Garden City, NY: Doubleday.

Morley, D. (1995) 'Television: Not so much a visual medium, more a visible object', in C. Jenks (ed.) *Visual culture*, pp. 170–189, London & New York: Routledge.

Morley, D. (1986) *Family television*, London: Comedia.

Morley, D. and Silverstone, R. (1990) 'Domestic communication—Technologies and meanings'. *Media, Culture & Society*, 12: 31–55.

Mouffe, C. (1992) *Dimensions of radical democracy: Pluralism, citizenship, community*, London: Verso.

Mouffe, C. (1997) *The return of the political*, London: Verso.

Okin, S. (1989) *Justice, gender, and the family*, New York: Basic Books.

Pateman, C. (1970) *Participation and democratic theory*, Cambridge: Cambridge University Press.

Pateman, C. (1989) 'Feminism and democracy', in C. Pateman (ed.) *The disorder of women*, pp. 210–223, London: Polity Press.

Phillips, A. (1991) Citizenship and feminist politics, in G. Andrews (ed.) *Citizenship*, pp.76–88, London: Lawrence and Wishart.

Rousseau, J.J. (1997/1762) 'Of the social contract or principles of political right', in S.M. Cahn (ed.) *Classics of modern political theory: Machiavelli to Mill*, New York, Oxford: Oxford University Press.

Schumpeter, J. (1976) *Capitalism, socialism and democracy*, London: Allen and Unwin.

Silva, E. and Smart, C. (eds.) (1999) *The 'new' family?* London: Sage.

Silverstone, R. and Haddon, L. (1996): 'Design and the domestication of information and communication technologies: Technical change and everyday life', in R. Mansell and R. Silverstone (eds.) *Communication by design: The politics of information and communication technologies*, pp. 44–74, Oxford: Oxford University Press.

Silverstone, R. and Hirsch, E. (eds.) (1992) *Consuming technologies: Media and information in domestic spaces*, London & New York: Routledge.

Silverstone, R. (1990) 'Television and everyday life: Towards an anthropology of the television audience', in M. Ferguson (ed.) *Public communication: The new imperatives*, pp. 173–188, London: Sage.

Spivak, G.C. (1985) 'Can the subaltern speak?: Speculations on widow sacrifice', *Wedge*, 7/8: 120–130.

Thomas, P. (1994) 'Participatory development communication: Philosophical premises,' in S.A. White (ed.), *Participatory communication: Working for change and development*, pp. 49–59, Beverly Hills, CA: Sage.

Tonkiss, F. (1998) 'Civil/political', in C. Jenks (ed.) *Core sociological dichotomies*, pp. 246–260, London, Sage.

Turow, J. and Nir, L. (2000) 'The Internet and the family: The view of U.S. parents', in C. von Feilitzen and U. Carlsson (eds.) *Children in the new media landscape: Games, pornography, perceptions*, pp. 331–348, Göteborg, Sweden: The Unesco International Clearinghouse on Children and Violence on the Screen at Nordicom.

Verba, S. and Nie, N. (1987) *Participation in America: Political democracy & social equality*, Chicago: University of Chicago Press.

10 An indispensable resource
The Internet and young civic engagement

Tobias Olsson

Since the mid- to late 1990s, the Internet's political significance has been a recurrent theme amongst researchers and in popular debates (cf. Holmes 1997; Hague & Loader 1999; Wilhelm 2000; Margolis & Resnick 2000; Blumler & Gurevitch 2001; Bentivegna 2002; Meikle 2002; Jenkins & Thoburn 2003). What is the Internet's significance for democracy? What new political movements can it bring about? In which ways can it remould people's role and identity as citizens?

These discussions—not least in the early days of Internet research—have had a theoretical, not to say speculative bias. Quite often they have started from an analysis of the new information and communication technology per se and have then tried to estimate its political significance—they have, so to speak, read the political significance of the new ICTs off the technology itself. For instance, the Internet's network structure has been seen as a forerunner to a politics following a network logic (Castells 1997), and the Internet's openness has been interpreted as a revitalizing factor in the late modern public spheres (Poster 1997; Tsagarousianou et al. 1998).

However, since the early days of Internet research, at least some of these discussions have been qualified by help from empirical research, not least of which has been the way in which research has begun to map the Internet's significance to the political process in a more empirical fashion. For instance, researchers have focussed on the political parties' self-presentation on the Internet (Nixon & Johansson 1999; Tops et al. 2000; Löfgren 2000), as well as citizens' use of the Internet as a tool for accessing political information. Another significant area of research has focussed on the use of the Internet in situations of political protest. For instance, we have seen, sometimes rather anecdotal illustrations of the use of the Internet by the Mexican Zapatistas (Castells 1997) and in the protests during the World Trade Organisation's (WTO) Seattle summit 1999 (Kahn & Kellner 2004). Besides that we have seen several statistical studies that have tried to present an overarching view of the political significance of the new ICTs through an analysis of access to and use of the Internet among various groups of users (cf. Wilhelm 2000; Quan-Haase et al. 2002).

But for the most part research has not told us much about the Internet's significance in the more modest, everyday life of political engagement that is not connected to specific social movements (such as the Zapatistas) or specific occasions of protest (such as the protests in Seattle). Neither has this dimension been salient in statistical studies of Internet use, which can only sketch an overarching picture rather than one that describes its everyday use. In other words, there is a need to know in what ways the Internet is a resource for politically active and politically interested citizens in their everyday lives: How is the new ICT perceived and used among already engaged citizens?

This chapter presents and discusses some of the main findings from such a study, based on interviews with and observations among 19 young (15–18 years old) Swedish people that are affiliated with the political parties' youth organizations (Olsson 2004). The chapter focuses on how the Internet is used in everyday life as a resource for their political engagement.

In this chapter we will in turn see how the Internet is a civic resource for young, politically active respondents in four different ways: (1) as a tool for monitoring society; (2) as a resource for organizational coordination; (3) as a resource for participation in the internal public spheres; and (4) as a tool for participation in the public forums of opposing political parties.

A TOOL FOR MONITORING SOCIETY

It is of course an important aspect of a citizen's identity to keep up to date on the society of which one is a part (cf. Gripsrud 2002). Media research has certainly made it clear that the traditional mass media have played an important role in this respect. It has made it obvious that the mass media are essential to the establishment of mutual frames of reference (Thompson 1995) and to people's ability to identify themselves with communities that are beyond their concrete everyday settings (Anderson 1983).

The traditional media are important resources also for this study's politically active, young people (Olsson 2004). The traditional mass media are obviously interpreted as important sources of information for their political engagement and they are also well incorporated into the structures of their everyday lives. Further, the respondents' use of the media tends to be rather adult—their preferred use of media content, such as news and current affairs, mirrors that typical of older generations (Olsson 2004).

The Internet has also been shaped into an important resource for helping the young respondents in monitoring society, and the analysis of the empirical material suggests that the practice of keeping abreast of societal development can mainly be divided into two components. Firstly, they use the Internet as a tool for daily *news updates*—quite often several times a day—on the traditional news media's websites. Secondly, they look for and visit various *first-hand information sources* on the Internet; for example, the political parties' web pages, in order to read about their suggestions, planned activities, and current campaigns.

The two kinds of practices connected to the respondents' efforts to monitor society through the Internet are presented in decreasing order, from the most to the least prevailing. It is very common to follow up the news via the Internet, but all respondents are not as likely to be active when it comes to searching for first-hand information on the Internet; that is, information that derives from other than the traditional media sources.

The empirical material holds multiple examples of the use of the Internet for *news updates*. When Peter (18 years) tells about his everyday life around the media, he mentions in passing that: '[T]hen I move onto the Internet, to check on *DN* (Daily News, the largest newspaper in Sweden) to see if something has happened. Then I...I guess I do that about twice a day.' Matilda (17 years) prefers to use the Internet at school (she is in high school), and she does that in order to: 'Check up on the news'.

Also Desirée (17 years) likes to check up on the news on the Internet:

Interviewer: Can you describe an ordinary day around the media?
Desirée: [...] And then I.... On my computer I always start with DN [Daily News], I've chosen it to be my starting page. Because I think it's good that it pops up as soon as I turn the computer on, then I can make a quick check on whether something particular has happened. But otherwise I'm not that much into the Internet. [...] And then if something really special has happened, like during the murder of the Swedish foreign minister [Anna Lindh] [...] then you look it up on the Internet, as a second step, because there you can usually find more information.

Desirée emphasises that she is not a heavy Internet user, notwithstanding the fact that she uses the *Daily News* web page as her starting page on the Internet and uses the Internet to '[C]heck up' on things. Further, she also uses the Internet to follow up on news, at least when something special has happened. She does all this on a regular basis even though she also states that she does not really use the Internet a lot. It is thus quite evident that she has integrated her use of the Internet into the routines of her everyday life.

Tina (16 years) reads her local morning paper at home every morning. She serves currently as an assistant for her political party and during office hours she also manages to read other newspapers on the Internet and to keep updated about the news. But Tina also applies the Internet to other uses when it comes to her efforts to keep updated—she regularly looks up political *first-hand sources* on the Internet:

Interviewer: In the afternoons then?

Tina: I used to watch TV-serials in the afternoon, on channel three and channel five [two commercial Swedish channels], but I don't have time anymore. Well, the news... I cannot say that I watch them a lot. Well, nowadays I do, because I usually arrive home just in time for them. But I do surf on the Internet... I do that quite a lot, like this community for young writers, and also my youth organization's web page. And then Club 28, the neo-nazis...I check up on what they're up to and...Oh, my god! But they don't have any chat rooms, so I just read their articles about how they want to kick ass with people like myself.

In this extract Tina tells about her everyday use of the media, and mentions that she regularly follows the right-wing extremists on the Internet (a group to which she does not belong). She does that in order to keep up-to-date on their plans and to get first-hand information about their whereabouts—a quite spectacular example of Internet use for keeping in touch with political first-hand sources. But Tina is not the only respondent to follow up on right-wing extremists on the Internet. Marcus (18 years) tries to track both right- and left-wing extremists.

Interviewer: Could you mention some of the web pages that you regularly follow on the Internet?

Marcus: Yes, well... I of course follow the other youth organizations' web pages, but then I also check up on... extremists on the political left as well as the political right. Especially the left-wing extremists [who] are growing fast and I try to understand why they do that. What kind of rhetoric are they using? What are they actually saying? And when it comes to the right-wing extremists I just check up on them and try to debate with them. But as soon as something happens [involving] these organizations, I usually go to their web pages to see what it's all about rather than trusting second hand information [the media], which usually isn't right.

Marcus starts by telling that he 'of course' follows the other youth organizations through the Internet, checking up on their campaigns and new arguments. But besides that, he also keeps himself updated about left- and right-wing extremists, not least when they are involved in the news. Then he goes to their web pages to get their perspective rather than solely relying on the traditional media's representation of the event. In this way, Marcus tries as hard as possible to get hold of first-hand political information.

In the literature around the new ICTs, where the Internet has been the example par excellence, its convenience as a civic tool has often been touched upon. Not least due to the Internet's global reach and its ability to be the source of a large amount of information all in one place—the computer screen. Thus, the Internet is a great resource for citizens who want to keep up to date about current issues and it also gives access to a diversified supply of information (cf. Hague & Loader 1999; Campbell et al. 1999; Coleman 2001).

But in most of the empirical studies (cf. Margolis & Resnick 2000; Wilhelm 2000; Olsson 2002), the shaping of this potential into reality has been questioned. The studies that so far have been undertaken have made it quite clear that the actual use of the new ICT has not lived up to expectations. Therefore the use of the Internet among the young, politically active respondents is really worthy of attention—to a great extent they present a use of the new ICT that very much resembles the hoped for civic use of the Internet. Firstly, they use the Internet for everyday news updates—they regularly follow the news through different newspapers on the Internet. Secondly, they also use the new ICT in order to get in touch with first-hand information about current issues. In short, what we see here is an ongoing and independent search for valuable information on the part of the young respondents in their roles and identities as citizens.

ORGANIZATIONAL COORDINATION

So far, the empirical illustrations have been few, but within the theoretical literature there has been thorough discussion of how the computer and the Internet can function as tools for political organizations. It has been stated that the Internet offers political organizations the chance to present themselves in a new context; on the Internet they can get plenty of space to present ideas and visions. Further, the interactive design of the new ICT makes it easier for interested citizens to get in touch with political organizations (Hague & Loader 1999; Campbell et al. 1999; Coleman 2001; Wring & Horrocks 2001).

Besides these public practices, where political organizations turn to the general public, or perhaps, rather, to individuals within the public, the Internet also offers administrative resources for the political organizations' internal affairs. The empirical material formed in the course of this study makes the Internet's advantages in this area rather obvious. To the young respondents, who all are members of the political parties' youth organizations, the Internet is an important coordinating tool.

The analysis of empirical data first suggests that the Internet is an important tool for the respondents' efforts to *keep up to date about current issues* within their political organizations. Sofie (18 years) specifically stresses the Internet's advantages in this respect:

Interviewer: Do you have any favourite pages that you often visit [on the Internet]?

Sofie: No, not really. If I'm on the Internet, and not on the organization's web page, I use the search engines. But I guess that I usually visit the party's homepage...or it's rather my starting page...and I don't really look very closely, I just check if there is something that I should look closer at.

Interviewer: What is that you find worthwhile paying closer attention to?

Sofie: Well, it is usually current issues: The party has said this or that, or now they have released a report, or they have put out a press release, that kind of things.

Interviewer: Does it feel important to you to follow up on what is happening on the web page when it comes to—for instance—attending internal meetings?

Sofie: Perhaps it's not so much for the internal meetings as.... Well, it's also important to the internal meetings...but also when you meet people, like in meetings with other political parties, and then: 'Yes, but why has your party done this and that'. And then you must.... Well, of course you do not have to agree with everything that your party does... but at least one has to know what they are talking about and why the party has said this or that. I have to be able to explain.

In the extract, Sofie tells that she uses the Internet to follow up on current issues within her political party and her youth organization. She uses the party's web page as her starting page, which makes her able to follow the party's whereabouts on a daily basis. There she follows the press releases and current political actions. The extract makes it quite obvious that the Internet is an important tool in Sofie's political engagement, not least in her efforts to be able to explain her party's policies to others. By regularly following the internal affairs and the party's political actions via the Internet, she is better able to explain the party's policies to others.

Sofie is by no means the only respondent to keep up to date via the Internet regarding the affairs of political youth organizations as well as the political parties' current affairs. Christian (18 years) is another example:

Interviewer: Uhu...then the Internet. Do you use the Internet for anything else, except for communicating with your friends?

Christian: I guess.... In that case...I use 'youthorganization.se' [faked address], but there's not too much to read.

Interviewer: Do you do that everyday?

Christian: Yes, pretty much everyday at least. Sometimes I plan not to use the computer, but I end up sitting there anyway.

Interviewer: You mentioned e-mail and then you mentioned the youth organization.... Is there something specific that you usually do on 'youthorganization.se'?

Christian: No, not really. Well, I mostly check up on it and read the articles to see if something new has happened.

Christian's interest in following his party's and the youth organization's activities is not really that big, which is made quite obvious by the remark: '[B]ut there's not too much to read.' Despite his rather weak interest, he regularly visits the web pages to check up on current issues and to read new articles that have been posted. To Christian, as well as to Sofie, the Internet is an important tool for keep up with the affairs of their respective political organizations.

Another example of the Internet's significance regarding respondents' efforts to keep up to date about the internal affairs of political and other organizations of interest, is apparent from the interview with Sandra (18 years). Sandra has been a member of the youth organization since she was 13 years old; she does not really use the Internet that much, she says. But then she realizes that it is actually an important tool for her when she prepares for her youth organization meetings. Besides that, she also suddenly realizes how important the e-mail based information system really is to her:

Interviewer: What about 'youthorganization.se' then?

Sandra: No, I don't visit it a lot, no.

Interviewer: That sounds like a policy.... Why not?

Sandra: Well, it's the youth organization, and it's not that.... Well, on the other hand, I find it useful in my preparations for the meetings. But I'd rather use the local information system. We've got our own [local] mailing list and on a weekly basis we distribute all necessary information through that.

Interviewer: Local information system... Could you explain that?

Sandra: Well, we've set up a...—I think it is Yahoo—mailing list, so if you need to send information to everyone on the local level you just send an e-mail to the list and then everyone gets it. So, for example, if there's a new meeting, you just tell about it on the list.

Interviewer: Do you do a lot of that?

Sandra: Yes we do, we do that quite a lot. It's the fastest and easiest way. If you need help with, for instance, painting a banderol tonight, you can easily get in touch with someone to help you. If you send an e-mail in the morning, you'll have help by the evening. It's fast and easy.

The extract, which starts with Sandra telling about how she seldom uses the information from her political party on the Internet, slides into a discussion about the Internet as a tool for *internal coordination* within her youth organization. To Sandra, who is a member of the youth organization's local board, the Internet does not appear as important in her efforts to connect with the youth organization's internal affairs as it is for her coordination of activities within the organization. Through the mailing list she keeps informed about local issues and can also easily coordinate various activities.

Sandra is not the only respondent to interpret the Internet as a useful tool for internal coordination. This dimension tends to reappear in particular in the interviews with the respondents who have especially central positions within their youth organizations. The interview with Abdi (18 years) is one example:

Interviewer: The Internet you say, do you use it yourself?
Abdi: Well…. The Internet… It's like… In the youth organization we've something that we call the local information system. Like if something has happened you send an e-mail there and then everyone gets to know about it: 'We've a demonstration here or there' and 'At that meeting we decided to….' Thus you can always be informed about what is happening. Besides that, I don't know if I use the Internet that much.

Abdi, who describes himself as 'more engaged than the average member of the youth organization', interprets the Internet's importance as a tool for coordinating internal affairs, just as Sandra did. Through the Internet, and more specifically the internal information system, he keeps updated about what is happening in and around the organization. He reads about current decisions and about planned activities: 'Like if something has happened you send an e-mail there and then everyone gets to know about it'.

It is thus quite obvious that the Internet has been shaped into a useful tool for the respondents' political engagement. But the Internet's usability does not end at *keeping up to date* about current events in the political organization and *coordinating activities*. The Internet also appears to be important to the internal debate within the youth organizations themselves and within the political parties they are connected to.

INTERNAL DEBATE ON THE INTERNET

Ever since the early years of the Internet, the question has been discussed as to whether or not it can contribute to a revitalization of the public sphere (Tsagarousianou et al. 1998; Bentivegna 2002). On the one hand, some commentators have seen the Internet as a new ICT capable of revitalizing the public sphere (Rheingold 1994/1999), but on the other hand, critical voices have said that the Internet will go along the same track of commercialisation as earlier media when they were new (McChesney et al. 1997).

The results from the empirical studies that have been undertaken so far have not really confirmed the Internet as being a revitalizing force in the public sphere. In the Swedish context, various studies have concluded that focussed discussions are not easily initiated on the Internet (Ranerup 2000a, 2000b), and that certain groups of users, for various reasons, feel excluded from the debate (Olsson 2002), and—from international research—that the discussions that do take place on the Internet hardly qualify as being worthy of the public sphere (Hill & Hughes 1999; Margolis & Resnick 2000; Jensen 2003).

But even though most empirical studies have tended to produce rather discouraging results, the new ICT, through its specific form, still holds all the possibilities suggested by the more optimistic scholars. It does supply access to a large array of debates and discussions that are easy for users to reach. This means that to users with the right resources, discursive ones and others, it is rather easy to get in touch with and participate in various public spheres on the Internet.

The present study's young respondents tended to participate in public spheres on the Internet, at least when it came to their political parties and youth organizations. The overall image from the interviews is that the Internet is an important public sphere for internal debate. With a few exceptions, all respondents are, at least to some extent, familiar with the current internal debate within their own political organizations on the Internet. Some of the respondents frequently participate in these debates, while others more just read the reports of the discussions in order to be able to follow up on them.

The empirical material suggests that the group of 19 respondents could be split into three different groups in terms of the extent to which they participate in the debates in the internal public spheres on the Internet (Olsson 2004). First, there is a group of respondents who rather frequently participate in the public spheres on the Internet; second there is a group of respondents who do not participate themselves, but who like to follow debates by reading reports of what has been said. Last, but not least, there is a rather small group of respondents who do not very often follow the debate at all. In this context, where we are specifically interested in the Internet as a resource for civic engagement, the first two of the three groups are put into focus.

One of the sixteen respondents who belongs in the first two groups is Matilda (17 years). To Matilda, the Internet has become an important resource for her political activities, especially for her participation in her political party's debates on the Internet. In the following extract she has just told the interviewer about her youth organization's web pages and the internal discussions they post there:

Interviewer: Do you go there regularly [to the youth organization's web page]?
Matilda: Oh, yes, I go there at least once a day.
Interviewer: Do you go there during school?
Matilda: Sometimes, but it can be at home as well. It depends on whether or not I've got time to do it in school.
Interviewer: What do you usually do on the net?
Matilda: I used to read the debates, and if there is something for me to react to, then I do it.

Every day Matilda reads her political organization's debate on the Internet. She does that mostly in order to keep track of what is happening, but also to actively participate in the debates. She notes at a later stage in the interview that the debates she participates in are local as well as regional and national.

Desirée also pays interest to the internal debate on the Internet:

Desirée: But on our BBS.... Or I never say BBS, I usually say FC, First Class... that is really... it is addictive! I mean I go there all the time. When I'm at home, I always keep the computer on, and I always keep the First Class window opened to see if something happens, to check up on the debate: who's out there? Is there anyone to talk to? [...] Are there mails to answer [...] and is something happening at the local level? Well, that's about it.
[...]
Interviewer: So you are always logged on [to First Class] then?
Desirée: Yes, I always keep it open, so I can go there and just click on; for example the internal debate. In the internal debate the party discusses internal affairs. Then we also have a separate, internal debate for the youth organization, but it's usually...usually it's not so much discussions going on there, so if you feel like debating, you hang out on the party's debate instead.

Desirée is 18 years old and is finishing her last year in high school. Since she started to follow her party's and her youth organization's internal debate on the Internet, she has become addicted to it, she says. Everyday she follows the internal debates on the Internet. Thus, her computer at home is always on and she frequently consults the internal First Class server in order to check on the updates. Aside from that, she is also a frequent participator in the internal discussion on the Internet: 'Are there mails to answer [...] and is something happening at the local level?' The quote makes it quite obvious that Desirée feels very much at home in the internal public spheres on the Internet, and indeed refers to herself as addicted to them.

Of course, Desirée is quite an extreme example. Not many of the respondents reported such heavy participation in the internal debates. Nevertheless, quite a few respondents report getting updates on current issues that are a part of the internal debate on the Internet, and about eight of the 19 respondents take an active part by mailing responses and answering others' mailings.

Some of the respondents frequently participate in the internal debates on the Internet, and almost all respondents at least check out the debates from time to time. These responses are interesting and important in at least two different ways. Firstly, they are important as an internal discussion per se, in which the party's policy is shaped. But secondly they are interesting as a space in which the young, engaged respondents *learn* about how to conduct a debate. This knowledge is of course valuable for future debates on the Internet, but not only on the Internet. These internal public spheres can also be understood as spaces in which more general debating skills are developed, skills that might be useful in other contexts, such as the respondents' future political engagement.

PRACTICING DEBATING IN ANTAGONISTIC PUBLIC SPHERES

The development of rhetorical skills does not exclusively take place in internal public spheres on the Internet. At least some of the young, politically active respondents also use the Internet regularly to participate in debates in public spheres connected to political parties other than the ones of which they are members. This participation accentuates the points made with reference to the respondents' participation in the internal debates: here we have an even more advanced practice for learning debating skills.

Stefan (18 years) is a good example:

Interviewer: The last time you participated in a debate [on the Internet], what was it about?
Stefan: Yes, well…it was the European monetary union. I discussed it with people on the [opposition party] website.
Interviewer: What do you think of that? When I visited your meeting…your idea of this campaign…it aims at reaching a lot of people, but the debates on the Internet—on the other side—hardly include any people?
Stefan: No, it is mostly for myself to test arguments and to see what kind of response I get. To try to ask a good question and see how they react to it.

Interviewer: How do they react then?

Stefan: It can be anything from not bothering to answer to a long answer stating how terribly wrong I am [laughter].

Stefan's use of the Internet is extensive. He uses it a lot in school and he is also a member of several Internet communities. Besides that he uses the Internet as a tool for his political engagement and in this extract he presents how he uses the Internet in order to improve his debating skills—he uses opposing political parties' public spheres on the Internet. It is quite interesting to note how Stefan deliberately looks for opposition in these discussions. He is not hoping to make his readers change their points of view. Instead, he is looking for counter-arguments, because they can help him to enhance his arguments and develop rhetorical skills.

Annika (16 years) has realized what use she can make of the Internet when it comes to developing her arguments and practicing debating skills:

Interviewer: Do you visit your political antagonists' web pages as well?

Annika: It happens. I've been to the antagonists web page a couple of times and that was quite fun, I was kicking up some fuss. It's especially good for testing one's arguments.... If you have an idea and you're not sure whether it will work out or not, then it's quite good. But sometimes people just do it in order to destroy the debate, that's no fun. [...] But I do think it's good that the debates don't get to internal and it's good for trying out arguments. [...] What do they answer if I say like this? You really get to learn quite a lot.

Even though Annika indicates that it is somewhat problematic with people from other parties attending her party's internal debate, she basically has a positive attitude to a more inclusive discussion on the Internet. She also adds that she herself from time to time uses the antagonistic parties' debates to get feedback on and develop her own ideas: 'If you have an idea and you're not sure whether it will work out or not, then it's quite good'.

Stefan and Annika are not the only respondents to spend time with this kind of activity. Marcus (18) has for instance tested his arguments about equal rights for homosexual people within a debate among the right-wing extremists on the Internet.

Even though not too many of the respondents engage in this kind of practice, it is worthwhile paying attention to, for one thing as an example of how the Internet can be shaped into a tool for the development of skills necessary for political debate, just as in the internal public sphere.

CONCLUSIONS

If we sum up the young, politically engaged respondents' Internet practises, that in one way or another are related to their political engagement,
it becomes quite obvious that what we are dealing with is almost ideal
citizens in the era of the Internet, at least in the sense that they very much
resemble the ideas about Internet citizens as they appear in the theoretical
literature on the subject. If the respondents' Internet use is compared to
what statistical studies suggest about average young people's Internet use,
the respondents might be understood as presenting *deviant behaviour*—
what kind of young people use the Internet in these ways nowadays?

The young citizens use the Internet as a tool to keep updated about current issues. They also use the Internet in order to be in touch with various
kinds of first-hand information and to coordinate internal affairs within
their political organizations. Further they use the new ICT in order to get
in touch with and to participate in various kinds of public spheres. They
certainly at least read and sometimes even participate in the (political
party) internal public spheres on the Internet, and some of the respondents
even use the opposition parties' public spheres in order to develop rhetorical skills. Thus, it is quite obvious that the Internet is an important everyday, not to say indispensable resource for political engagement among the
young, politically active respondents.

In the light of these empirical results, technologically skilled citizens,
as the literature has posited, certainly seems to gain advantages for their
functioning in everyday life as a direct result of their Internet involvements.
Among politically active young citizens the new ICT has become a civic
resource, inscribed into the everyday structures of their political engagement. What we have seen here could thus be interpreted as a forerunner of
a heavily digitalized politics of the future, interactive, and easy to access.
But of course it is not that simple, especially not since we are dealing with
such an open technology as the Internet, open in the sense that it has a
wide variety of possible uses (Woolgar 1996; Mackay 1997). The Internet's
open character makes the users' preceding resources especially important
to what kind of use the ICT is put (Olsson 2002; Golding & Murdock
2004), and that point is certainly made obvious by the group of already
politically engaged citizens who are discussed in this paper.

If looked upon as a group, the 19 respondents definitely have the right
resources for shaping the Internet into a civic tool. They have good access
to the Internet both at school (or work in some cases) and at home. Furthermore, they are part of that generation of young Swedes (they were all
born 1985–1987) that has always had access to computers, the Internet,
and even had computer education at school. Thus, the respondents may be
said to be formally educated in terms of Internet use. To this we can also

add the fact that all but two of the respondents are pursuing high school academic programmes, and so make extensive use of the Internet in their school work and have many reasons and opportunities to become pretty advanced Internet users.

Apart from access to the technology per se and skills in using it, other factors also contribute to the young respondents' shaping of the Internet into a civic tool. One such factor is the rather obvious fact that they are already politically active. They already know a great deal about politics and are also especially interested in the subject. Seen from this point of view their use of the Internet as a civic tool is a logical extension of their already established interests and practises.

Their already established political interest results in other features that are useful for the shaping of the new ICT into a civic tool. For instance, they have plenty of social contacts with people within their own political parties as well as with young people in opposing parties. This of course encourages the young respondents to keep up their "political exchanges" on the Internet as well. With the young respondents' political engagement and their interaction with other young and engaged citizens also helps develop their political vocabulary, or discourse, enabling them to participate in debates and discussions.

Conceptualising the necessary resources

The importance of various kinds of resources for the shaping of new ICTs among different social and cultural groups of users has already been highlighted within research for quite sometime. As early (at least in an Internet context) as 1992 media researchers Graham Murdock et al. analysed how access to and the use of computers depended on the users' access to *material* as well as *social* and *discursive* resources (see also Golding & Murdock 2004).

Material (economic) resources are not only decisive in determining whether an individual—or a household—can acquire information and communication technology, but once purchased, material resources also determine how the ICT is used. For example, by limiting the purchase of computer programs and Internet connections, the lack of material resources thus contributes to further shaping of the ICT among its users.

The concept of *social resources* refers to the user's social network. Murdock et al. argue, with specific reference to computers as ICTs, that knowledge of computers within the network is important to the user's re-shaping of the information and communication technology.

Furthermore, the notion of *discursive resources* in this context is closely related to the French sociologist Pierre Bourdieu's concept of cultural capital (Bourdieu 1984). As such it pays attention to such intellectual elements as the educational, cultural, and language resources, which users draw upon in order to make the information and communication technology both meaningful and useful.

More recent research has confirmed the importance of these resources (cf. Miller & Slater 2000; Olsson 2002) for shaping computer and Internet use and has also further developed the analysis (Warschauer 2003) by ascribing even greater influence to the social resources. But with reference to this specific study, there is obviously a need for further, more fine-grained conceptualisation around these issues. Because even though the politically active young citizens included in this study have access to material as well as social and discursive resources, these resources cannot by themselves explain the civic use of the new ICT. If such were the case, pretty much all young middle-class Swedes would present a similar use of the Internet as this study's respondents, since they are fairly equal to these respondents in terms of access to material as well as social and discursive resources. But just a quick glance at statistical studies of Internet use definitely suggests that this is not the case.

Therefore it might be reasonable to add another concept to the set of concepts, namely *political resources*, which adds dimensions such as political interest, political knowledge, and political experiences to the flora of resources that might have to be considered for our understanding of how new ICTs in general and perhaps the Internet in particular are shaped and re-shaped by various users. Of course, the concept of political resources is in need of further elaboration, but for now can merely be left as a suggestion. It might be valuable to consider what some of its implications would be for our understanding of young people and digital citizenship.

The above mentioned material, social, and discursive resources refer to pre-existing resources among the Internet users. Similarly, the concept of political resources points towards the reproduction of an already well known social problem: new ICTs increase rather than decrease gaps between social groups in terms of knowledge and societal influence. This means that already powerful social groups become even more powerful as a consequence of the development of new ICTs. The specific group that has been focused on here makes up quite a good example—what we have seen might basically be how an already rather powerful group of young people, who also have access to the right kinds of resources, shape and re-shape the Internet into a civic tool in their everyday life. Meanwhile, we can also quite easily imagine that the shaping of the new ICT looks completely different among groups of less privileged users (Olsson 2002).

This notion also points towards discussion of the *digital divide*: however, it is fair to say that it puts a slightly different emphasis to it. So far the discussion on the digital divide has been biased by a focus on issues of access to ICTs (cf. Loader 1998; Norris 2001), but the idea of preceding resources with which users shape and re-shape new ICTs encourages researchers to rethink the idea of the digital divide and focus on the ways in which ICTs are used. By doing that, and understanding the uses of the ICT as dependent on the users' access to preceding resources, we are also forced to understand how the civic participation through the new ICT is mapped onto already existing social structures—the civic capacity of the ICT per se does not matter as much as the resources upon which the users draw in their shaping of the ICT. This also means that the question of the Internet's civic elements is less a question of features in the new ICT than it is a question of the general distribution of social and cultural possibilities within the society.

REFERENCES

Anderson, B. (1983) *Imagined Communities: Reflections on the Origin and Spread of Nationalism*, London: Verso.

Bentivegna, D. (2002) 'Politics and new media', in L. Lievrouw and S. Livingstone (eds.) *The Handbook of New Media*, London: Sage, pp. 50–61.

Blumler, M. and Gurevitch, M. (2001) 'The new media and our political communication discontents: Democratizing cyberspace', *Information, Communication and Society*, 4: 1–13.

Bourdieu, P. (1984) *Distinction. A Social Critique of the Judgement of Taste*, London: Routledge & Kegan Paul.

Campbell, A., Harrop A., and Thompson, B. (1999) 'Towards the virtual parliament—What computers can do for MPs', in S. Coleman, J. Taylor, and W. van de Donk (eds.) *Parliament in the Age of the Internet*, Oxford: Oxford University Press/Hansard Society for Parliamentary Government.

Castells, M. (1997) *The Information Age: Economy, Society and Culture. Vol. 2: The Power of Identity*, London: Blackwell.

Coleman, S. (2001) 'The transformation of citizenship', in B. Axford and R. Huggins (eds.) *New Media and Politics*, London: Sage, pp. 109–126.

Golding, P. and Murdock, G. (2004) 'Dismantling the digital divide: Rethinking the dynamics of participation and exclusion', in A. Calabrese and C. Sparks (eds.) *Toward a Political Economy of Culture*, Lanham, MD: Rowman & Littlefield, pp. 244–260.

Gripsrud, J. (2002) *Understanding Media Culture*, London: Arnold.

Hague, B. and Loader, B.D. (eds.) (1999) *Digital Democracy: Discourse and Decision Making in the Information Age*, London: Routledge.

Hill, K. and Hughes, J. (1998) *Cyberpolitics: Citizen Activism in the Age of the Internet*, Lanham, MD: Rowman & Littlefield.

Holmes, D. (ed.) (1997) *Virtual Politics: Identity and Community in Cyberspace*, London: Sage.

Jenkins, H. and Thorburn, D. (eds.) (2003) *Democracy and New Media*, Cambridge, MA: MIT Press.

Jensen, J.L. (2003) 'Virtual democratic dialogue? Bringing together citizens and politicians', *Information Polity*, 8: 29–47.

Kahn, R. and Kellner, D. (2004) 'New media and Internet activism: From the "Battle of Seattle" to blogging', *New Media and Society*, 6: 87–95.

Loader, B.D. (ed.) (1998) *Cyberspace Divide: Equality, Agency and Polity in the Information Age*, London: Routledge.

Löfgren, K. (2000) 'Danish political parties and new technology: Interactive parties or the new shop window', in J. Hoff, I. Horrocks, and P. Tops (eds.)

Democratic Governance and New Technology: Technologically Mediated Innovations in Political Practice in Western Europe*, London: Routledge/ ECPR Studies in European Political Science.

Mackay, H. (1997) 'Consuming communication technologies at home', in H. Mackay (ed.) *Consumption and Everyday Life*, London: Sage/The Open University.

Margolis, M. and Resnick, D. (2000) *Politics as Usual: The Cyberspace 'Revolution'*, London: Sage.

McChesney, R., Wood-Meiksins, E., and Foster-Bellamy, J. (eds.) (1997) *Capitalism and the Information Age: The Political Economy of the Global Communication Revolution*, New York: Monthly Review Press.

Meikle, G. (2002) *Future Active: Media Activism and the Internet*, London: Routledge/Pluto Press, Australia.

Miller, D. and Slater, D. (2000) *The Internet: An Ethnographic Approach*, New York: Berg.

Murdock, G., Hartmann, P., and Grey, P. (1992/1994) 'Contextualizing home computing: Resources and practices', in R. Silverstone and E. Hirsch (eds.) *Consuming Technologies: Media and Information in Domestic Spaces*, London: Routledge, pp. 46–160.

Nixon, P. and Johansson, H. 'Transparency through technology: The Internet and political participation', in B. Hague and B. Loader (eds.) *Digital Democracy: Discourse and Decision Making in the Information Age*, London: Routledge, pp. 135–154.

Norris, P. (2001) *Digital Divide: Civic Engagement, Information Poverty, and the Internet Worldwide*, Cambridge: Cambridge University Press.

Olsson, T. (2002) *Mycket väsen om ingenting: Hur datorn och internet undgår att formas till medborgarens tekniker* [Much ado about nothing: How the computer and the Internet miss their promise as tools for the citizen], PhD thesis, Uppsala: Uppsala University Library.

—— (2004) *Oundgängliga resurser: Om medier, IKT och larande bland partipolitiskt aktiva ungdomar* [Indispensable resources: On media, ICTs and learning among young, politically active people], Lund: Lund Studies in media and communication.

Poster, M. (1997) 'Cyberdemocracy: Internet and the public sphere', in D. Porter (ed.) *Internet Culture*, New York: Routledge, pp. 201–218.

Quan-Haase, A., Wellman B., Witte, J., and Hampton, K. (2002) 'Capitalizing on the net: Social contact, civic engagement, and the sense of community', in B. Wellman and C. Haythornthwaite (eds.) *The Internet in Everyday Life*, Oxford: Blackwell, pp. 291–324.

Ranerup, A. (2000a) 'On-line forums as an arena for political discussions', in T. Ishida and K. Isbister (eds.) *Digital Cities. Technologies, Experiences, and Future Perspectives*, Berlin: Springer.

—— (2000b) 'Local government policy toward virtual public spheres', in Proceedings of the *DIAC 2000. Shaping the Network Society: The Future of the Public Sphere in Cyberspace*, Seattle, WA, May 20–23, 2000.

Rheingold, H. (1994/1999) 'The virtual community', in H. Mackay and T. O'Sullivan (eds.) *The Media Reader: Continuity and Transformation*, London: Sage/The Open University, pp. 272–286.

Thompson, J.B. (1995) *The Media and Modernity: A Social Theory of the Media*, Cambridge: Polity Press.

Tops, P., Voerman, G., and Boogers, M. (2000) 'Political websites during the 1998 parliamentary elections in the Netherlands', in J. Hoff, I. Horrocks, and P. Tops (eds.) *Democratic Governance and New Technology: Technologically*

Mediated Innovations in Political Practice in Western Europe, London: Routledge/ECPR Studies in European Political Science.

Tsagarousianou, R., Tambini, D., and Bryan, C. (eds) (1998) *Cyberdemocracy: Technology, Cities and Civic Networks*, London: Routledge.

Warschauer, M. (2003) *Technology and Social Inclusion: Rethinking the Digital Divide*, Cambridge, MA: MIT Press.

Wilhelm, A. (2000) *Democracy in the Digital Age: Challenges to Political Life in Cyberspace*, New York: Routledge.

Woolgar, S. (1996) 'Technologies as cultural artefacts', in W.H. Dutton (ed.) *Information and Communication Technologies: Visions and Realities*, Oxford: Oxford University Press. pp. 87–102.

Wring, D. and Horrocks, I. (2001) 'The transformation of political parties', in B. Axford and R. Huggins (eds.) *New Media and Politics*, London: Sage, pp. 191–209.

11 Mobile monitoring

Questions of trust, risk and democracy in young Danes' uses of mobile phones

Gitte Stald

THE UBIQUITOUS MULTIMEDIA MOBILE PHONE

It may seem banal to start yet another presentation on the uses and meanings of a digital communication technology with the notion that it has, within a short period of time, become omnipresent and important.[1] There is, however, nothing banal about the impact of mobile communication devices as tools for personal use, and across levels in society (institutions, systems, citizens) and levels of interpersonal relations. The potentials of the mobile phone are to be distinguished at several levels of functionality and meaning: One level is the technological solutions on the market; another is the level of diffusion and integration. At the level of use and meaning, the personal ownership of the mobile phone provides direct, personal access to individuals. The user achieves instant access to information on broadly perceived news from 'the world' and from social network/relations. Through practical interconnectedness, meaningful at the level of micro-coordination as well as at a symbolic level, the mobile phone enhances development and maintenance of social relations, cultural practices, and psychological identity. Finally, the mobile phone functions and has an impact in addition to and as an expansion of other media.

At the present time, most mobile users either have a rather primitive[2] mobile phone or an advanced phone which they do not exploit fully. The number of advanced phones is increasing rapidly as Danish users exchange their mobile phones on average every 9 months. Within the next two years almost all phones in use will be advanced multimedia phones with a lot of data capacity, numerous services, wireless applications, and so forth. Even more advanced and affordable technology has already been developed;[3] currently, the realisation of mobile potential is a question of adjusting the transmission system to new demands and getting mobile phone owners to make maximum use of their potential.

MOBILITY, INFORMATION, AND PACE

We move between many localities in everyday life (homes, urban space, school/work, sports facilities). We move over larger geographical distances (travel). We move locally and globally in symbolic rooms; for example, by making use of computer media. Digital media provide us with the locality and space for interaction, exchange, and proximity. But, first of all, *information* has become genuinely mobile.

In a way media, media content, and people have always been mobile, that is, we have been able to travel, to get access to mediated experience, and to communicate over time and distance. Along with media development the pace and rate of access to information have increased and with the Internet we have become capable of abstracting from limitations in time and space. This isn't a new development, but with the mobile phone always on,[4] the pace of exchange and liberation from limitations has been radically intensified.

At a general level, our now automatic use of mobile phones is relevant. A few out of many examples regarding pace of change at various levels of meaning include developing and ever-changing linguistic media codes (especially in youth or sub-cultures), changes in permitted communication styles at various institutional levels and levels of interpersonal relations; rapid changes in trends regarding content and styles of use; still decreasing time limits of expected access, reaction, and response; and, most essential, the meaning of the instant capture of moments and ways of communicating them.

Some of the questions we should ask are how these radicalized potential information exchanges impact our way of living and our way of understanding ourselves and the world. Is it just more of the same? Can we—and especially can young people—in fact grasp so much factual and symbolic information—from the simple message between friends to larger amounts of mediated information—and to also transform it into the experience of meaning, attitudes, and action? Is it possible to balance the amounts of information with the need for absorption and reflection? Or is it simply a matter of learning the methods to use in order to deal with new meanings and new ways and new norms? Will new ways of interacting influence (not necessarily for the worse) our habitual ways of exercising social life at all levels plus the values as we know them—and how will this take place?

Obviously this chapter cannot discuss let alone answer all these complex questions. The aim here is to discuss the use of the mobile phone, especially by young people, and the potential connection between everyday uses and issues of trust, risk, and democracy.[5] The title of this chapter, 'Mobile Monitoring', refers to the many ways, good and bad, in which mobile phones may be used for checking up, tracking, control, surveillance. With the mobile phone to hand, ear, and eye, the individual users may check up on information of all kinds, track the whereabouts of friends and family, check up on appointments, status, moods, activities of others—yet also monitor and document events, activities, and incidents in public space. The title also refers to society's ways of monitoring individual citizens' opinions and activities versus citizens' ability to access public information, institutional activity, and not least, to exchange all information instantly. Monitoring in this broad definition triggers questions of trust, risk, and citizenship in relation to the use of mobile phones.

YOUNG USERS

The point of departure here is young Danes' uses of the mobile phone, but the general themes are relevant across age brackets. First of all, democracy, risk, and trust, and the meaning of media in democratic processes are, in principle, equally important to all citizens, regardless of age. Second, almost all Danes have a mobile phone (note 1). Third, our basic professional and personal needs regarding our use of media are basically the same. We all depend on being informed, being able to communicate, and being entertained. Fourth, for all of us, form and content develop on a continuing basis and the potential ways of transcending the borders between virtual and physical spaces are becoming increasingly sophisticated.

Still, a number of aspects are typical for the young users. Children and young people have grown up with the digital media that are most essential in our everyday lives— multimedia computers, the Internet, portable music devices, and mobile phones. When a medium is perceived as a natural part of life, its functions and meanings impact the way in which we integrate it into our lives and how we experiment with its uses in terms of communication and experience. And not least, young people are also a significant and interesting group in regard to how their practices of democracy and citizen rights impact on their everyday lives. It is thus important to study how young people's uses of communication technologies influence their way of living, their meaning making, and their concepts of and ways of participating in modern democracy.

DEMOCRACY AND MOBILE YOUNG CITIZENS

At a general level the integration of mobile media in modern society and in our personal lives is important as a process of change in regard to our perceptions of democracy and citizenship. We increasingly have the option of using digital media for individual participation at various institutional and societal levels, to participate in social groups and networks, to state our opinions and to participate in polls, to vote, and so on. We use the phone to be heard, or to convince ourselves that we are heard. This combined with direct Internet access to and from the mobile device radically enhances the potential for personal engagement, participation, and interaction in various contexts of public, commercial, and private activities.

DEMOCRACY AND CIVIC TALK

'...the term "democracy" has several (competing) models and should not be reduced to a mantra' (Dahlgren 2003: 43), is obviously a wise notion. Yet, it seems that in public discourse, among citizens, 'democracy' is used exactly as a mantra that will protect citizens' rights and which connotes trust in the system. 'Democracy' is thought of as the system that protects public rights to vote, general elections, parliamentary responsibility, and, not least, freedom of speech.

Yet, what happens when digital media are used in democratic practices, from distributing information to interaction between large institutions, and in the exercise of citizen rights? Do digital media alter the concepts and practices of democracy and if so, in what ways? The jury is still out on such large, overarching questions, but in the current situation, I share Hacker and van Dijk's view that 'digital democracy' points to new variation of relations between system, citizens, and media, but as a complement: they do not herald a replacement of traditional 'analogue' political practices (Hacker and van Dijk 2000: 1).

Van Dijk also suggests in his model of plebiscitary democracy that such direct channels of communication can amplify the voice of the citizenry (2000: 42). The citizen is no longer the anonymous voter—especially not in his or her own perception. Direct interaction implies being a part of a process at the micro level that can impact the system at a macro level. Van Dijk also states that 'The strongest appeal, perhaps, of digital democracy is the potential reinforcement of interactive politics between citizens, representatives, governors and civil servants' (2000: 47). Dahlgren, in looking to the future, also sees democracy under development: 'Today's democracy needs to be able to refer to a past, without being locked in it. New practices and traditions can and must evolve to ensure that democracy does not stagnate' (2003: 60). The use of mobile phones may facilitate such new practices, even if thus far the Internet has offered clearer examples. Young people's generally explorative uses of digital media are likely to pave the road for new forms of civic interaction.

Of course, people talking together in mediated spaces need not automatically enhance democracy; Wilhelm (2000: 44)[6] warns of the pleasure of interacting with others in conversation, rather than addressing or solving problems. Yet, it can be argued that even socially pleasant collective communication can be seen as a prerequisite for democracy. John Durham Peters[7] (Peters 2003: 7) underscores the importance of formats that allow many individuals to take part simultaneously: singing, voting, dancing, striking, worshipping, protesting, cheering, or petitioning. This broad, communal conception of civic activity and democratic potentials puts the mobile phone in focus as a medium for formal and informal interaction, for sharing social spaces, and for mobilising, for example, demonstrations, happenings, or sports in public spaces.

CITIZENSHIP AND MOBILE MEDIA

At the same time, we should be alert to the possibilities of problematic developments. Bryan Turner describes cultural citizenship as 'cultural empowerment, namely the capacity to participate effectively, creatively and successfully within a national culture' (2001: 12). Crossley notes[8] that citizenship is bound to the intersubjective nature of human beings and conditional upon recognition of and respect for the communal view (Crossley 2001: 36–37).

Fortunati, however, claims that as the mobile makes it possible to exercise the individual right to mediated communication at a widespread and articulated level, it may trigger unchecked appropriation of public space, 'with all the anti-democratic behaviour that this process implies. The triumph of individual rights, even if on a mass scale, is opposed to the rights of others' (Fortunati 2003: 249). It is to be hoped that young mobile users will largely belong to specific micro-level communities with ethical frameworks that acknowledge the rights of others. Castells (2001: 144–45) suggests that while at the general level of society the solidarity factor might be quite low, the use of digital communication media enhance specific network cohesion at the micro-level of participation.

It is obvious, however, that traditional democratic institutions are challenged by these developments (Jarnerö et al. 2003: 341). Institutions, movements, politicians, and individuals have to deal with the fact that information is mobile, users are mobile, and democratic actions are more individualized because of personal digital media. At this point, Fortunati is a step ahead of most researchers when she claims the mobile phone to be a fundamental means of democracy in modern society: 'Its having become a new information frontier and a crucial means of interaction with Public Administration makes it an even more fundamental instrument of constructing citizenship in postmodern society' (Fortunati 2003: 241–42). Thus, the mobile phone is significant to young people in helping them to identify themselves as citizens, 'as members and potential participants with efficacy in social and political entities' (Dahlgren 2003: 59).

In our study it appeared that young people often view the mobile phone as a cheap, always available 'citizen tool'. Danny, 20, for example, would like to use his mobile for interacting with the local authorities:

> It would be really great if you could use it to correct your estimation of taxes, I mean SMS is a medium in line with email and Messenger,

and it is kind of fun that it is the only medium which the local authorities have left over. They even use, not exactly Messenger, but other chat-formats.[9]

Danny has participated in the EU project 'mobile citizens', which made him consider the meaning of the phone number as an alias that facilitates the connection between the physical and the represented self (even if he may forget that we are already digitized as citizens through our civil registration number). To him the mobile phone number is the code which facilitates his interaction and communication across time, space, and physical borders; it signals the rise of a new kind of citizen.

While a large part of mobile communication today is still what Rich Ling calls horizontal discussion, that is, communication with local friends (Ling 2004: 111), this may change, as Mobile Social Software and 3G accelerate the extension of the mobile Internet (Innovation Lab, 2005) into an expansive many-to-many network. Shared knowledge is the condition for collectivity, citizenship, and democracy (Nyiri 2005: 299). The most inclusive and extensive mediated space for sharing knowledge is the Internet, which is now being enhanced by the mobility factor.

Mobile phones function in the circuits of the public sphere even as personal media. At present, micro-public spheres (Keane 2000) are particularly interesting in the context of young people's uses of digital media and mobile phones. Keane argues that micro-public spheres, such as computer games and debates in networks, even if they appear to be 'private', and distanced from public life, may challenge the existing power 'exactly because they operate unhindered in the unnewsworthy nooks and crannies of civil society' (Keane 2000: 78).

TRUST AND RISK

Perceptions of trust and risk in relation to the use of mobile media are related to the general functions and perceptions of trust and risk in society. If the personal mobile multi-medium fosters numerous ways of immediate interaction and of exchange of information, it also facilitates numerous ways of control, monitoring, and surveillance. These are considered positive options in various situations, yet it also raises important questions of privacy and publicity, democracy, and citizen rights. One essential question to be asked is whether young people, who have adapted the technologies and transformed them into local usefulness, consider the risk of being under surveillance at various levels of their everyday lives—or consider the general potential surveillance of citizens, among others based on an increased public and political awareness of potential risk factors during the past few years.

Risk and trust in the correlation between society, citizens, and media, yet also between persons and media, are interdependent. The absence of expressions of risk may be interpreted as expressions of trust. According to Stig Hjarvard (Hjarvard 2002: 78)[10] 'trust' is a functional, rational, and useful 'activity', which enables agency in complex, social systems. It relates also to systemic-personal and interpersonal relationships:

> By trusting a person, you expect him/her to act in specific ways, thereby eliminating the possibility that he/she will act otherwise. Similarly, by trusting a system, you expect it to perform in specific ways and thereby avoid the insecurity of not being able to predict the outcome. Trust is a mechanism that allows individuals to act in complex social systems. (Hjarvard 2002: 78)

That is, trust is a precondition for optimal or at least obvious use of the mobile phone, just as it is the case for our informants. Probably few of our informants have experienced risk at a collective level of society in relation to mobile phone use and in general they trust society's ability to secure citizens' rights. They most likely know the mobile phone as tool for surveillance or as a tracking device from anecdotes, news stories (Thorsen/Tradssagen),[11] or fiction (Ørnen).[12] Risk today is of a different nature than it was in earlier epochs—the last general upheaval of citizen rights in Denmark (World War II, the German occupation) did not take place in their lifetime. In the 21st century threats towards our system and norms are getting closer but so far systems of surveillance and control are generally seen as protection rather than violation.

SURVEILLANCE

In the final chapter of *Smart Mobs,* Howard Rheingold discusses whether we are in fact facing a situation of 'always-on panopticon' or 'cooperation amplifier'. He claims that 'surveillance technologies become a threat to liberty as well as dignity when they give one person or group power to constrain the behaviour of others' (Rheingold 2002: 183). He envisions how new technology may be the tools by which human societies are reorganised to a higher level of cooperation[13] and ends with the notion that people will have to learn how to exploit the technologies as cooperation amplifiers.

A Danish study on attitudes towards surveillance[14] demonstrates that the majority of the informants think that surveillance is a safety precaution and that it may prohibit crime. This is supported by Mann's findings that 'Certain kinds of rule violation can be deliberately used to engender a new kind of balance. They show public acceptance of being videoed as an act of surveillance in public places' (Mann et al. 2002: 346). Global political crises and threats by terrorists have upped the limits for levels of acceptable control.

The balance which Mann et al. mention is based on neutralization; that is, if everybody is using surveillance, the surveillance itself becomes unnecessary (2002: 347).[15] The claim is that the balance between surveillance and what can be called 'sousveillance'[16] generates an 'awareness of the disempowering nature of surveillance, its overwhelming presence in western societies, and the complacency of all participants towards this presence' (2002: 347). The idea of awareness of surveillance is inspired by the concept of the panopticon—self-surveillance as the ultimate description of the modern person's psyche regarding behaviour and self-control, as discussed by Foucault (Deleuze 1992).

In our study the positive attitudes and expectations towards the potentials were clearly outnumbering the anxiety about potential risk factors related to uses of digital media/the mobile phone. One explicit example is Anders, 22 years, who, in response to a question about what it may mean, answers, 'I have a feeling that you are trying to coax me into something about surveillance society and something? Actually, I really don't care'.

To most of our informants the problem of surveillance at the societal level does not exist at all. They would mainly discuss issues of surveillance and control at the level of interpersonal relations. Apart from the lack of personal experience with systemic surveillance, the explanation for this may be found at various levels of experience and understanding: first of all trust is quite firmly established by collectively shared attitudes fostered by ongoing praise of our national Danish culture. Anything which threatens our culture and systems is considered 'un-Danish'. Very importantly, media are creating trust partly by reminding us about our cultural foundations but first of all by monitoring and revealing any flaws in the system. Hence, 'if social systems are monitored in order to expose and eliminate undesirable performance, the individual is able to trust the system' (Hjarvard 2002: 78).

Finally, our findings are influenced by the fact that our informants represent a broadly defined group of average young Danes. Had we interviewed among others young "autonomies" or poorly adapted young immigrants or third generation Danish welfare users the picture might have been different. In that hypothetical situation, however, the distrust would be related to distrust of the system more than it would be related to the idea of digital media as potential tools for yet another way of surveillance, control, and suppression.

PERSONAL LEVEL—UPDATE, SAFETY, CONTROL

One of the risks for the user of personal communication devices is that personal freedom disappears in some sense as it becomes increasingly impossible to maintain a sphere of privacy and to disappear, both at the level of society and in relation to others (Haggerty and Ericson 2000: 619).[17] The coalescence of practices and technology makes it 'increasingly difficult for individuals to maintain their anonymity, or to escape the monitoring of social institutions' (2000: 619).

The notion of disappearance of anonymity is contradicted by Hjarvard who says that 'the "global metropolis" allows for anonymity' (Hjarvard 2002: 73). This, however, is changing as all information about us may be observed, recorded, and transmitted no matter where we are. And we and our activities can be readily retrieved through the digital traces we leave everywhere.

Contradicting Hjarvard, Haggerty and Ericson claim that there has been an exponential multiplication of visibility on city streets. In contrast to Baudelaire's flâneur who was unobtrusively and anonymously scrutinizing the city's significations, modern citizens are now by means of various media 'increasingly transformed into signifiers for a multitude of organized surveillance systems'. Benjamin (1936/1955/1966) recognised 'how the development of photography helped undermine the anonymity which was central to the flâneur by giving each face a single name and hence a single meaning' (Haggerty and Ericson 2000: 605–6). The development of the mobile camera phone almost a century later enforces Benjamin's claim, but surveillance today does have certain voyeuristic entertainment value (Haggerty et al. 2000: 616), perhaps especially to more time-wealthy adolescents.

POWER POTENTIALS

Young mobile phone (and Internet) users, gain new power and influence by their media use, in particular those who are outside of or new to democratic institutions. According to Ling (2004: 119) 'The mobile phone changes the power equation'. There is the mutual monitoring as constant update not only on activities in public spaces but also on people in networks and there is the potential emancipation, primarily experienced by the youngest users, in their relationships to parents and the world in general. Mobility and freedom of movement in physical terms and psychological/symbolic ways may be enhanced by the use of mobile phones (also found by Stald 2000).[18] Ironically, part of the emancipation is warranted by the control mechanisms of the mobile—the check-up, call-in-emergency-potentials; that is, the emancipation is not built on an increase of parental trust in the offspring but in the the young person's use of the technology.

SOCIAL POTENTIALS

The mobile phone is a core tool, especially by young people, to keep and develop social networks by creating communicative spaces and keeping the contact system updated and vibrant. This coordination of 'Social networks of the individual along with the various webs of reciprocity' (Ling et al. 2003: 359) produce social capital; in short, groups and individuals are empowered by being included in social, shared spaces and also having the power to exclude others, if necessary. Part of the empowerment is that information is spread rapidly in mobile networks. Hence, participants influence social and cultural practices and representations almost instantaneously.

A concept on the rise[19] is so called MoSoSos (Mobile Social Software). MoSoSos are designed to establish contact between users in networks and to track users with shared interests, in short, by use of the Internet or Bluetooth. The software is programmed to fit the individual user's interests and needs and to open up for new encounters, but with the consent of the user at chosen levels of accessibility (Innovation Lab Newsletter July 2005). MoSoSo software facilitates creation of what Dahlgren (and Rheingold) call 'ad hoc networks', hence they create 'spaces in which citizens belonging to different groups and cultures, speaking in registers or even languages, will find participation meaningful' (Dahlgren 2003: 49). The empowerment involves the ability to participate even more directly and with new expressions and great visibility in the development of new civic cultures.

It is still today most common that mobiles are used for cultivation of friendships and for support and maintenance of local networks in horizontal discussion (Ling 2004: 111). This is supported by our findings which document that young mobile users call or text friends and families most.[20] In another article Ling et al. claim that the Internet is a generator of social networks where they are already strong, supporting a 'the rich gets richer'—argument, which means that 'the net itself does not generate social capital; it only facilitates already existing tendencies' (Ling et al. 2003: 361).

The mobile phone, however, is also a useful tool to try out new relations (e.g. boyfriends/girlfriends) because it is less 'dangerous' than f2f contact. As an icebreaker SMS is very useful. Some young users are better at being bold or intimate on the screen or on the phone. But, when it is serious, one *has* to have eye contact with one another.

SMART—OR JUST—MOBS?

One of the power potentials of the mobile is the use of it as a mobilising social instrument (Rheingold 2002: 160). Massive cooperation and gathering (also virtually) isn't new but mobile technology many double the communicative and organising potentials. No other medium could raise the swarming effect as instantaneously as the mobile phone. In *Smart Mobs* Rheingold focuses on variations of political, 'critical mass' smart mobs, that is, organisation of protest at all levels.

However, most of the smart mob phenomena, which the average young mobile user experiences, are locally organised spontaneous gatherings. One example is clashes between youth groups of a criminal type or more casual conflicts where a situation suddenly arises, for example, at a party or other kind of social gathering, and the opposing parties call associates who gather instantaneously. These kinds of spontaneous mobilisation create situations which are difficult to control by other citizens/adults/authorities. A less threatening but equally powerful kind of smart mob is the instant organisation of gatherings, emerging as local invitations to join the group at a specific place, and spreading instantaneously through the ramifications of the network. 20-year-old Marie says:

> And then there are also these SMS parties—it's a wildly big problem.... 'We are at some beach at this or that time' to everyone on your phone list and then suddenly you have 120 dead drunk young people there.... Well, there isn't that much control when it is about SMS-ing; perhaps it is more casual, less committing in a way....

What seems to be an essential difference between the mobilisation of citizens in demonstrations and movements, and locally, instant smart mobs, is that the first are based on a predefined purpose and reflection (even if the participants may redefine this), and that it ramifies widely among strangers. The second is based on spontaneous and occasionally emotionally motivated ad hoc organisation where the distance between the nodes and links in the network is not big. The common factor for these kinds of smart mobs is that, through visibility and seemingly organized agency they have an impact on society and on other people's experience of demonstrations of power, for better or for worse.

DOCUMENTATION AND SOUSVEILLANCE

Mobile phones function as personal mobile logs, that is, a kind of life diary which saves experiences, memories, thoughts, or moments in visual and textual form. The SIM-card documents your life-story. Not only SMSs, photos, and videos, but also icons, call tunes, music lists, the diary, the address book, and the alarm clock all save and display expressions of the user, documenting his or her life as mediated via the mobile. Moblogging is not so far very popular in its developed form but all kinds of representations in/on the mobile phone function as a private moblog because they may be forwarded and shared with friends. Sharing is a form of self-exposure of one's personal life in the moment. The mobile phone documents one's immediate story as logs have to be erased with a frequency matching the extension of use and limitations of capacity. Or we may chose to save bits of our story by logging onto our pc. Or we may want to transfer our 'story' when we change mobile phones.

So, the mobile is the digital diary which is gladly shared with friends, but it may also, according to Haggerty and Ericson (2000: 611),[21] be perceived as the 'data double', the mobile extension of the body and mind, a kind of 'additional self'. This McLuhanian and Harrowayian line of thought is, however, not completely shared by Green and Smith who argue that even if the mobile phone is regarded as a *personal* device it is simply a *device*. The *representation* of the user is not the user (Green and Smith 2004: 580–81).[22] Seen from a less academic level it seems that the users are divided between being in a kind of symbiosis with their mobiles,[23] because these represent but also mediate essential experience and meaning in their lifeworlds, while others clearly perceive the mobile as a useful tool. Apparently, however, the shell, the device itself, holds no or little affective value— it may be exchanged for a newer model. It is primarily the content and the representations which format the meaning of the mobile.

CASE: PERSONAL MONITORING AND CONTROL

One example of documentation of everyday life is the use of the mobile for maintaining private moments. Karen, aged 21, answers to the question about her attitude towards having her photo taken at a party when she is drunk and embarrassing:

Karen: (laughs) *In the situation you probably don't care, but the day after I'll probably think: 'Oh no! Do* they have photos of that?'
Int.: Have you ever experienced something like that?
Karen: No, actually not. Well, I assume that my real friends and who have a camera *phone wouldn't be so cowardly* as *to take pictures and so on (laughs).*

The main issue here is not the provoked attitudes towards potential exposure of embarrassing situations, but the fact that Karen has faith in her friends. If they would exploit the situation to make fun of or to mob her she clearly does not consider them true friends. Another example is the small, everyday control. Rikke, 24, tells that her friends sometimes check their boyfriends' mobile phones and she finds that such actions transgress the limits of privacy:

You know, it's like a very private thing and I think it transgresses the borderline. I myself would get cross [...] that is if it is private, when you check up on one another in some way.

In both examples the users define clear ethical and moral frames for behaviour in relations of trust. If the relation is strong there is no risk related to use of the mobile, but distrust of the boyfriend may drive the individual to act 'wrong'. The mobile phone facilitates control and at the same time endangers the trust between individuals.

Always being available, always in contact also facilitates a more constant, ongoing state of controlling and being controlled. Seventeen-year-old Lisa enhances both aspects, telling that the mobile gives a feeling of being safe when you come home alone at night. At the same time complaints from friends and family if you choose to shut off your phone for a while 'is also a kind of control over you all the time, because you have this gadget which makes it possible for everyone to contact you'. This confirms the notion of the mobile as a kind of panopticon amplifier.

CASE: THE STREET REPORTER

An issue which may turn out to be of great importance is the potential shift in the individual (perhaps especially young) citizen's status from being a common citizen to being able to appropriate part of the executive power. One example is the possibility that citizens, by using the mobile camera phone, register illegal, criminal activity and persons who behave in a strange, threatening, illegal way and at once transfer the information to the police. Another example is the citizen becoming private paparazzo who registers 'interesting' celebrities as well as unknown people, with the possibility of selling photos and other information to weeklies and other media, willing to pay for the best story. In certain cases it enforces the role of the press as the fourth state power, as seen in an example from the 1224 campaign of the Danish tabloid, *Ekstra Bladet*: "1224—if you know something", where the readers are encouraged to become street reporters and photographers,[24] if they 'experience something exciting, dramatic, funny everyday events, injustice'. This marks a shift for the citizen from being the ordinary curious citizen flâneur, who monitors his or her environment, to becoming a semi-professional hunting *the story*. The paper pays a symbolic amount of money for the tips and material which is used. In contrast, the weekly magazine *Se & Hør* pays up to 100.000 DKR[25] for the best story. This encourages the readers to be more aggressive as kind of bounty hunters who with hidden cameras and endless inventiveness chase the good stories.

At a different level in relation to the system, but equally a matter of the individual's integrity and of the blur of the boundaries between public and private spaces, are the situations mentioned above when the mobile user documents other people's private activities in order to pass on or sell the information. The use of the mobile phone is particularly interesting in the context of this article, because the mobile compared to the latest mini digital cameras is likely to be found in most citizens' pockets regardless of time or location. This facilitates immediate recording and forwarding of a photo or video, by means of which the actuality is intensified and the distance between situation and reaction is radically diminished. A highly topical example is the case of private mobile photos from situations in relation to the terror bombings in London, July 7, 2005, when passersby on the spot took photos and videos with mobile phones and sent them to news media.[26]

It is relevant to ask whether we can actually talk about a genuine democratisation of media or if it is an asserted democracy. The media do in fact use the information delivered by citizens and the agenda is defined by level of sensation and the fascination of preserving the radical 'now', which motivates the use. Haggerty and Ericson argue that while citizen sousveillance is 'not a complete democratic levelling of the hierarchy of surveillance, these developments cumulatively highlight a fractured rhizomatic criss-crossing of the gaze such that no major population group stand irrefutably above or outside the surveillant assemblage' (2000: 618).

The phenomenon 'citizen documenting' and 'citizen reporting' raises questions of journalistic reliability and quality, but it also moves moral boundaries. In line with the popularisation of the public will to document it may become increasingly more difficult for the individual to judge when, for example, the limits of private life are transgressed, and to make more subjective evaluations of the fairness of exhibiting others in situations which the media will pay to get access to. The question remains whether young people are perhaps less likely to look at the ethical and moral standards in cases like this, because they have become accustomed to transgressing traditional borders of behaviour, especially through their behaviour and interaction in cyberspace and geographical public space with the help of digital media.

DEMOCRATIC POTENTIALS

The case reported below is related to traditional concepts of democratic practices—it turned out to be quite difficult to make our informants think about future uses and potentials as they base abstraction or attempts at creative thinking on what is familiar to them. At least the case demonstrates that young citizens in Denmark are generally quite interested in democratic practices.

Case: The mobile as ballot paper and voting device

One of the issues discussed in the interviews is the potential use of the mobile phone as payment device[27] or as a medium in democratic processes such as voting or at the polls. On the one hand the potential use of the mobile phone as 'credit card' or 'ballot paper' is viewed as practical, simple, time saving—if security is reliable. On the other hand, diverse perceptions are represented as well: it is too easy to vote by SMS, security precautions are too complicated, and SMS-voting expresses laziness plus breaking of traditions.[28]

Not all the young mobile phone users in our study see the device as a potential means for interaction with the system when it comes to serious business like voting in general elections. Voting in television programmes or opinion polls is considered to be less serious, whereas tax registration or banking business considered rather serious.

Most of our informants mention security as a main topic. Some would mention the Internet as a safer way of voting electronically, which is interesting because it points to a perception of the Internet as more integrated and reliable while the mobile phone is still considered to be the personal device where everyone can access you and hence perhaps easily hack your codes for interacting with the system/institutions. A few years ago the same scepticism characterized attitudes towards the Internet but now frequent users feel confident about using it for all kinds of purposes, including net banking, shopping, etc.[29]

One example of scepticism towards mobile security is the potential manipulation of the incoming electronic votes.[30] Another mentioned 'risk' is that the vote didn't go through—which sounds amazingly familiar from popular TV show votes like MGP or Idols.

Surprisingly, in light of the obviousness with which most of our informants integrate new technology in their everyday lives, almost half of the informants mentioned tradition and ritual as an argument against electronic, distanced voting compared to fear of lack of security. A number of informants simply think that the action of voting by using SMS would lose its special touch of active participation in democracy, perhaps even lose its solemnity and aura. Many, however, express a 'both-and' attitude, talking about atmosphere and tradition as well as about the practical potentials of distance voting.

An essential topic is illustrated by 17-year-old Lisa who concludes that digital voting is too convenient or comfortable, which is likely to cause voters to miss studying the basis on which they are voting. She expresses indirectly her sentiment that the foundation for democracy would be weakened:

> I don't think I would vote via SMS. I also think it would be a bad idea to vote via the Internet. If you have got yourself up and put the mark on the ballot paper, you really mean it, it is something you want to do. It is too easy to enter the Internet,... I think that many more who don't want to vote properly simply put a mark, that they don't familiarize themselves with the ideas.

Hence, voting as the ultimate expression of democratic process should not be too easy. It is especially interesting in the light of the discussion of attitudes towards surveillance and trust, when it could be concluded that our informants in that context would take civil rights and democratic systemic guarantees more or less for granted. In the context of voting, that is, electing the ultimate system of political power, the view was that we have to work for it. The question is, of course, if there is a direct relation between the activity related to actually voting and engagement in studying the various political agendas. But, the two informants who were positive towards electronic polls because they considered themselves to be too lazy to get down to the polling station, are in fact the confirmation of Lisa's pessimistic predictions and prejudices. Yet, they also demonstrate the wide range of combined experience, attitudes, and personal reflection and emotion which is represented in our study.

Another topic is the question of the limitations of the mobile phone regarding content formats, services, and capacity. Sune (21), who participated in a SMS opinion poll about the future of Christiania,[31] thinks that those kind of polls are not accurate because they are too selective and hence do not provide a clear impression of popular opinion. He also thinks that it would be difficult to participate in debates on social matters via SMS because there are too few signs at the user's disposal. The medium limits the validity due to its own limitations because it is difficult to ensure that those who do answer represent a population and that they vote on a solid basis of information.

SPEED AND ACCESS

Two issues are particularly relevant in analysis of the impact of digital media on society, culture, and personal living: the significance of increasing pace and the quantity of accessible information. In his book *Tyranny of the Moment. Fast and Slow Time in the Information Age* Thomas Hylland Eriksen discusses the meaning of time—the consequences of its speed and consequently absence, as he sees it, as well as the luxury of having time in modern, digitalised society. Another core point he makes is the luxury of lack of information; that is, the potential shutting off of channels of information in order to achieve the time and quiet for contemplation and reflection. According to Eriksen, unavailability is a new human right because we are now theoretically online 24 hours a day. One of his claims is that the extensive growth and use of digital communication technologies, among which is the mobile phone, are to blame for the intensified pace of social spaces and in society at all levels.

A counter argument towards the line of thought in Eriksen's book, however, is exactly the fact that mobile phones are providers of access(ability), information exchange, and instant communication. Along with other digital communication media it provides citizens with potentials for dialogical, horizontal communication and for vertical exchange in institution–citizen relations; and for shared social spaces which may be seen as the bottom-up democratic civic potentials. To some degree it also facilitates, among other issues, possible interaction and active citizen influence because it has become very easy to mobilise not only opinions but also movements. And doesn't the mobile also allow for coordination of everyday life which gives more time with friends and family? Our informants do not mention being overwhelmingly stressed by their mobile phone—bur rather being stressed by its absence, which of course to some degree seconds Eriksen's point. The average users in our study seem to be rather laid-back regarding their mobile phone, even if it is the obvious, ubiquitous, yet also 'invisible' device, and to some, an extension of their body and soul. Since 1998, when mobile phones began their rise as popular, personal communication media in Denmark, we have experienced ongoing shifts in behaviour; these shifts include getting used to living with it but also creating new norms, new ways of limiting the stress factor. We are probably balancing on the edge between two equally valid positions.[32]

Clearly, this chapter raises as many questions as it provides answers, but: '...given the pace of change—social, political, and technological—we should not expect to soon arrive at some simple, definitive answer to the questions' (Dahlgren 2003: 1). Nyiri (2005b) points out, as an unconscious comment to Eriksen, that we should not measure our ideas of mobile phones' future impact on society and processes by today's uses, even if we have some indications of the future: We as researchers should not take as our point of departure our own experience if we are conservative users. What are the particular points of relevance regarding young people?

Peter, 20, thinks that technology is the future and you have to start at an early age to be able to manage. At the same time he offers a solution for all the troubles and even a way to get the luxury of being offline and with no information; 'Well people can choose to close their phone if they don't want to available'. A few self-assured boys I have talked to demonstrate control by leaving the phone at home, risking lack of info, update, or access. But in general it seems that the very difficult thing is exactly to be without the phone or, even at night, to turn it off.[33]

Lise, 17, says in answer to the question as to whether she is likely to be happy about the future smart mobile:

> I don't know, but as I said, you follow the trends and then you are likely to accept it. But you can't just predict that you are going to be a user—you probably just take it as it comes. You may have a lot of prejudices before the devices have been invented, right? And then you end up being a user because it has become a need.

This rather pragmatic attitude is shared by the majority of our informants but it does not mean that young users of digital personal media simply take what comes and integrate it according to the expected use. Even if Lisa and most other young mobile phone users may not consciously reflect much upon or experiment with potential new services their attempts to make the mobile useful in social spaces and in identity building foster small changes and new practices and not least an acceptance of the usefulness of the phone in increasingly more situations. Development, integration, experience, practices, and attitudes are influenced collectively by everyday experiments with form and content of the mobile phone and the many various ways its uses are integrated in ever changing cultural and social practices. Thereby young mobile users and up and coming citizens, who have grown up with digital communication media, and who still have to exploit the potentials optimally, are the collective carriers of future development and change.

NOTES

1. According to *Danskernes kultur- og fritidsaktiviteter 2004—med udviklingslinier tilbage til 1964* (Trine Bille et al. 2005) 83% of the informants (total population) used a mobile phone in 2004 (compared to 53% in 1998). More than 90% of the 16- to 49-year-old group use a mobile phone; 93% of the 13- to 15-year-olds and 10% of the 7- to 9-year-old group have their own mobile phone. Finally 42% of people who are 70 and over use a mobile phone. The coverage among the youngest and oldest has increased rapidly. In the second half year of 2004, the number of fixed network subscriber lines decreased to 64, 2 per 100 inhabitants. The number of mobile subscriptions increased to 95, 5 per 100 inhabitants.
2. 'Primitive' compared to the first mobile phones and to digital communication systems in general just a few years ago.
3. According to Innovation Lab Denmark, http://www.innovationlab.dk. The combination of telephone text messaging, music device, gaming device, Internet access, diary, notebook, address book, camera, and the quality and capacity of today's mobile phones is indeed primitive compared to the devices which are waiting for the market to be ready.
4. We still experience landscapes with dead, 'no signal', zones and phones which cannot communicate, plus of course practical matters of being able to pay for the services and understanding how to use the phone and understanding the information we access via the phone. But, we are talking about a rapidly increasing part of the global population since Asian countries beyond Japan and Korea have experienced an immense growth in mobile phones.
5. This paper is partly based on findings from previous studies on young people's uses of digital media, partly on a new empirical study on 15- to 24-year-old Danes' uses of mobiles in social and cultural contexts. The empirical part of the project was conducted in the fall of 2004.
6. With a reference to Schudson.
7. With a reference to Giddens.
8. With a reference to G.H. Mead.

9. In fact governments and the EU do focus on mobile devices, e.g., this initiative: http://www.icmg.mgovernment.org/euro.html. And still more systemic institutions make use of mobile services, like the Danish Foreign Ministry which used SMSs in a counter campaign in the case of the Mohammed drawings. Another example was demonstrated at a conference prior to the elections for the EU parliament: the Italian participants received a SMS from their home district authorities that they should remember to vote.
10. With reference to Luhman.
11. One of the biggest cases about financial crime in recent times in Denmark. Tracking of mobile phone calls, both as to content and the location of the phone user, was the decisive factor in find the accused guilty.
12· Danish television crime series from 2004. The advanced 3G phones, which were used in the episodes, were dummies, and didn't even function at the time—let alone with the apparent quality.
13. With a reference to Wright.
14· This is interesting in the light of a new study which shows that nine out of ten Danes are negative towards television surveillance when it gets close to the private sphere, while 97% think that television surveillance of banks and shops (and train stations) are acceptable. Det Kriminalpræventive Råd: TV-overvågning. Fakta om TV-overvågning i Danmark, februar 2005. http://www.crimprev.dk/sw2436.asp.
15. Based on W. Gibson.
16. We call this inverse panopticon "sousveillance" from the French words for "sous" (below) and "veiller" (to watch). (Mann et al. 2003: 332)
17. With a reference to George Simmel.
18. With a reference to Meyrowitz.
19. At least new in Denmark. It has been realised in variations in Japan and the USA, for example.
20. According to our survey 75% of our informants primarily talk to or SMS with people they see daily
21. With reference to Poster.
22. Inspired by Sadie Plant 2002.
23. One example from our study is the young woman who puts her phone on her pillow beside her at night—not to be able to monitor activities but because she doesn't have the heart to put it on the table or floor.
24. http://ekstrabladet.dk/VisArtikel.iasp?PageID=299437. Latest CBS has also started recruiting what they call 'citizen journalists', following the terror bombings in London in July 2005. (Broadcasting & Cable 7/20/2005). The largest example of the mobile as the personalized news medium where everyone can document (photo, video, text) and post news is the Japanese MyNews which has millions of contributors.
25. A little less than £1,000 sterling.
26. According to the newspaper Politiken 12.7.05, the BBC on Friday July 8 in the afternoon—the day after the bombings—had received 1,000 photos, 20 amateur videos, 4,000 SMSs, and 20,000 e-mails. Something like this has been the case in relation to other dramatic events like September 11, the hostage situation in Beslan, and the Tsunami catastrophe. It is astonishing that people think of documenting in such a situation, like reporters in a war zone. We are getting used to recording our lives.
27. Which has yet to be seen in Denmark, compared to Japan, for example.
28. In our qualitative study, 27 out of 48 discussed the possibility of voting via their mobile phone. Nine were positive, 10 were negative, and 8 said maybe, almost equally divided by gender. The oldest respondents were a little more

positive than the youngest. The data only shows some tendencies, as it is collected through qualitative interviews and is by no means representative.

29. According to a study by MasterCard the money spent by Danes on Internet-shopping has increased with 91% in one year, which places Denmark at the top of the list of European countries regarding Internet trade.

30. Disregarding the fact that ballot papers, as history has shown, may also be very easily be manipulated.

31. Christiania is a free town, situated in a former military area in central Copenhagen, which was occupied by activists many years ago. The question of the legitimacy and existence of Christiania divides the population.

32. Time studies would give insight into the complexity and elements of importance and the processes.

33. Seventy-eight percent in our survey have the phone on around the clock. The average number of hours with the mobile on is 22. Most commonly our informants would put it on mute, perhaps with a vibrator, in order to be: available!

REFERENCES

Benjamin, Walther (1936/1955/66): *Das Kunstwerk im Zeitalter seiner technischen Reproduzierbarkeit*. Frankfurt am Main, Suhrkamp Verlag.

Castells, Manuel (2001): *The Internet Galaxy*. Oxford: Oxford University Press.

Crossley, N. (2001: 'Citizenship, Intersubjectivity and the Lifeworld', in N. Steventson (Ed.), *Culture and Citizenship*. London: Sage.

Dahlgren, Peter (2003): 'Internet, Public Spheres and Political Communication: Dispersion and Deliberation'. Working Paper, No. 8, Theme Issue, *Media Convergence, Mediated Communication, and the Transformation of the Public Sphere*, University of Copenhagen: Modinet.

Deleuze, Gilles (1992): 'Postscript on the Societies of Control'. *OCTOBER*, winter: 3–7.

Eriksen, Thomas Hylland (2001): *Tyrannny of the Moment. Fast and Slow Time in the Information Age*.

Fortunati, Leopoldina (2003): 'The Mobile Phone & Democracy: An Ambivalent Relationship', in Kristóf Nyirì (ed.): *Mobile Democracy. Essays on Society, Self and Politics*. Vienna: Passagen Verlag.

Green, Nicola & Sean Smith (2004): 'A Spy in Your Pocket? The Regulation of Mobile Data in the UK'. *Surveillance & Society*, 1(4), 573–587

Hacker, Kenneth L. and Jan van Dijk (2000): 'What Is Digital Democracy?', in Kenneth L. Hacker & Jan van Dijk (eds.): *Digital Democracy*. London: Sage.

Haggerty, Kevin D. & Richard V. Ericson (2000): 'The Surveillant Assemblage'. *British Journal of Sociology*,. 51 (4), 605–622.

Hjarvard, Stig (2002): 'Mediated Encounters. An Essay on the Role of Communication Media for the Creation of Trust in the "Global Metropolis"', in Stald og Tufte (eds.): *Global Encounters: Media and Cultural Transformation*. Luton: University of Luton Press.

Innovation Lab Newsletter July 2005: 'Mobil mening til masserne' (Mobile meaning for the masses) http://www.innovationlab.dk/sw8498.asp?trackingid=532&newsletterid=187

Jarnerö, Dan, Daniel Folkesson, & Per Flensburg (2003): 'Can Mobile Communication Make Democracy More Available?', in Kristóf Nyirì (ed.): *Mobile Democracy. Essays on Society, Self and Politics*. Vienna: Passagen Verlag.

Keane, John (2000): 'Structural Transformations of the Public Sphere', in Kenneth L. Hacker & Jan van Dijk (eds.): *Digital Democracy*. London: Sage.

Ling, Rich, Birgitte Yttri, Ben Anderson, & Deborah DiDuca (2003): 'Mobile Communication and Social Capital in Europe', in Kristóf Nyirì (ed.): *Mobile Democracy. Essays on Society, Self and Politics*. Vienna: Passagen Verlag.

Ling, Rich (2004): *The Mobile Connection. The Cell Phone's Impact on Society*. San Francisco: Morgan Kaufmann.

Mann, Steve, Jason Nolan, & Barry Wellman (2002): 'Sousveillance: Inventing and Using Wearable Computing Devices for Data Collection in Surveillance Environments'. Retrieved August 2003 from: http://www.surveillance-and-society.org/articles1(3)/sousveillance.pdf

Nyiri, Kristof (2005): 'Collective Thinking', pp. 299–304 in *Seeing, Understanding, Learning in the Mobile Age*, Conference Papers. Budapest: The Institute for Philosophical Research of the Hungarian Academy of Sciences.

Peters, John Durham (2004): 'Conversation, Democracy and Communication Technology'. Working Paper, No. 8, Theme Issue, *Media Convergence, Mediated Communication, and the Transformation of the Public Sphere*. University of Copenhagen: Modinet.

Rheingold, Howard (2002): *Smart Mobs. The Next Social Revolution*. New York: Basic Books.

Stald, Gitte (2003): 'Outlook and Insight: Young Danes' Uses of the Internet, Navigating Global Seas and Local Waters', in Andrea Kavanaugh & Joseph Turow (eds.) *The Wired Homestead*. Cambridge, MA: MIT Press.

Stald, Gitte (2000): 'Telefonitis. Unge danskeres brug af telefonen I IT-tidsalderen', pp. 4–22 in *særnummer af MedieKultur* nr.31. Aarhus: Sammenslutningen af Medieforskere i Danmark.

Turner, Bryan S. (2001): 'Outline of a General Theory of Cultural Citizenship', in Nick Stevenson (ed.): *Culture & Citizenship*. London: Sage.

Van Dijk, Jan (2000): 'Models of Democracy and Concepts of Communication', in Kenneth L. Hacker & Jan van Dijk (eds.): *Digital Democracy*. London: Sage.

Wilhelm, Anthony G. (2000): *Democracy in the Digital Age*. New York & London: Routledge.

12 Social networks and young people's activism and cultural practices

Dominique Cardon, Fabien Granjon, and Jean-Philippe Heurtin

Political participation depends heavily on the existence of social networks. Many recent works insist on the importance of personal relationships in the nature, duration, and orientation of activism in political parties and trade unions (Diani and McAdam 2003). Personal networks have played a crucial role in recent transformations of political involvement, where individualization, multi-engagement, and specialisation characterize the rise of a network culture (see Lance Bennett's contribution in this volume), which is prominent in the youth political culture in the alter-global movement. In this paper we compare two different analyses of the articulation between on the one hand, social networks and cultural practices, and on the other hand, between social networks and political involvement. Our premise is that on a methodological level, political activities can be considered as a cultural practice and observed with the same descriptive tools. We raise this question in juxtaposing the results of two different research projects on which we have collaborated in recent years. One deals with cultural and leisure practices, and the other with political involvement; both use the methodology of personal networks to represent social relationships among small groups of young people.

The objective of the first study is to build methodological tools for the description and interpretation of the relations between three types of activities that are often studied in isolation: the practices of communication, the personal network of contacts, and cultural and leisure activities (Cardon and Granjon 2003). In this perspective we have conducted a qualitative study of the social networks of 20 young French students. A typology of three configurations linking social networks and cultural practices has been developed in order to analyse the different uses of communication tools. The second study tries to analyse the place and the role of new technologies of communication in the building of the alter-global movement. In this perspective we pay specific attention to new forms of political involvement and to the role of new technologies in transnational activist networks (Aguiton and Cardon 2004). We have conducted network analysis of the relationship of a small group of 10 young activists by using the same methodological protocol of personal networks.

Though these two different research projects had no direct connection, their juxtaposition highlights many aspects of the transformation of youth political culture. In order to set up this comparison, we treat civic activism as a cultural practice. Recent transformations of young civic involvement towards what we call 'network culture' also suggest that we can understand the rise of this new organizational form among activists using tools derived from social network theory. In this way, we attempt a different approach to the main features that many observers have depicted as characteristic of 'network political culture': namely, we emphasize the interaction of personal and political dimensions, membership in many different organizations, the critique of delegation processes, the consumption of traditional and alternative media, and the use of the Internet. We suggest that one consequence of the intensive use of Internet in youth political groups is to strengthen the articulation between friendship and political activities, a link that has characterized many student mobilisations in the past.

CULTURAL PRACTICES AND SOCIAL NETWORKS

What connection can be established between the cultural and political practices of young people and their systems of relationships? By applying certain methodologies of the sociology of social networks to the sociology of cultural practices, we construct descriptive tools enabling us to explore the relational dimension of cultural and recreational activities.

The personal network methodology

Individuals' cultural and recreational activities can be seen as starting points for investigating their networks of relationships (Lavenu 2002). Many social relations are constructed, in different ways, around cultural and recreational activities (without necessarily being limited to them). The reasons are multiple: these activities are often performed in a group, they provide subject matter for conversations, they are the object of common tastes, and, finally, relevant objects are exchanged (books, magazines, CDs, audio, or videotapes, etc.). We therefore chose, in an ethnographic spirit, to apply the methodology of personal networks developed by the network analysis approach. In this methodology (Gribaudi 1998; Eve 2002) the respondents were first asked to keep a record of all the individuals they contacted and all their media-related, cultural, recreational, and communication practices over a period of two weeks. These data, recorded in a notebook, enabled us to identify regular or occasional relations as well as their context of activation. They also allowed us to make an inventory of daily cultural and political practices. We then constructed a matrix of relations between people who know one another. The analysis of the different information provided by the notebooks and the matrix then served as a basis for long biographical interviews that enabled us to articulate the respondents' cultural profiles to their relationship patterns.

This approach does not enable us to work on large corpuses or representative samples. Since our aim was to obtain individual portraits of participants in a *screen culture* (Jouët and Pasquier, 1999)—in this case, computers—we opted for a qualitative sample based on a particular social group with seemingly rich and varied combinations of forms of sociability and cultural engagement. We selected 10 young people of both sexes, in the 19 to 24 age group, with extensive use of computers, with Internet access (at home, at their parents' home, at university, etc.), use of various functions of mobile telephony, and attendance at institutions of higher education. Since the distribution of cultural practices and social networks corresponds, cumulatively, to an individual's cultural capital (Héran, 1988), the weight of the cultural capital inherited from their social background and acquired from higher education institutions makes this group particularly well-suited for this type of research.

The 19 to 24 age group corresponds to a life period in which experimentation tends to be more extensive than in earlier phases (Galland, 1995; Dubet, 1996). It is thus a key period in the construction of personal networks. During these years a more elective and interpersonal logic in 'choices' of relationships gradually replaces a contextualized logic centred on shared places and activities (Bidart, 1997), and relationships tend to be linked to cultural and recreational practices. The cultural orientations of this group are characterized by a decrease in the consumption of 'established culture' and more consumption of information, along with a greater variety of activities (Mendras, 1988). Students show more broad-mindedness as they shift their focus from a single 'genre' characteristic of adolescence, to an eclecticism accompanied by the 'discovery' of formerly less popular genres (Patureau, 1992; Donnat, 1994). This student eclecticism can be seen, for instance, in the typical repertoire of outings, situated precisely at the intersection of characteristically juvenile practices (cinema, discos, bars, sports events), more 'mature' cultural activities (theatre, opera, museums, exhibitions), and essentially family-oriented activities (walks, fun fairs, etc.) (Lahire 2004; Jouët and Pasquier 1999).

Three types of relation between sociability and cultural/ political practices: Specialization, distribution, polarization

We applied a descriptive tool to our sample in order to identify the person's individual ways of configuring certain segments of their network of relations, based on their cultural practices. Three different situations were identified, in which: (1) a specific type of cultural practice is reserved (quasi-)exclusively for a type of relational network (*specialization*); (2) a type of cultural practice is shared with several circles of the person's relational network (*distribution*); and (3) several types of cultural practice involve the same relational network (*polarization*). In order to illustrate this typology, we will now consider the portrait of three of our respondents corresponding to these three types of configuration. In our approach the production of relational mapping was designed as a continuation via interviews with the respondents. During the final interview we showed them their respective relational maps and asked them to identify the different circles of relations and to describe each of these groups. The clarifications offered in the interviews highlighted the three types of sociability and practices (Maillochon 1998).

Polarization of the Goulven clan and free parties 'galaxy'

We illustrate the method with Goulven, 24, a part-time student in a technical university in Rennes where he is taking a degree in socio-cultural leadership. He also has a subsidized job as an assistant educator. Goulven's father is from a working-class background while his mother is from the lower middle-classes. Goulven has a passion for music and his taste has developed and broadened with time. His network of contacts has also evolved considerably in recent years. Schematically it is represented by concentric groups of contacts. Like Russian dolls, his groups of friends fits into larger networks of relations related to music and so-called free parties (open social gatherings).

Goulven lives in an independent flat in his father's home with his brother Serge whose friends are present more or less permanently. Goulven's immediate gang, or clan, is thus comprised of his 21-year-old brother, who had repeatedly failed at school and two of his friends, Julien and Lolo, both doing a course in horticulture. They more or less live together in the flat and spent their evenings smoking, playing video games, listening to music, and watching TV. On weekends the clan often goes to concerts, especially to listen to reggae and rap at a club where Goulven occasionally works as a DJ. The parties he goes to and the people he meets have gradually changed the clan's taste in music from reggae and rap to techno. This change in their centre of interest has prompted them to go out and move about far more, looking for free parties. Every weekend he and the clan frequent the larger collectives, or galaxies, of those offering free parties. In this context he met Anthony and Stéphan, from Lorient, who opened a door for him. They were to act as gateways to Goulven's deeper involvement in the techno community, where he sees himself as a future organizer of events.

Goulven's relational dynamics

Co-presence is a crucial feature in the *polarization* dynamic. This dynamic can be defined as a tendency to focus on a set of distinct cultural practices that are shared within a clan. The clan, a close-knit core that initially thrives on gregarious togetherness, nevertheless remains open and also participates in larger galaxies (Bidart, 1997). Thus, Goulven and the members

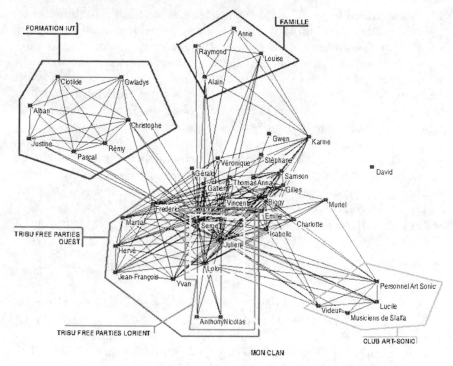

Figure 1 Goulven's polarized network.

of the clan with whom he practices multiple 'internal' activities (music, videogames, TV, the growing and use of cannabis, etc.), are also engaged in 'external' activities such as concerts and free parties. These external activities lead them to broaden their small circle to other people that they then contact occasionally by phone and meet personally at concerts and parties. The youth culture galaxies, that often revolve around public places in which people can meet without making appointments (e.g., bars and night clubs), have found particularly fertile ground for their deployment in the development of urban cultures and, more specifically, in the so-called free parties movement (Racine, 2002), a form of open-house socialising. Hence, the expansion of practices in the *polarization* dynamic is collective rather than individual. It is the clan as a whole that socialises, accumulates knowledge, and develops competencies. In the case of Goulven's group, the expansion of the clan's interest in free parties will lead them together to become the organizers of techno events and activists for the free parties' movement.

The distribution of Nina's festive sociability

Nina is a 23-year-old master's student at Rennes University and lives alone in a small flat in the city. She is from an upper-class family and spent her childhood in Nantes (a big urban centre in the west of France) and at the family's holiday home in La Baule (a holiday town close to Nantes). Nina is an assiduous student, loves TV and the Internet, is sporty, and enjoys having fun with her friends. The degree of interconnection between different groups of relations is very high in her case; she has dense networks. Characteristically, her family network is not isolated from her friendships. At the time of the survey Nina had maintained regular contact with all the people with whom she had formed relationships throughout her life. This high level of interrelations between the different segments of her network is characteristic of the social ease with which Nina has established contact between these different groups of friends (especially by attending parties). She has gradually overlapped and shifted her different circles of relations without ever creating a sudden break. This has enabled her to maintain bonds with different circles of friends while progressively transforming the modalities and forms of contact with them.

Nina's relational dynamics

With the *distribution* dynamic, there is a strong tendency to shift a cultural or recreational activity to other circles, leading to connection and inter-relations between the different circles. This is the case with Nina, who distributes her taste for outings, parties, and television among all her groups of friends, irrespective of the origin of the group (family, holidays, student life, brothers' network, etc.). In fact Nina's activities are not instrumental in the creation of new relations. They neither change nor impact significantly on the forms of relationship between members of the different circles, which are often multiple. Nina conceives of her different groups of relations as 'private clubs' among which she distributes her tastes for 'parties' and TV, while specifying particular ways of *doing things* with each of them (drinking parties, dance parties, more intimate parties; TV series, DVD, general-interest programmes).

When, due to geographic distance (among other criteria), the members of these various circles are unable to attend the same festive events, Nina tries to share the atmosphere of the parties held with certain individuals (e.g., her mother and her best friend). She allows them access to the dedicated website that she manages, centralizing the photos, videos, and various multimedia objects constituting the visual memory of that particular circle. The wish to share experiences, emotions, and points of view with people who did not participate in the activities can also be seen in regular conversations on 'My parties with the others' and 'What I watched on TV'. In this respect it is striking to note a particularly marked use of the telephone (in Nina's case, mobile: voice and text) to discuss past and future parties or TV programmes with best friends. The distribution of activities in a highly multiplexed network corresponds to a form of social capital

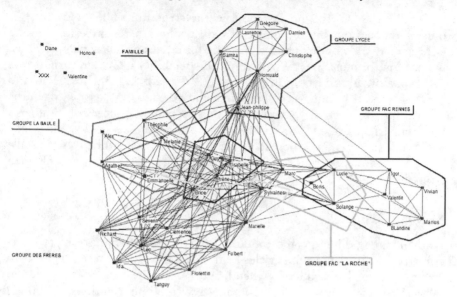

Figure 2 Nina's distributed network.

that corresponds with the social skills usually found among the middle and especially the upper classes.

Nathan's specialized virtual relations

Nathan is from Arcachon. His mother is a teacher and his father is retired from the air force. Apart from the family network that plays a minor part in the construction of Nathan's 'new social world', the actors of his relational network clearly belong to four poles related to specific territories and individuals. The first pole consists of the other students that he met in the private student residence. The university is the second way in which Nathan met people. The third part of Nathan's network consists of the "virtual" relations that he maintains with various people on the Internet. He subscribes to various newsgroups on computing, films, music, and video games, and his online activities are structured around forums on *mangas*, hacking, and video games. He has also created a "pirate" website from which he allows websurfers to upload software and files that are under copyright, free-of-charge.

These electronic relations can be divided into two categories: on the one hand, a majority of individuals with whom he has only electronic contact and, on the other, two people with whom Nathan has developed a closer relationship: Jean-Pierre, a friend with whom he has a lot in common, and Anne, his girl-friend whom he met through chatting and with whom he maintains different forms of communication on a daily basis.

Finally, the fourth and last pole in the structure of his sociability is music. Throughout his life music has always been a resource for making (strong or weak) contacts and enhancing his circles of relationships. Thus, his passion for music partly structures his sociability which, in turn, draws on it to grow and develop (e.g., he plays in a jazz band with David and Jean—his 'best' friends—and sings in a choir). Nathan's passion for music is distributed differently, depending on the people concerned. With his musician friends he exchanges pieces by unknown specialized musicians found on the Internet, whereas to his university friends he gives (or sells) compilations of pop music from throughout the world, also downloaded from the Net.

Nathan's relational dynamics

Nathan manages his social capital on his own. Rather than trying to inter-connect the different social circles he frequents, he keeps potential links to a minimum, as he used to do when he previously lived in New Caledonia. Nathan's social network thus contains few multiple relations. Although some of his friends in a particular group (e.g., his fellow students) know other friends in other circles (e.g., his musician friends), Nathan purposely keeps these different relational spaces separate. For instance, none of the members of his network know his girl friend, his musician friends have not met his student friends, and his family knows virtually none of the people he has met in Rennes. For all these reasons, his social network can be described as specialized.

The specialization dynamic is characterized above all by a strong tendency to select and to separate circles of sociability, each of which is associated with a specific activity. This is the case of Nathan, who has specialized circles of friends: his musician friends and his Internet friends, fans of mangas, and video games. Nathan closely manages his social capital, essentially by creating 'relational niches' over which he exercises tight control. His tastes and activities serve less to unite these different relational worlds in a common space of shared activities than to isolate them. The specialization of his practices has an increasingly strong selective impact on possible people he meets. Opportunities for contact become rarer as the information, competencies, and learning required for the accomplishment of the activity become more specialized. That is probably why frequentation of virtual communities seems far more developed in the specialization dynamic than in the other two. When no interlocutor can be found close by, interaction on the Internet is an essential resource for creating communication spaces in specialized areas.

Between the members of the specialised circles a form of 'differentiated' friendship develops that, as Simmel (1991: 34) put it, 'each time concerns only one aspect of the personality without interfering with the others'.

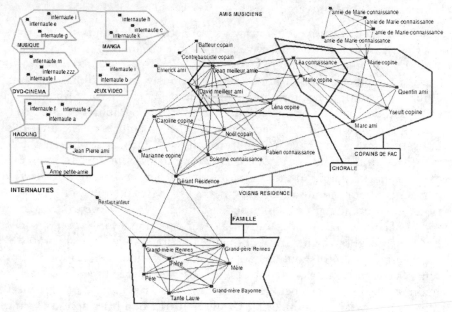

Figure 3 Nathan's specialized network.

They do not meet in other places and their conversations are oriented by their shared activity. These groups are thus formed in the same way as amateur clubs, fan clubs, or communities of conviction (Le Guern 2002). Yet the formal diversification of the link and more personal conversations do sometimes appear as a necessary step in maintaining and enhancing the initial relationship.

SOCIAL NETWORKS AND ACTIVISM

Especially since the 1999 demonstrations in Seattle against the World Trade Organization, the rise of the alter-global movement has been tremendous. This new form of international activism is characterized by the cooperation of a large diversity of organizations: trade unions, NGOs, social movements, local associations, think tanks, etc. (Keck and Sikkink 1998; Della Porta, Kriesi, and Rucht 1999; Riles 2001). This constellation of actors is exemplary of a large-scale network structure organized, from a local to international level, by the coordination of thousand of individuals and groups with heterogeneous properties (Florini 2003). Among many others, two dimensions of this new kind of international mobilization must be underlined for our purpose: the uses of Internet-based communication tools and the role of young activists in the shaping of the movement.

The alter-global movement as a network

The building of transnational networks of activists demands specific tools for the co-ordination of collective actions, the circulation of information, and the running of multipolar structures. For this reason the networks against neo-liberal globalization, called variously the no-global, the anti-globalization, or the alter-globalization movements, have developed an early and decisive use of the Internet. Separated geographically and rarely having the opportunity of meeting each other, members of the alter-glo-balisation movement have incorporated the web into most of their activi-ties (McCaughey and Ayers 2003; Downing 2001). Internet technologies are thus participating in the constitution of a new repertoire of collective action (calls for mobilisation, alert networks, virtual sit-ins, on-line peti-tions, mail-bombing, etc.). Internet distribution lists also encourage new forms of co-operation and circulation of information. Many observers have been surprised by the intensity of the use of cooperative electronic tools by transnational activists: online cooperative publication, syndication of con-tents between websites, lists of discussions with procedures for decision making, audio and videoconferencing, and the growing use of chat meet-ings, etc. (Costanza-Chok 2003; Granjon 2001). In a brief period of time, the web has become the principal area of visibility for the thoughts and actions of the alter-global movement. Even if its audience remains limited to a nebula of activists and interested journalists, the coverage on the web of counter-summits (Seattle, Prague, Quebec, Genoa, Porto Alegre, Flor-ence, etc.) is radically different from that of traditional mass media. Even though the distinction is somewhat artificial, it is not difficult to remark that this alternative production of online information is more documented, better illustrated, more controversial, and far more focused on globalisa-tion issues than that produced by the professional press (Cardon and Gran-jon 2002).

The Internet appears not only as a useful tool but also as a technical infrastructure that shares the same organizational form with this new web of activists. The Internet has increased the opportunity to connect actors distributed among the world; it helps to promote alternative media opened to the participation of the public; it offers specific resources to share infor-mation during an international campaign; it provides the possibility of forming global networks that bypass central authority, and further, espe-cially significant for resource-poor organizations, Castells (2001) suggests that we can compare the form of international activism with the structure of the World Wide Web. The organization of the World Social Forum in Porto Alegre is exemplary of a network mobilization of international social movements (Sen, Anand, Escobar, and Waterman, 2004). The way they are organized presents clear differences in comparison to former techniques of mobilisation used by social movements.

First, the World Social Forum is an open space with no strong criteria to select its participants. One of the main political goals of its promoters is to preserve the diversity of its participants and to remain open to newcomers. Left-wing Marxist organizations, Christian associations, academics, professional NGOs, and others are linked together in the forum coordination structure. Therefore, we can understand why a network-based organization has been chosen as the best solution to organizational diversity without promoting a central leadership. The network appears as much as a technical configuration having its own geometry as a political imperative establishing a particular discipline for the actors who participate in it (Boltanski and Chiapello 1999).

Secondly, there are no real political discussions between the leading figures of the forum in order to shape a political platform or to draw a strategic agenda. Nobody can speak on behalf of the forum. The Forum's Charter of Principles strongly opposes the assignment of any kind of direction or leadership inside it. The building of the forum is mainly procedural and its main objective is to give the opportunity to various actors to create contacts, debates, and local coordination on specific issues. Instead of hierarchical mass organizations led by delegates, new social movements are built by the coordination of small collectives who refuse delegation processes, specialize in their objective, and prefer direct and symbolic action to representative politics. Even though there is a strong heterogeneity inside the alter-globalisation movement, central actors and leading figures are representative of this new form of activism: more flexible, more individualistic, and more oriented towards international struggles. Among the different generations of activists in the alter-global movement, youth activism is certainly the most characteristic actor in this new frame of mobilization.

Young activists in the alter-global movement

Since demonstrations in Seattle in December 1999, young activists have played an important role in the alter-global movement. Even though youth activism is not the main feature of the rise of these new forms of mobilization, young people nonetheless figure prominently in the organizations (environmentalists, alternative media, homeless and unemployment organisations, etc.) and are very active in street demonstrations. They've also developed original and visible techniques of mobilization that are very attractive for the media (zap, haktivism, army of clowns, etc.). In a quantitative survey dealing with the identity of participants to the European Social Forum (ESF) in November 2003, Agrikoliansky and Sommier (2005) showed that 28 percent of the participants were less than 25 years old and 22 percent were between 25 and 35 years old. During demonstrations against the meeting of the G8 in Evian in June 2003, there was also a very high proportion of young activists among the participants, and in Annemasse during the G8 protest, ten thousands of young activists gathered from all over Europe to experiment in a self-organized way of living in two large youth camps.

The involvement of young activists in the alter-globalisation movement has a few specific characteristics. Some youth organizations are linked to NGOs such as the student's group from ATTAC; others belong to political parties and trade unions. But young citizens are often attracted by new forms of involvement and refuse the vertical and hierarchical structure of traditional political parties or large NGOs. The most active elements of young activists in the alter-globalisation movement create new forms of collectives that are more closely linked to the main concern of the international struggle against neo-liberalism, such as associations of unemployed, homeless, and immigrant people, as well as developmental and environmentalist associations. They prefer to use the term 'collective' or 'network' than to be identified as a traditional organization.

In Europe, new collectives of activists of this sort appeared at the end of the nineties, such as Reclaim the Street, Aarrrg! (Apprentis Agitateurs pour un Réseau de Résistances Globales), VAMOS, and MRG (Movimiento de Resistencia Global) (Bircham and Charlton 2001). Without regard to their ideological differences, such organizations gather and coordinate individuals belonging to different collectives. For example, the Network of Global Resistance is an international coordination of youth movements linking German, Argentine, Brazilian, Canadian, Chilean, Spanish, French, Indian, Italian, and Portuguese individuals and organizations. They meet during World Social Forums and have a close electronic coordination (Datchary and Pagis, 2005). In France, the Intergalactic Network is a constellation of very different youth organisations (Catholic, Marxist, anarchist, ecologist, etc.) that prepares specific events during the different social forums. Individual commitments play a more important role than organizational belongings.

The individualization of political involvement appears clearly in youth organizations of the alter-globalisation movement. This feature is linked to the sociological profiles of participants. Most of them are highly educated and are students in the best universities. It explains their abilities to communicate, to write texts, messages, and manifestos. Their use of the Internet is highly intensive. However, it seems that only few of the activists, the most committed, actually produce some kind of formal texts on the Internet.

Sociability and political involvement

If both social networks and political participation are closely linked to the distribution of cultural capital among individuals, social networks play nevertheless a crucial role in the process of individual participation in social movements (Diani and McAdam 2003). As we noted above, McAdam and Paulsen (1993) have shown that organisational links are a strong predictable variable of political involvement. Networks have multiple functions and intervene at different moments in the process of individual participation. A social network approach offers new perspectives in the understanding of the sensitivity of actors for different public issues, the dynamic of their involvement, its intensity, and its duration. The social networks in which actors interact convey meanings (e. g. symbols, rituals, narratives) that build and solidify identities and shape the actors' cognitive frames, thereby enabling them to interpret social reality and to define a set of actions that involve them in this perceived reality (Passy 2003). As one might expect, it is often the case that the duration of the involvement depends on the density of the links that have been woven inside the organization. It has also been shown that, in the case of young people's commitments to civic organizations, a strong link associates friendship and activism. Civic, environmentalist, and feminist student mobilizations have always created friendship cliques built on deliberative democracy.

This model of political cooperation and radical equalities, which has characterized youth political participation since the sixties, has often also been criticized for its closeness and its exclusivity:

> When a movement old guard is made up of friends, its effort to incorporate newcomers may be compromised by the subtle ways in which members reaffirm their bonds with each other, inadvertently excluding newcomers. In addition, friends tend to choose friends who are like them, in terms of both their values and beliefs and their demographic characteristics. They probably do this both to minimize their own discomfort with difference and to avoid threatening the existing network of friends. [...] Another danger: if friends are generally likely to agree on major issues, profound disagreements may be experienced as emotional betrayal. (Poletta 2002: 154)

The paradox of friendship has often been seen as a threat for the destiny of young political groups and a reason why many of them have failed or have transformed themselves into hierarchical and professional organizations. The hypothesis that we want to explore here is that a change has occurred in the manner young activists view friendship in new social movements. With a more individualistic perspective, partly imported form behaviours in consumption and leisure activities, friendship seems to be more differentiated and opportunistic.

Although this interpretation has received a lot of criticism (Collovald et al., 2002), different studies indicate that changes in the relationship between sociability and political participation in parties and trade unions have occurred over the last fifteen years (e.g., Ion 1997). The links between familial political orientations and political participation have loosened their importance. To the same extent, the close connection between socio-professional inscription and political participation has not the same importance as in the past. Many other factors have played a role in this shift: the loosening power of political and unionist organizations; the fragmentation of protest into many specialized and partly contradictory issues; and the disappearance of integrating ideological mainframes. Activists' social networks are not so imbedded in familial and professional networks as they used to be in regard to the building of left-wing party participation. New forms of participation, mainly in NGOs and new social movements, show a relative de-connexion between these spheres of social relations.

Nevertheless, this transformation appears to be more complex than a simple shift from a strong determination of political participation by familial and professional relationships to an individual choice conducted with elective friends. We want to suggest that the different configurations of social networks also determine, and are shaped by, the type of involvement in different social movements. In short, we hypothesize that the network-like forms of the protests appear as an opportunity structure of relational bonds that fits well with the transformations of sociability. New opportunities for participation offered to young people by the network structure of the alter-globalisation movement and the uses of communication tools in order to extend and strengthen their social networks are two determinant features of the reorganisation of activist sociability that we must consider together. The development of web-based relationships enhances the emergence of weak ties in individuals' networks and accordingly affords multiple, short-term, and overlapping co-ordinations.

We want to explore this hypothesis by looking at three cases extracted from a study using quite the same network methodology we introduced above in regard to networks of culture and leisure. Judith, Louis, and Alexia belong to organizations or collectives representative of the new social movements that appeared in France during the 1990s in opposition to traditional parties, trade unions, and hierarchical NGOs and who see themselves as part of the alter-globalisation movement. Even if the methodological protocol of this survey is slightly different, we have still basically mapped their personal network of relations on the basis of the contacts (face-to-face, phone, e-mail) they recorded during the two-week research period. In this study, the focus on cultural practices has been replaced by an exploration of civic involvements and political practices. But, as we will see, we can use the same formal typology of configurations of social networks to understand the distribution of civic activities among their repertoire of social contacts.

The first characteristic of this sample of activists is the intensity of their sociability. Unlike classical observations of the decline in the number of social contacts that normally follow with age, we observed that the number of contacts is increasing with age within this very specific population. In the sample of activists, interviewees are older (from 20 to 29 years old) than in the young students' sample, but significantly, they appear to have a larger network of relationships. A second characteristic is the active role of new tools of communication in the management of this large amount of social relationships. All interviewees are active users of e-mail and discussion lists. They spend a lot of time coordinating activities by using electronic tools. Online and offline contacts are closely articulated in the organisation of their daily activities, mainly because online coordination is an instrument that is used for organising face-to-face meetings or demonstrations. Civic involvement increases social capital by raising the number of weak ties and the ability to reach very distant contacts in order to coordinate them.

Judith, in a polarized network

Judith is 26 years old. Her father is professor at the university and her mother teaches in a school. They are not committed to any political parties (her mother is a member of a trade union), but discussions about left-wing political concerns have always been strong in the family. Judith discovered civic participation in high school when she took part in anti-racist mobilizations. After her studies at the university, she spent one year in Italy with her sister where she occasionally had a few activities in Rome's Social Centre. When she came back to France to become a young teacher, one of her friends brought her to the occupation of a church in Paris led by a collective that supported illegal immigrants. Even though Judith had no particular interest in this issue and had no specific knowledge about Chinese immigrants' situation, she discovered a new political experience and decided to commit herself passionately to this mobilisation.

Within a few months, she participated in three different collectives: Cargo (a small affinity group who demand a universal minimum income); a collective of Chinese illegal immigrants; and AC! (Action contre le chômage; a collective of unemployed workers). Judith also had a lot of contacts with Act-Up and the trade-union, Sud. Over a two-year period, she jumped from one mobilization to another. She helped illegal immigrants to produce files in order to get official papers, she participated in many occupations of buildings in Paris with homeless people, she was strongly active in the unemployed's struggle against the reform of unemployment allocation, and she took part in multiple zaps organized by Act-Up against pharmaceutical companies. Belonging to multiple activist groups is one feature of new social movements that has appeared since the mid-nineties in France. Judith illustrates this flexible structure of interlinked relationships well. She doesn't create any kind of separation between all her spheres of engagement. Everybody knows everyone. And she has multiplex relationships with everyone. Friends and activists are linked to one another and for Judith, it can't be otherwise. Her boyfriend is also an activist and Judith

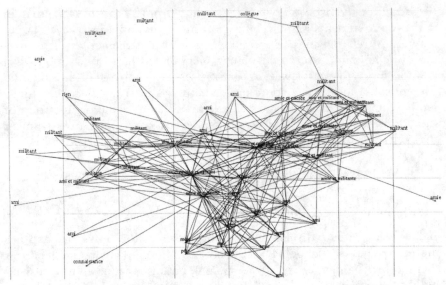

Figure 4 Judith's polarized network.

doesn't have many relationships outside this large circle of friend-activists. 'Affinity groups' are essentials in Judith's civic experiences.

Louis, in a specialized network

Unlike Judith, the structure of Louis' network is clearly specialized. Louis is unemployed and belongs to different collectives. He has joined an association of unemployed people (MNCP, 'Mouvement national des chômeurs et des précaires') and had some participation in a small group of young anarchists. But his main involvement is in technology for activism. He belongs to RAS, an association that provides Internet services for activists of social mobilizations (websites, e-mail lists, etc.). He spends a lot of time giving technical advice to other activist structures, and he moderates some discussion lists. In his network, Louis clearly establishes a separation between activists and friends. Only a few activists are both declared 'activist and friend'. His 'true' friends are constituted by another group of people who have no connection with his activist world. They share another passion, archaeology, and have different opportunities to meet each other and to discuss and practice archaeology.

Alexia, in a distributed network

Alexia's distributed social network keeps the memory of the different stages of her life. Her parents are employees and communist activists in a small town in Brittany. During her studies in high school in Rennes, she was

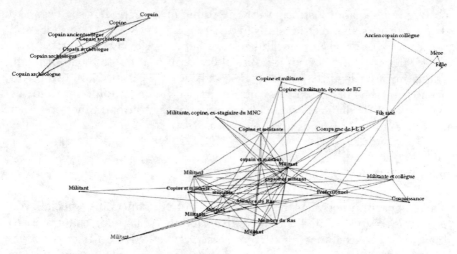

Figure 5 Louis's specialized network.

strongly connected with a closed group of activists belonging to the youth communist party organization (JC : 'Jeunesses communistes'). The 16 to 19 years period was a very intense period of Alexia's life. Friendship, political, sexual, and cultural activities were closely shared in this small community of young activists. This polarized clan is still a group of reference for her, even if nearly all of them have stopped their political involvement in the communist party. Alexia has named them 'friends'. She always has a lot of face-to-face and phone contacts with them. After the 'polarized' period of her student life in Rennes, she went to university in Paris where she participated in a communist party section and worked as assistant in

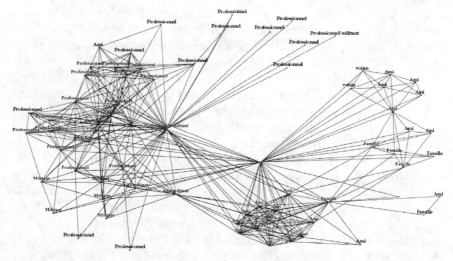

Figure 6 Alexia's distributed network.

regional public administration for the communist party. But she began to distribute her social relationships in different circles. Activist comrades and professional relations are not linked together and Alexia constitutes different circles of relations even if political concerns are shared by all of them. She is involved in different struggles and creates special relationships for each of them. This network structure appears more traditional than the two others. Alexia has built a clear division of the role and function of her different circles of friends and comrades.

A FEW COMPARATIVE HYPOTHESES

The comparison between the six networks of Nathan/Louis (specialized), Nina/Alexia (distributed), and Goulven/Judith (polarized) enables us to identify a few attributes for each of these networks dynamics in the organization of sociability and activism. These categories must nevertheless be understood as de facto configurational dynamics representing trends in the different ways that individuals share their cultural practices or civic activities with their circles of friends. Accordingly, these dynamics should not be seen as too deliberate. They are essentially the unintended result of an accumulation of minor acts, choices and refusals, inclinations and repulsions that make sense only in the overall result produced by the notebook methodology. Also, we should not assume that these individuals are confined to a single configuration.

These relationships between civic involvements, cultural practices and the organization of networks of sociability in the 19 to 24 age group highlight several types of phenomena. First, in order to identify the multiple figures of political participation, it is necessary to consider the full spectrum of an individual's relations. In some cases individuals set limits on an active involvement in a particular circle and distribute more ordinary civic practices to other segments of their relational network. Second, these modes of cultural/political organization of sociability also have to be understood in a dynamic perspective. Since they correspond to specific moments in any individual's relational trajectories, they necessarily evolve with time, as those individuals' representations and relationships are renewed. These categories define the characteristics of individuals and their social milieu, and specific times in their life cycles.

We can also posit that the *polarization* dynamic corresponds to a phase closer to the experiences of high-school pupils and to the 'total' involvement in affinity groups, while the *distribution* dynamic corresponds to entangled sequences of student life and the succession of short-term involvements. Finally, the *specialization* dynamic marks an individualization of practices necessitated by the time constraints of family and working life. It fits particularly well with the rising of expert engagement in new forms of social protest. This temporal organization obviously varies from one individual to another. This dynamic transformation can also be observed in the transformation of youth political commitments. After the 'affinity' group period, they tend both to specialize and distribute their political networks. However, this argument suggests that it would be useful to develop a longitudinal and dynamic approach to transformations of individuals' systems of relationships, in relation to changes in their political practices—something that calls for further study.

However, we want to conclude with a more hypothetical interpretation of possible transformations of the youth activist culture. Briefly, it seems that the risk of exclusivity in the networks of young, polarized activists is counterbalanced by network articulations offered by the shape of new social movements. The coordination of multiple issues, the intertwined building of public campaigns, and the changing distribution of multiple belongings reclaim circulation and openness. Even if this 'network culture' is only reserved for upper and middle-class students, it is becoming a major concern inside political groups involved in alter-globalisation movements. Further, and importantly, we suggest that new communication tools have an important role in this dynamic. Mobility and specialization are the two main characteristics of network activism. And, as our examples suggest, mobile phone and communication with the Internet are key instruments for distributed and specialized social networks. Democratic behaviour is not an organizational objective but an imperative for the management of network structures. Transparency is not only claimed inside the organization, as in student mobilization of the sixties, but also outside and between organizations. Significantly, a lot of youth organizations have decided to give access to their internal discussion to outsiders. The minutes from meetings are accessible on their websites, discussion list archives can be read by everyone, and activists are very sensitive on the issue of their openness to outsiders.

Francesca Poletta (2002) has compared the internal life of Direct Action Network (DAN), a group of young American activists who played a leading role in the demonstrations in Seattle, and previous American feminist and civic organisations Poletta shows that the role of friendship has changed in the building of internal democracy. In the new forms of protest, the multiplication of the bonds, the necessity of multi-polar coordination of collective action between people who have sometimes nothing in common but the issue of the mobilization, and the imperative of transparency as a condition of democratic behaviours, all serve to disperse even the more polarized affinity groups. Even if trust, intimacy, and proximity are always strong values in affinity groups, the new models of commitment emphasize individual circulation to join one issue after another. Given the variety of multiple and short-term commitments in single-issue mobilizations, affinity is becoming more spotty if not less intense, less exclusive, and less attentive to ideological differences. In a network context, we can hypothesize that, in the Simmel's words (1991), 'undifferentiated' friendship is becoming more 'differentiated'.

REFERENCES

Aguiton, C., and Cardon, D. (2004) 'Activism and Information Technologies: Networks and Democracy', communication for *4S et EASST Meeting*, Paris, 25–28 August.

Agrikoliansky, E., and Sommier, I., eds. (2005) *Radiographie du mouvement altermondialiste. Le deuxième forum social européen.* Paris: La dispute.

Bidart, C. (1997) *L'amitié. Un lien social.* Paris: La Découverte.

Bidart, C. and Le Gall, D. (1996) 'Les jeunes et leurs petits mondes. Relations, cercles sociaux, nébuleuses', *Cahiers de la MRSH*, 5(juin), 57–76.

Birchman, E. and Charlton, J. (2001) *Anticapitalism. A Guide to the Movement.* London: Bookmarks.

Boltanski, L. and Chiapello, E. (1999) *Le nouvel esprit du capitalisme.* Paris: Gallimard.

Cardon, D. and Granjon, F. (2002) 'La radicalisation de l'espace public par les média-activistes. Les pratiques du web lors du second Forum social mondial de Porto Alegre', Communication au VIIe Congrès de l'Association française de science politique, Table-ronde 'La radicalisation politique', Lille, 18–21 septembre 2002.

Cardon, D. and Granjon, F. (2003) 'Eléments pour une approche des pratiques culturelles par les réseaux de sociabilité', in Donnat, O. and Tolila, P., eds., *Les public(s) de la culture.* Paris: Presses de Sciences Po, pp. 93–108.

Castells, M. (2001), *La galaxie Internet.* Paris: Fayard.

Collovald, A., Lechien, M.-H., Rozier, S., and Willemez L. (2002) *L'humanitaire ou le management des dévouements.* Rennes: PUR, 2002.

Costanza-Chok, S. (2003), 'Mapping the Repertoire of Electronic Contention' in Opel, A. and Pompper, D., eds., *Representing Resistance. Media, Civil Disobedience and the Global Justice Movement.* Westport, CT: Greenwood.

Datchary C., and Pagis J (2005), ??????, *Réseaux*, n° ?,

Della Porta, D., Kriesi, H., and Rucht, D., eds, (1999) *Social Movements in a Globalizing World.* London, Macmillan, pp. 206–222.

Diani, M., and McAdam, D., eds. (2003), *Social Movements and Networks. Relational Approaches to Collective Action.* Oxford: Oxford University Press.

Donnat, O. (1994), *Les Français face à la culture, De l'exclusion à l'éclectisme.* Paris: La Découverte.

Downing, J.D.H.), 2001, *Radical Media. Rebellious Communication and Social Movements.* London, Sage.

Dubet, F. (1996), 'Des jeunesses et des sociologies. Le cas français', *Sociologie et sociétés*, 28 (1), 23–35.

Eve, M. (2002), 'Deux traditions d'analyse des réseaux sociaux', *Réseaux*, 20, (115), 183–212.

Florini, A. M. (2003) 'Transnational Civil Society', in Edwards, M. and Gaventa, M., eds., *Global Citizen Action*, Boulder. CO: Lynne Rienner.

Galland, O. (1995) 'Une entrée de plus en plus tardive dans la vie adulte', *Économie et statistiques*, 283–284 (3–4), 33–52.

Galland, O., ed. (1995) *Le monde des étudiants.* Paris: PUF.

Granjon, F. (2001) *L'Internet militant. Mouvement social et usages des réseaux télématiques.* Rennes: Apogée.

Gribaudi, M., ed. (1998) *Espaces, temporalités, stratifications. Exercices sur les réseaux sociaux.* Paris :EHESS.

Héran, F. (1988), 'La sociabilité, une pratique culturelle', *Économie et statistiques*, 216 (décembre), 3–22.

Ion, J. (1997) *La fin des militants?* Paris: Éditions de l'Atelier.

Jouët, J., and Pasquier, D. (1999) 'Les jeunes et la culture de l'écran. Enquête nationale auprès des 6–17 ans', Réseaux, 17 (92–93) ; CNET/Hermès Science Publications, pp. 27–102.

Keck, M. and Sikkink, K. (1998) *Activists beyond Borders. Advocacy Networks in International Politics.* New York: Cornell University Press.

Lahire, B. (2004) La culture des individus. Dissonances culturelles et distinction de soi. Paris: La Découverte.

Lavenu, D. (2002) 'Activités du temps libre et sociabilité de jeunes à la sortie de l'adolescence', *Loisir et société/Society and Leisure*, 24 (2), 403–428.

Le Guern, P., ed.(2002) *Culture fan et œuvres cultes.* Rennes: PUR.

Maillochon, F. (1998) 'Réseaux utopiques: Formes de relation et pratiques spatiales à Paris', in Gribaudi, M., ed. (1998) *Espaces, temporalités, stratifications: Exercices sur les réseaux sociaux.* Paris, EHESS, pp. 169–205.

McAdam, D., and Paulsen, R. (1993) 'Specifying the relationship between social ties and activism', *American Journal of Sociology*, 99, 640–667.

McCaughey, M., and Ayers, M. D., eds. (2003) *Cyberactivism. Online Activism in Theory and Practice.* New York: Routledge.

Mendras, H. (1988), *La seconde Révolution française.* Paris: Gallimard..

Passy, F. (2003) 'Social Networks Matter. But How?' in Diani, M. and McAdam, D., eds. *Social Movements and Networks. Relational Approaches to Collective Action.* Oxford: Oxford University Press, pp. 21–48.

Patureau, F. (1992) *Les pratiques culturelles des jeunes.* Paris: La Documentation française.

Polletta, F. (2002) *Freedom is an Endless Meeting. Democracy in American Social Movements.* Chicago: University of Chicago Press.

Racine, E. (2002) *Le phénomène techno. Clubs, raves, free-parties.* Paris, Imago.

Riles, A., (2001) *The Network Inside Out.* Ann Arbor: University of Michigan Press.

Sen J., Anand A., Escobar A., and Waterman, P. (2004) *World Social Forum Challenging Empires.* New Dehli: The Viveka Foundation.

Simmel, G. (1991) *Secret et sociétés secrètes.* Paris: Circé.

Contributors

Jo-Ann Amadeo is an evaluation specialist for the Arlington Public Schools in Virginia and a researcher with the IEA Civic Education Research Group at the University of Maryland, College Park. She is the lead author of *Civic Knowledge and Engagement: An IEA Study of Upper Secondary Students in Sixteen Countries* and co-author of numerous articles on the civic attitudes and activities of adolescents. Dr. Amadeo holds a PhD in Human Development from the University of Maryland.

Lance Bennett is Ruddick C. Lawrence Professor Communication and Professor of Political Science, as well as the founder and director of the Center for Communication and Civic Engagement at the University of Washington in Seattle. His work on the news media and political communication has appeared in many leading scholarly journals. The author of several books, including *News: The Politics of Illusion*, 6th ed., he is also co-editor of the Cambridge University Press series 'Communication, Society, and Politics', which includes his co-edited volume *Mediated Politics: Communication in the Future of Democracy*.

Liesbeth de Block is a lecturer in Media and Cultural Studies and a research officer in the Centre for the Study of Children, Youth and Media at the Institute of Education in London. Her special interest is in the role of media in children's lives in migration and in the processes of settling. She has conducted and coordinated research projects in this area for the last eight years, often using children's media production as a research tool.

David Buckingham is professor of education at the Institute of Education, London University. He is the founder and director of the Centre for the Study of Children, Youth and Media, and has pioneered research in media education in the UK, especially analysing children's and young people's interactions with television and electronic media. He is the author, co-author, or editor of many books, and an extensive number of articles and book chapters. Among his recent books are Computer Games: Text, Narrative and Play (co-authored), Toys, Games and Media (co-edited), and

Media Education: Literacy, Learning and Contemporary Culture, which was translated into six languages.

Bart Cammaerts is a political scientist and media researcher lecturing on media, citizenship, and democracy at the Media & Communication Department of the London School of Economics and Political Science, University of London. He chairs the Communication and Democracy Section of ECREA. His research focuses on alternative political movements and their use of new media. He is the co-editor of *Reclaiming the Media: Communication Rights and Democratic Media Roles* and author of the forthcoming *Transnational Civil Society Activism and Media Strategies*.

Dominique Cardon is a sociologist in the research section of France TelecomR&D, as well as associate researcher in the Centre d'Études des Mouvements Sociaux at l'École des Hautes Études en Sciences Sociales in Paris. He is working on the transformation of the public space and the uses of new technologies. He has published a large number of articles on the role of new technologies in the alter-globalization movement, on alternative media, and on the socio-cultural process of bottom-up innovations in the digital world.

Nico Carpentier is a media sociologist working at the Communication Studies Departments of the Catholic University of Brussels (KUB) and the Free University of Brussels (VUB). He is co-director of the KUB research centre CSC, a member of the VUB research centre CEMESO, and a board member of the European Consortium for Communication Research (ECCR). He has published numerous articles and reports on media, democracy, and engagement, and is the co-editor of *Reclaiming the Media: Communication Rights and Democratic Media Roles*.

Stephen Coleman is professor of political communication at the Institute for Communications Studies, University of Leeds. He was previously professor of e-Democracy at the Oxford Internet Institute and senior research fellow of Jesus College, Oxford. He has written extensively on new forms of political communication and democratic representation, exploring the relationship between popular and political culture.

Peter Dahlgren is professor of media and communication at Lund University, Sweden. His research focuses on democracy, the evolution of the media, and contemporary socio-cultural processes. Most recently he is looking at how young citizens make use of new communication technologies for democratic engagement and identity work. He has published on journalism, television, the public sphere, and civic culture. His forthcoming book is *Media and Civic Engagement*.

Fabien Granjon is a sociologist in the laboratory SUSI of the research and development section of Orange-France Telecom. His researches deal with alternative media, collective action in connection with ICTs, and the evolution of cultural practices.

Uwe Hasebrink is director of the Hans Bredow Institute for Media Research and Professor for Empirical Communication Research at the University of Hamburg. His main research interests include individual patterns of media use, development of the media, and patterns of audiences' media use in Europe. His work also focuses on programme quality and the public service function of media.

Ingrid Paus-Hasebrink is professor and head of the Department for Communications at the University of Salzburg, as well as professor of Audio-visual Communication. Her particular interest is related to young audiences and to media content targeted to children and young people; media education, media literacy, and protection of minors in the evolving information society.

Jean-Philippe Heurtin is professor of Political Science at the University of Nice-Sophia Antipolis. He published in the fields of social criticism, media sociology, and social movements; his recent book deals with the parliamentary public sphere. His current research deals with political criticism and activists' sociability. He is member of the Groupe de sociologie politique et morale (Paris, EHESS) and on the editorial board of the journal *Politix. Revue des sciences sociales du politique.*

Sonia Livingstone is professor of Social Psychology and a member of the Department of Media and Communications at the London School of Economics and Political Science. She has published widely on the subject of media audiences. Her recent work concerns children, young people, and new media in domestic, familial, and educational contexts. Among her many books are the recently published *Young People and the New Media*, the co-authored *Harm and Offence in Media Content: A Review of the Literature*, and the co-edited *Handbook of New Media*. She is President-elect of the International Communication Association.

Tobias Olsson is a postdoctoral researcher at Lund University, where he works on the project Young Citizens and New Media. He is also a lecturer in Media and Communication Studies at Växjö University. He has published a number of journal articles, book chapters, and reports from the project, as well as made a number of presentations at international conferences.

Henk Vinken is a sociologist and affiliate of OSA, Institute for Labour Studies, Tilburg University, Tilburg, Netherlands and Faculty of Liberal Arts, Sophia University, Tokyo, Japan. Until recently he was visiting professor at Komazawa University, Tokyo, Japan. He is a vice-president of the International Sociological Association (ISA) Research Committee Sociology of Youth RC34 and founder of Pyrrhula BV, a company specializing in research on cultural and political change produced by generation formation. He has published many journal books, articles, book chapters, and reports on these and related issues.

Index

Page numbers in italics refer to figures or tables.

A

Abusive power, collusion, 24
Access, mobile phones, 220–222
Accountability, 29
Action *vs.* organisation, 89
Affectivity, significance, 34–35
Agency, citizenship, 8–9
Alter-global movement
  Internet, 236–237
  social networks, 235–244
    sociability and political
      involvement, 238–241
    young activists in, 237–238
Alternative politics, 6–7
American DotNets, 60, 66
Animation, 153
Australia, civic education, 64–65
Austria
  civic engagement, 81–84, *85*
  civic participation, 81–84, *85*
  information and communication
    technologies, patterns of new
    media use, 84–88, *87, 88*
  Youth Report, 86
Authoritarianism, 25
Authority, collusion with manipulative,
  21

B

Belgium, 167–183
Big Brother (TV show), participation,
  21, 26, 27–37
Bricolage, identity construction, 92
Bulletin boards, 151

C

Career orientation, Dutch young
  people, 46

Children in Communication about
    Migration, 148–162
  adapting approach, 158–159
  after-school clubs, 149
  animation, 153
  bulletin boards, 151
  burden of representation, 155–158
  children making videotapes about
    their lives, 148–162
  delays in distributing, 154
  football, 153
  intercultural communication,
    149–162
  Internet, 149, 150–151, 154–155
  languages, 154
  logistical difficulties, 150
  music, 151–153
  objectives, 148
  poem, 152
  rap, 152
  sex, 153
  successful instances, 150–153
  websites, 150–151
Chile, *144*
  Internet, 132–142
    civic knowledge, attitudes, and
      engagement, 136–137
    to get news about politics, 132–
      133, *133*
    online student characteristics,
      133–135, *134, 135*
    predictors of future engagement,
      139–140, *140*
    students' expected participation
      and political actions, *138,*
      138–139
Citizenship
  agency, 8–9

Citizenship (*continued*)
  changing definitions, 60–61
  as communication practice, 71–73
  education for, 48–49
  information and communication
      technologies, 47–53
  minimal definition of, 49
  mobile phones, 209–210
  new media, 47–53
Civic agency
  civic culture, 9–10
  role, 9
Civic culture
  civic agency, 9–10
  defined, 9–10
  learning, 10
Civic education
  actualizing citizen model, 62–64, *63*
  Australia, 64–65
  bringing civics back in, 74–75
  challenge, 62–64
  in changing democracies, *59–75*
  communication-based model, 65–66
  content, 60
  dutiful citizen model, 62–64, *63*
  information and communication
      technologies, 71–73
  recognizing changes in citizenship,
      75
Civic engagement
  Austria, 81–84, *85*
  changing life courses, 41–54
  declining, 1
  generation, 52
  Germany, 81–84, *85*
  identity formation, civic identity,
      129–130
  information and communication
      technologies
    links between, 88–91
    new forms, 89–91
  Internet, 52, 103–122
    functions, 90
    indispensable resource, 187–202
  learning, 8–10
    attributes, 9
Civic identity, construction, 129–130
Civic incapability
  consumption, 48
  media use, 48
Civic interests, Internet, 115, *116*
Civic networks, participation,
      translating communication skills
      into, 73–74

Civic participation
  Austria, 81–84, *85*
  information and communication
      technologies
    links between, 88–91
    new forms, 89–91
Civic talk, democracy, 208–209
  models, 208
Class identification, 5–7
Collective framing, 67
Collusion, abusive power, 24
Commitment, Internet, 51
Computers, as tools for political
      organizations, 191
Consumerism, 4
Consumption, civic incapability, 48
  higher competence, 48
Creativity, Internet, *114, 115*–116, *117*
Crowds, 24
Cultural citizenship, 209
Cultural practices, social networks,
      228–235
  distribution, 229–230, 231–233,
      233, 242–244, *243*
  personal network methodology,
      228–229
  polarization, 230–231, *231*, 241–
      242, *242*
  screen culture, 229
  specialization, 229–230, 233–235,
      235, 242, *243*
Culture of sobriety, politics, 35
Cynicism, 2

D
Debates, Internet, antagonistic public
      spheres, 197–198
Democracy
  civic talk, 208–209
    models, 208
  concept, 182
  floating signifier, 182
  information and communication
      technologies, relationship,
      175–176
  Internet, 1
    early optimism, 1
    impact, 1–2
    role in democratic life, 7–8
  as learning experience, 168–170
  mobile phones, 207–208
  mobility, 207–208
  politics of definition, 168
  young citizens, 5–7

Democratic familyship, negotiated
practices
acquisition, 177–181
conflict, 176–178
dealing with, 181
over use-time, 177–179
dialogue, 176–178
educational or work uses, 176
expertise, 176–178, 179–181
family contexts, 174
information and communication
technologies
(dis)integrative role of, 174
user practices, 167–183
necessary requirement, 175
negotiation, 179–181
North-Belgian youngsters, 174–183
opportunity for, 175
widespread, 176
Democratic learning, family, 170–172
Democratic practices, mobile phones
case: mobile phone as ballot paper
and voting device, 218–220
limitations, 220
Demography, political participation
of exclusion, 32–33
rebalancing, 32–33
Denmark, *145*
Internet, 132–142
civic knowledge, attitudes, and
engagement, 136–137
to get news about politics, 132–
133, *133*
online student characteristics,
133–135, *134, 135*
predictors of future engagement,
139–140, *140*
students' expected participation
and political actions, *138,*
138–139
mobile phones, 205–222
Determined technology, 147
Digital democracy, 208
Digital information sphere, 70
Direct Action Network, 245
Disengagement, 21
Distributed network, 229–230, 231–
233, 242–244, *243*
Documentation, mobile phones,
215–216
case: personal monitoring and
control, 216–217
Dutch young people
career orientation, 46

dynamic life course model, 46–47
generation, 46
Duty, participation, 22
Dynamic life course model, 46–47
Dys-socialization, 52

E
Ecological cognition, 131–132
E-democracy, 7
Electoral communication, 68–69
Empowerment
limits, 159–162
migrant children, 147–162
adapting approach, 158–159
after-school clubs, 149
animation, 153
bulletin boards, 151
burden of representation, 155–158
children making videotapes about
their lives, 148–162
delays in distributing, 154
football, 153
intercultural communication,
149–162
Internet, 149, 150–151, 154–155
languages, 154
logistical difficulties, 150
music, 151–153
objectives, 148
poem, 152
rap, 152
sex, 153
successful instances, 150–153
visual symbolism, 149–162
websites, 150–151
new media, 147–162
Engagement
characterized, 21–22
consequences, 22
engaging youth *vs.* engaging with
youth, 36–37
etymology, 36
problematised, 21
uncritically normative fashion, 21
England, *145*
Internet, 132–142
civic knowledge, attitudes, and
engagement, 136–137
to get news about politics, 132–
133, *133*
online student characteristics,
133–135, *134, 135*
predictors of future engagement,
139–140, *140*

England (*continued*)
    students' expected participation
        and political actions, *138,*
        138–139
Entertainment media, political
    influence, 69–70
EUYOUPART, 83–84, *85*, 88
Experience, 94
Extra-parliamentarian political
    engagement, 4–5

F
Family, 167, *See also* Democratic
        familyship
    democratic learning, 170–172
    power struggle for technology,
        172–183
    as site for democratic learning,
        168–170
Fear, 29
First-hand sources, Internet, 189–190
Football, 153

G
Generation
    civic engagement, 52
    Dutch young people, 46
        Mannheim's theory, 45–46
        membership, 46
        shared sense of belonging, 45
        younger Dutch cohorts, 46
    Internet, 52
Germany
    civic engagement, 81–84, *85*
    information and communication
        technologies, patterns of new
        media use, 84–88, *87, 88*
    Shell Youth Survey, 82–83
Global perspective, 89
Government
    governance, contrasted, 27
    models, 27
Governmentality
    concept, 27
    self-disciplining nature, 27
    surveillance, 28–29
Group mind, 24

H
Habitus, 94
Hidden transcripts, 32
Human rights, unavailability as,
    220

I
Identity, 94
Identity formation, 81–97
    bricolage, 92
    civic engagement, 129–130
    Internet, 125
    media, 125
    young people, theoretical
        approaches, 91–93
Immigrants' rights, support for, 146
Individualism, 4
Information
    mobility, 206–207
    pace, 206–207
Information and communication
        technologies, *see also* Specific
        type
    Austria, patterns of new media use,
        84–88, *87, 88*
    citizenship, 47–53
    civic education, 71–73
    civic engagement
        links between, 88–91
        new forms, 89–91
    conceptualising necessary resources,
        200–202
    democracy, relationship, 175–176
    discursive resources, 200–201
    domestication, 172–174
    Germany, patterns of new media use,
        84–88, *87, 88*
    learning preferences, 72, 72–73
    material resources, 200–201
    participation, 33
    perceived as natural part of life,
        207
    political resources, 201
    reshaping modern life, 7
    social resources, 200–201
Interactive media, mass media,
    contrasted, 103–104
Interactivity, 29–30
    Internet, 113, *114*
International activism, 235–244
International Association for the
        Evaluation of Education
        Achievement, Civic Education
        Study, 131–142
    civic knowledge, attitudes, and
        engagement, 136–137
    countries involved, 132
    dataset, 132
    ecological theory, 131–132

to get news about politics, 132–133,
   133
online student characteristics, 133–
   135, *134, 135*
predictors of future engagement,
   139–140, *140*
situated cognition, 131–132
students' expected civic participation
   and political actions, *138,*
   138–139
theoretical framework, 131–132,
   150–151
access, 105
alter-global movement, 236–237
Chile, 132–142
   civic knowledge, attitudes, and
      engagement, 136–137
   to get news about politics, 132–
      133, *133*
   online student characteristics,
      133–135, *134, 135*
   predictors of future engagement,
      139–140, *140*
   students' expected participation
      and political actions, *138,*
      138–139
civic interests, 115, *116*
commitment, 51
convenience as civic tool, 190–191
creation of multiple identities, 50–51
creativity, *114,* 115–116, *117*
debates, antagonistic public spheres,
   197–198
democracy, 1
   early optimism, 1
   impact, 1–2
   role in democratic life, 7–8
Denmark, 132–142
   civic knowledge, attitudes, and
      engagement, 136–137
   to get news about politics, 132–
      133, *133*
   online student characteristics,
      133–135, *134, 135*
   predictors of future engagement,
      139–140, *140*
   students' expected participation
      and political actions, *138,*
      138–139
early research, 187
embedded in everyday life, 105
England, 132–142
   civic knowledge, attitudes, and

engagement, 136–137
to get news about politics, 132–
   133, *133*
online student characteristics,
   133–135, *134, 135*
predictors of future engagement,
   139–140, *140*
students' expected participation
   and political actions, *138,*
   138–139
explicit political or civic intentions,
   128–129
first-hand sources, 189–190
generation, 52
ideal citizens, 199
identity formation, 125
interactivity, 113, *114*
news updates, 188–189
participation, 104–106
   benefits of participation, 107–108
   civic-minded, *118,* 119
   disengaged, *118,* 119
   giving youth their say, 106–107
   institutional structures
      importance, 111–112
   interactors, 117, *118*
   lack of regard for youth, 109–110
   listening to young people, 108–112
   optimism, 106–107
   peer-to-peer, 113
   politics as boring, 108–109
   from producers' perspective,
      106–107
   typology of young people online,
      116–117, *118*
   varieties of participation, 112–113,
      114
   varieties of participators, 116–117,
      118
   website aesthetics, 111
political culture, 51
political engagement, 52, 103–122
   civic knowledge, attitudes, and
      engagement, 136–137
   countries involved, 132
   dataset, 132
   ecological theory, 131–132
   functions, 90
   to get news about politics, 132–
      133, *133*
   indispensable resource, 187–202
   online student characteristics,
      133–135, *134, 135*

Internet (*continued*)
    predictors of future engagement,
        139–140, *140*
    situated cognition, 131–132
    students' expected civic
        participation and political
        actions, *138,* 138–139
    theoretical framework, 131–132
    use patterns, 125–142
    political organizations, 191–194
        current issues, 191–192
        internal debate, 194–197
        tool for internal coordination, 191,
            194
    reasons for accessing, 128
    social identities, 51
    symbolization of selves, 50–51
    tool for monitoring society, 188–191
    as tools for political organizations,
        191
    usage rates, 127–128
    uses, 188–189, 199

J
Journalism, evolution, 2–3

L
Learning preferences
    information and communication
        technologies, 72, *72,* 72–73
    new, 71–73, *72*
    traditional, 71–73, *72*
Life courses
    absence of pedagogically inspired
        institutions and agents, 53–54
    de-standardized, 41–43
    post-industrial, 41
    traditional three-phased model, 42
    transitions, 41, 42

M
Mass media
    interactive media, contrasted,
        103–104
    participation, traditional framings,
        103
Media, *see also* Specific type
    adoption in hospitals, 173
    attention to, 126–129
    changes in types, 126–127
    civic incapability, 48
        higher competence, 48
    identity formation, 125
    mediatization of everyday life, 4

political disengagement, 2–5
socio-cultural change, 2–5
thematic competencies, 84–88, *87*
traditional, 188
uses, 126–129
Media literacy curriculum, 69–70
Media research
    concepts, 92–93
    ethnographic research, 172–173
    practical meaning as basic concept,
        93–96
    usage study, United States, 127
Migrant children
    empowerment, 147–162
        adapting approach, 158–159
        after-school clubs, 149
        animation, 153
        bulletin boards, 151
        burden of representation, 155–158
        children making videotapes about
            their lives, 148–162
        delays in distributing, 154
        football, 153
        intercultural communication,
            149–162
        Internet, 149, 150–151, 154–155
        languages, 154
        logistical difficulties, 150
        music, 151–153
        objectives, 148
        poem, 152
        rap, 152
        sex, 153
        successful instances, 150–153
        visual symbolism, 149–162
        websites, 150–151
    new media, 147–162
Millenial generation, social change,
    60–61
Mobile phones
    access, 220–222
    appropriation of public space, 209
    citizenship, 209–210
    as citizen tool, 209–210
    democracy, 207–208
    democratic practices
        case: mobile phone as ballot paper
            and voting device, 218–220
        limitations, 220
    Denmark, 205–222
    documentation, 215–216
        case: personal monitoring and
            control, 216–217
    horizontal discussion, 210

pace, 206
power, 213
  case: the street reporter, 217–218
  as mobilising social instrument,
    214–215
  risk, 210–211
  disappearance of anonymity,
    212–213
  security, 219
  social potentials, 214
  speed, 220–222
  surveillance, 211–212
  trust, 210–211
  ubiquitous, 205
Mobility
  democracy, 207–208
  information, 206–207
MoSoSos (Mobile Social Software),
    214
Motivation, 67
Music, 151–153

N
National citizenship, 59
Negotiated practices, democratic
    familyship
  acquisition, 177–181
  conflict, 176–178
    dealing with, 181
    over use-time, 177–179
  dialogue, 176–178
  educational or work uses, 176
  expertise, 176–178, 179–181
  family contexts, 174
  information and communication
    technologies
    (dis)integrative role, 174
    user practices, 167–183
  necessary requirement, 175
  negotiation, 179–181
  North-Belgian youngsters, 174–183
  opportunity for, 175
  widespread, 176
Network culture, 228
New media
  citizenship, 47–53
  empowerment, 147–162
    adapting approach, 158–159
    after-school clubs, 149
    animation, 153
    bulletin boards, 151
    burden of representation, 155–158
    children making videotapes about
      their lives, 148–162

delays in distributing, 154
football, 153
intercultural communication,
    149–162
Internet, 149, 150–151, 154–155
languages, 154
logistical difficulties, 150
music, 151–153
objectives, 148
poem, 152
rap, 152
sex, 153
successful instances, 150–153
visual symbolism, 149–162
websites, 150–151
as learning process for participation
    in society, 175
migrant children, 147–162
new media culture, 3–5
pedagogic dimensions of young
    people's engagement, 148
potential, 147
News
  Internet updates, 188–189
  media's political influence, 69–70
  quality, 3
Nineteen Eighty-Four (George
    Orwell), 23–29
Non-participation, 21
Norms, 23

O
Online media culture, 125
Orientation, 94–95

P
Pace
  information, 206–207
  mobile phones, 206
Participation
  Big Brother (TV show), 21, 26,
    27–37
  civic networks, translating
    communication skills into,
    73–74
  decline, 59
  duty, 22
  dystopian images, 26
  information and communication
    technologies, 33
  Internet, 104–106
    benefits of participation, 107–108
    civic-minded, *118*, 119
    disengaged, *118*, 119

Participation (*continued*)
　giving youth their say, 106–107
　institutional structures
　　importance, 111–112
　interactors, 117, *118*
　lack of regard for youth, 109–110
　listening to young people, 108–112
　optimism, 106–107
　peer-to-peer, 113
　politics as boring, 108–109
　from producers' perspective,
　　106–107
　typology of young people online,
　　116–117, *118*
　varieties of participation, 112–113,
　　114
　varieties of participators, 116–117,
　　118
　website aesthetics, 111
march through institutions, 50
mass media, traditional framings,
　103
motivations, 22
new forms, 50
Nineteen Eighty-Four (George
　Orwell), 23–29
participatory norms, 21–23
participatory pathologies, 23–26
postponed, 44
rationales, 22
social networks
　effect of friendships, 239
　sociability and political
　　involvement, 238–241
Western European countries, 60
Party politics, 2
Peer-to-peer, 113
Performance, surveillance, 28–29
Personal network methodology,
　228–229
Plebiscitary democracy, 208
Poem, 152
Polarized network, 230–231, *231,*
　241–242, *242*
Political, defined, 103
Political communication, 68–71
Political culture, 22
　definition, 22
　entertaining participatory forms,
　　35–36
　Internet, 51
Political disengagement
　media, 2–5

socio-cultural change, 2–5
Political engagement
　democratising, 30–32
　Internet
　　civic knowledge, attitudes, and
　　　engagement, 136–137
　　countries involved, 132
　　dataset, 132
　　ecological theory, 131–132
　　to get news about politics, 132–
　　　133, *133*
　　online student characteristics,
　　　133–135, *134, 135*
　　predictors of future engagement,
　　　139–140, *140*
　　situated cognition, 131–132
　　students' expected civic
　　　participation and political
　　　actions, *138,* 138–139
　　theoretical framework, 131–132
　　use patterns, 125–142
　rules, 30–31
Political identity, standpoint issues,
　66–68
Political information environment,
　navigating, 68–71
Political organizations, Internet,
　191–194
　current issues, 191–192
　internal debate, 194–197
　tool for internal coordination, 191,
　　194
Political participation
　demography
　　of exclusion, 32–33
　　rebalancing, 32–33
　new models, 31
Politics
　as boring, 108–109
　culture of sobriety, 35
　decentralized, 7
　decentred, 7
　interest in, 82
　personal, 60–61
　popular images, 26
　as uncool, 111
　young citizens, 5–7
　　cross-national trend origins, 60–62
Politics of definition, democracy, 168
Power, mobile phones, 213
　case: the street reporter, 217–218
　as mobilising social instrument,
　　214–215

Power struggle, within family for
    technology, 167–183
Pragmatism, *vs.* ideology, 89
Public culture, fragmentation, 3
Public discourse, 49
Publicity orientation, 90

R
Rap, 152
Reflexive biographization, 43–45
    de-standardization of life courses,
        42–43
Reflexive generation, 45–47
Reflexivity, 44
    competences, 44–45
    self-destruction, 45
    sociology, 45
Refugee children, *See* Migrant children
Repressed expression, 32
Rhetorical skills, development,
    197–198
Risk, mobile phones, 210–211
    disappearance of anonymity,
        212–213

S
Screen culture, 229
Security, mobile phones, 219
Self-destruction, reflexivity, 45
Self-socialisation, 92
Sex, 153
Sexual politics, 170–171
Shared interests, social identities, 51
Shell Youth Survey, Germany, 82–83
Situated cognition, 131–132
Smart mob phenomena, 211, 215
Social action, 94
Social activities, institutional context,
    83
Social change, 60
    millennial generation, 60–61
Social identities
    Internet, 51
    shared interests, 51
Socialization, 5–6, 43
    changing focus, 43–44
Social milieus, 94
Social networks, 227–246
    alter-global movement, 235–244
        sociability and political
            involvement, 238–241
        young activists in, 237–238
        comparative hypotheses, 244–246

cultural practices, 228–235
    distribution, 229–230, 231–233,
        233, 242–244, 243
    personal network methodology,
        228–229
    polarization, 230–231, *231,* 241–
        242, *242*
    screen culture, 229
    specialization, 229–230, 233–235,
        235, 242, 243
participation
    effect of friendships, 239
    sociability and political
        involvement, 238–241
Social science, affective turn, 34
Socio-cultural change
    media, 2–5
    political disengagement, 2–5
Sociology, reflexivity, 45
Specialized network, 229–230, 233–
    235, *235, 242, 243*
Speed, mobile phones, 220–222
Standpoint issues, political identity,
    66–68
Student Voices, 73–74
Surveillance
    as accountability, 33–34
    governmentality, 28–29
    mobile phones, 211–212
    performance, 28–29
Sweden, 187–202

T
Tabloidization, 3
Technological determinism, 147
Television, role, 173
Totalitarianism, 25
Trust, mobile phones, 210–211

U
UCLA World Internet Project, 128
UK Children Go Online, 106–122
United States, media usage study, 127

V
Voice, 148–162

W
Websites, 150–151
    aesthetics, 111
Western European countries,
    participation, 60
Women's rights, support for, 146

Work, work *vs.* non-work time, 42
World Social Forum, 236–237

Y
Youth
  democracy, 5–7
  lack of regard for, 109–110
  participation, normative discourse,
    22–23

politics, 5–7
  cross-national trend origins, 60–62
  voting decline, 59–60
Youth Report, Austria, 86
Youth research
  concepts, 92–93
  practical meaning as basic concept,
    93–96